Successful Coaching for Leaders and Managers

The rapid pace of change in the post-COVID world has made it more important than ever for managers to coach individual employees and teams effectively both online and face to face. This book draws on research from around the world and shares good practices to help managers become effective leaders in face-to-face, virtual, and hybrid workplaces.

The book examines how the coaching skills of observation, listening, questioning, goal-setting, feedback, and reflection can be used effectively with individuals and teams. Boxes offering scenarios and practical activities help the reader understand how to apply these skills in real life. The book goes on to explore coaching at the organisational level, bringing in systems thinking, coaching culture, cross-cultural coaching, and coaching in multinational organisations. Finally, the book considers ways for managers to evaluate and improve their coaching, including how to use technology and GenAI to support coaching.

This book synthesises different strands of research to help managers develop their coaching skills both face to face and online. HR managers will find ideas for how best to support managers in developing their skills. Researchers and educators interested in managerial coaching and successful leadership in the post-COVID hybrid workplace will also find food for thought.

Grace McCarthy is Dean of Business at University of Wollongong Australia. A pioneer of research into leaders as coaches, she has written numerous articles and the acclaimed book *Coaching and Mentoring for Business*. Grace sits on the editorial board of the *International Journal of Evidence-Based Coaching and Mentoring*.

'This is a "must read" book for managers and leaders who would like to embrace the concept of coaching their employees, both individually and in teams, as well as at the organizational level, and develop and improve their requisite coaching skills in the process. Detailed guidance on how to engage in coaching, build and enhance coaching skills, and create a culture of coaching are provided and illustrated with real-world vignettes. Grace McCarthy explores these concepts in a variety of contexts that are traditional face-to-face workplaces and in remote work arrangements which proliferated during the Covid pandemic and in its aftermath. She also considers the emergence of artificial intelligence (AI) and its relevance in supporting managers' and leaders' coaching endeavors. This book is well written, and supported with best evidence drawn from credible sources. It is a significant contribution to the ongoing dialogue about managerial and leadership coaching and is a most valuable resource for aspiring coaches, and a most worthwhile practical investment of "reading" time. It will help managers and leaders reap the rewards and benefits from becoming and being effective coaches in their ever-changing world of work.'

Andrea D. Ellinger, Professor Emerita, The University of Texas at Tyler, USA

'I can't think of a better person than Prof. Grace McCarthy, one of the leading international authorities on Managerial Coaching, to write this comprehensive book on a leadership approach every leader and manager needs to aware of. In today's world a smooth transition between virtual, hybrid and face-to-face managerial coaching is needed and this book gives leaders crucial insights in how to leverage these key managerial skills.'

Julia Milner, Professor of Leadership, EDHEC Business School, France

'Once again, Grace McCarthy has produced a book of enormous practical relevance for those with an interest in managerial and workplace coaching. The past 5 years has seen a radical redefinition of the "workplace", along with an acceleration of social interaction technologies. Whilst both have huge implications for the delivery of coaching, little practical guidance has been available for leaders and managers seeking to maintain a coaching approach in virtual or hybrid environments. As such, Grace has made another valuable contribution to coaching practice!'

Gordon Spence, PhD, University of Sydney, Australia

GRACE MCCARTHY

Successful Coaching for Leaders and Managers

How to Blend Virtual and Face-to-Face Coaching Effectively for Today's Hybrid Workplaces

Routledge
Taylor & Francis Group

LONDON AND NEW YORK

Designed cover image: Getty Images

First published 2025
by Routledge
4 Park Square, Milton Park, Abingdon, Oxon, OX14 4RN

and by Routledge
605 Third Avenue, New York, NY 10158

Routledge is an imprint of the Taylor & Francis Group, an informa business

British Library Cataloguing-in-Publication Data
A catalogue record for this book is available from the British Library

Library of Congress Cataloging-in-Publication Data
Names: McCarthy, Grace, author.
Title: Successful coaching for leaders and managers : how to blend virtual and face to face coaching effectively for today's hybrid workplaces / Grace McCarthy.
Description: Abingdon, Oxon ; New York, NY : Routledge, 2025. | Includes bibliographical references and index. | Identifiers: LCCN 2024041193 (print) | LCCN 2024041194 (ebook) | ISBN 9781032145372 (hardback) | ISBN 9781032145365 (paperback) | ISBN 9781003239826 (ebook)
Subjects: LCSH: Employees—Coaching of. | Personal coaching.
Classification: LCC HF5549.5.C53 M378 2025 (print) | LCC HF5549.5.C53 (ebook) | DDC 658.3/124—dc23/eng/20240906
LC record available at https://lccn.loc.gov/2024041193
LC ebook record available at https://lccn.loc.gov/2024041194

ISBN: 9781032145372 (hbk)
ISBN: 9781032145365 (pbk)
ISBN: 9781003239826 (ebk)

DOI: 10.4324/9781003239826

Typeset in Joanna
by codeMantra

*To Tim, Fiona and Seán, for your love and support,
when we're together and when we're apart, thank you.*

Contents

WORKING FROM ANYWHERE – THE CONTEXT OF THIS BOOK

During the pandemic, many organisations who had had no previous experience with remote working suddenly had to find effective ways of doing so, investing huge sums in videoconferencing and collaboration technology. Although remote teams had been the norm for multinational teams pre- COVID-19, virtual teams in the COVID-19 world often comprised people living in close proximity but working from home because of lockdown regulations. Many of these workers had no experience of remote working. Nor had their managers any experience of managing people remotely.

With the rapid responses required by the pandemic now behind us, it is a good time to reflect and make conscious decisions about our workplaces, to learn lessons from the pandemic, and to value the human as well as the technological aspects of work in the 21st century. In this new world of work, we can and must separate 'work' from 'workplace'. Understanding individual employee needs and preferences is key to success in the 'never normal' environment post COVID-19 (1). This book aims to help managers with the skills required to be successful leaders in this new normal world, illustrating how coaching skills can be used face to face, online, and in the hybrid workplace where employees do some of their work from home and some on site.

In this preface, we outline key debates around remote and hybrid work as well as the health and well-being concerns that emerged during the pandemic. Readers may of course choose to go straight to Chapter One, or whichever chapter is most relevant to them.

REMOTE AND HYBRID WORK

The experimentation with different forms of work and workplaces that began during the pandemic has continued into the mid-2020s, with organisations trialling different versions of the length of the working week and varying the balance between working from home and working in a fixed workplace. Variations in the working week, with three days in the office an increasingly common requirement (2), can help employees to manage their responsibilities outside the workplace, for example caring for children or for older relatives. While technology was implemented quickly during the pandemic to enable videoconferencing and online collaboration, leadership styles in some organisations have been slower to adapt. The pandemic also highlighted the global nature of supply chains, leading to an ever-increasing need for people to work efficiently across time zones and cultures.

Working from Anywhere

Many tasks nowadays can be carried out remotely, particularly if they are computer based. The combination of information and communications technology has freed people to work from anywhere. This new freedom was not available to earlier generations, apart from in a small number of roles such as sales representatives. Instead, the norm since the Industrial Revolution has been to bring employees together to work on office-based tasks, just as they had worked together in the Middle Ages on agricultural tasks such as sowing and harvesting.

People can now collaborate effectively from anywhere in the world. Collaboration can be synchronous where people work together at the same time, such as in meetings. Or it can be asynchronous where people work in their own time zone on shared documents, for example. It is important to decide which tasks are best done together and which as individuals, which tasks are best achieved synchronously and which asynchronously, and which tasks are best done face to face, and which may be done as well or possibly better online.

Benefits of Working from Anywhere

Despite the concerns of some managers about the potential downsides of remote and hybrid working, the trend is predicted to increase. Freedom to choose where to work gives both employers and employees multiple benefits (3), including higher levels of autonomy and motivation, more employee engagement, potentially lower costs due to reducing the amount of office space required, as well as ensuring that organisations can hire and retain the best talent available, wherever that talent resides (4). Employees can live somewhere affordable and appealing for their families without a long commute every day, thereby also reducing environmental impacts.

The resulting flexibility offers many advantages for companies. For example, companies can choose to operate customer service centres in three different time zones, providing 24/7 customer service without paying higher labour rates for night work. Companies can also choose to have much of their office work completed in countries with lower labour costs – not only manufacturing as happened in earlier decades. Many professional tasks such as architectural drawing, management accounts, and human resource transactions (e.g. payroll) are already being outsourced to different countries.

There is also the potential for local collaborative workspaces where employees of different companies work together, rather than travel to a larger city. Such hubs provide social connection. Some, such as the Impact Hub in Cork, Ireland,[1] also provide equipment and access for people with neuro-physical disabilities, which might be costly for individual small companies to accommodate. In the virtual workplace, technology places everyone on an equal footing. As working from home has become normalised, people with disabilities can take advantage of adaptations that make it possible for them to work effectively and to avoid some of the problems of inappropriately adapted workplaces or potential problems with public transport.

This freedom to work from anywhere has significant implications for recruitment practices, allowing organisations to hire the best people regardless of where they are located. Managers who can lead effectively using technology thus have access to a bigger talent pool. This is particularly important at a time when there is a war for talent. The World Economic Forum recently reported that a skills shortage and the inability to attract talent were the biggest barriers to business transformation (5). CEOs who allow flexible working are more than three times as likely to feel ready for recruiting and retaining staff compared with other CEOs (6). The software company Atlassian found that the number of applicants per role doubled since introducing their work from anywhere policy and furthermore that this did not result in any negative impacts on productivity (7).

The ability to work from anywhere also has implications for staff retention as employees can be tempted to work for other organisations they would previously not have considered, because they can work from home at least some of the time and do not need to relocate for a better job. This is a strong argument for implementing coaching in the workplace, as coaching by managers has been shown to have a positive effect on reducing staff turnover (5) and to enhance trust, which is particularly important in a remote working environment (8, 9).

Not everyone enjoys working remotely and some people do not want to work remotely all the time. Working remotely can be isolating. People may miss the social connections that emerge from casual corridor conversations, side conversations before or after in-person meetings, or the opportunity simply to have a cup of coffee with colleagues. Chat technologies can provide a partial alternative but for many, the social side of work requires at least some face-to-face time with others.

People working from home may find it difficult to set boundaries and leave their work behind at the end of the day. Yet the ability to switch off from ideas and thoughts related to work problems or opportunities is crucial to well-being (10). Knowing the possible issues allows us to put in place practices that support well-being, such as a virtual commute (e.g. a walk at the beginning and end of the day) and virtual social gatherings to help create a sense of belonging. There is emerging research that indicates a rise in loneliness and in mental health issues (11), although some of the increase may be due to more awareness and a lessening of the stigma of declaring a mental illness (12). As leaders, we have a responsibility to support our employees wherever they work. This includes ensuring that policies and procedures to promote safe workplaces, for example to prevent or deal with bullying or harassment, are implemented equally as effectively online as in the office. This requires managers to have the skills needed to have difficult conversations online.

Other difficulties with remote working have also been identified. On-boarding new employees can be more difficult in a totally remote work context. New employees have fewer opportunities for socialisation and acculturation, for understanding the culture and unwritten norms of an organisation, and learning what is and is not regarded as acceptable behaviour (13). More of an organisation's tacit knowledge needs to be made explicit in the virtual workplace than in a fully face-to-face environment. One suggestion is to have employees initially spend more time in the office being mentored by senior employees and later for employees to have more freedom about where to work once they have settled in. It is also important to be explicit about the purpose of bringing people together periodically, such as an innovation day or strategy day.

There are also challenges that relate to the long-standing belief in the need to be with someone in person when having a difficult conversation. Meeting in person allows managers to interpret non-verbal cues and to choose a physical location conducive to the nature of the conversation

(14). It can be more difficult in the online environment to give low-key informal feedback or have 'corridor coaching' conversations (15), as meetings have to be pre-arranged which automatically makes them appear more formal.

We are still in the early stages of large-scale remote and hybrid working. Much of the experience people have had with remote working was during pandemic conditions with additional difficulties such as lock-down restrictions and home schooling. Some of the possible downsides of remote/hybrid working may dissipate over time as we become more familiar with optimal ways of using technology. For example, Lee and Kim found that when leaders communicated that they cared for their employees' family situations, they fostered positive relationships and creativity among employees working from home (16).

Return to Office Mandates

Some organisations struggle with remote and hybrid leadership and have mandated that employees return to the office. They thereby run the risk of losing their best employees and being left with poor performing employees who unhappily comply (17).

Workers seem particularly keen on the hybrid model, while some managers are less convinced (18). Recent research in Australia, New Zealand, the UK, the US, and Canada suggests that options for hybrid and remote working are more likely to be made available to highly paid workers and less likely to be available for low-paid workers (19). This has the potential to alienate a large part of the workforce, especially if no reason is given.

Examples of negative consequences for remote or hybrid workers include being deliberately blocked from promotion or development opportunities, financial penalties, and even their positions being made redundant (20). Recently there have been reports of managers ignoring return to office mandates and continuing to allow employees to work from home in order to encourage employees to stay with their current organisation (21). These reports suggest that tasks requiring focused concentration and meeting deadlines are in fact better performed remotely. Hence, organisations need to consider carefully how and why they mandate any form of office-based working and communicate their rationale clearly.

Innovation

While it has previously been suggested that innovation, both planned and serendipitous, is more likely to result from co-located employees, more recent analysis of the data available suggests that this may be changing as people get used to using collaboration tools (22). In fact the number of patents filed increased during the pandemic (23). MIT suggests modelling the minimum amount of time spent working together in the office to ensure innovation thrives, and re-designing office spaces to encourage collaboration and innovation (24). Xu warns that "when researchers are forced to adhere to office presence schedules, ostensibly to improve creativity through serendipity and brainstorming, this can backfire and have the opposite effect due to the attendant loss of access to real drivers of creativity" (25, p. 10). They note the importance of solitude, suggesting that time apart improves the time that is spent together and stress that a nine to five working day five days a week may not be the optimal environment for innovation. Organisations need to experiment to find what works in their context.

The Productivity Question

One of the common reasons for demanding a return to full-time working in the office is linked with concerns about productivity and managers not feeling in control if they cannot see work in progress. Some admit that this is based on their judgement, rather than on data (20). A study of 1612 employees in a multinational company found that hybrid working improved employee satisfaction and retention, with the improvement in staff retention most significant in female employees and those with long commuting times (26). Despite the initial fears of managers, there were no negative impacts on performance.

Other studies have also found that return to office mandates have not improved productivity or performance and in fact have had a negative impact on employee satisfaction (27–29). This may be because the true cause of lower productivity is not whether or not people are in the office but whether or not they are engaged (30). As Lipman points out, "The normal challenges of in-person management are amplified by distance, poor communication, feelings of isolation and disconnection, and others" (31). Coaching has been shown to increase employee engagement (32, 33). We now have to develop our skills to be equally effective whether coaching in the online or hybrid or fully remote environment.

Recommendations from Research

Rather than a return to the office mandate, developing a shared understanding of expectations of the work itself and of how managers and employees communicate and work together is more likely to lead to improvements in engagement and result in productivity improvements (27). In some companies, putting in long hours was (and perhaps still is) deemed equivalent to commitment and motivation. This equation disadvantaged employees (particularly caregivers, often women) who were unable to stay longer in the office due to their responsibilities in the home. Nowadays women are more likely to take advantage of the new options for flexible working as they allow them, for example, to pick up their children after school and do some of their work later when their children are asleep (34). A survey of 5000 female workers around the world found that 'genuine flexible work options are non-negotiable when it comes to attracting and retaining female employees' (29). It has been suggested that managers find it easier to lay off remote workers, because they have less of a personal relationship with them, regardless of the business rationale for selecting which workers to make redundant (35). It is important as we navigate the new world of work that we do not continue to disadvantage some people over others.

Transparent guidelines for promotions, salary increases and professional development opportunities are an important part of developing a positive culture in a hybrid workplace (36). One of the reasons for people who take advantage of flexibility doing less well when it comes to promotion is proximity bias as illustrated in Box P.1.

Box P.1 Out of Sight

When Jo announced her resignation, her manager, Tom, knew he had a difficult decision to make. There were two other employees who worked alongside Jo in the office, both of whom he felt could be promoted, given some time to upskill. Mary was very strong in the analytical side of the job but often rubbed people up the wrong way. Jim, on the other hand, got on great with everyone but was not an expert in handling the analytics software. In the end, Tom decided that it would be easier to give Jim more training in the software. Before announcing the new appointment to the team, he decided to discuss with Mary the fact that he had considered her, the reason he had not appointed her, and to give her specific recent examples of how she had alienated her colleagues. He would also suggest finding a mentor who could help her work on her people skills.

In all his deliberations, Tom never once considered Sandy, who worked from home on the same software. While Sandy's work was exemplary, Tom had no sense of a personal connection with her, with their interactions mostly by email and in group meetings. Her name simply did not occur to him when considering a replacement for Jo.

When Tom announced Jim's appointment to the team, there were no questions in the meeting. However, later that day, one of Tom's long-time colleagues mentioned to him that he was hearing comments about a lack of transparency and favouritism, with those in the office being preferred over those who worked from home, regardless of how well the remote workers were performing.

That Friday, Sandy emailed her resignation, much to Tom's surprise. When Tom called to discuss, Sandy explained that the company she was moving to had specific policies in place to ensure all vacancies were advertised internally and that all employees regardless of whether they worked in the office or remotely were considered. Sandy had spoken to some employees who worked from home and who had been promoted. She talked about several things the company did to make remote employees feel that their work was visible and recognised and that they were well positioned to take advantage of opportunities that arose. While Sandy did not think there was anything deliberate in not being considered as a possible replacement for Jo, she did think her new company was far ahead in terms of getting the best from all their employees, regardless of how much time they spent in the office.

Tom realised that he had directly contributed to the company losing a valuable employee and that this could happen again unless he made changes. He determined to learn more about how to work effectively in the hybrid space to ensure that all employees felt valued. He determined to spend some time with managers who seemed to be doing this well to work out how he could do things differently.

For organisations and employees to be sustainable in the long term, it is important to switch from a focus on productivity to measures including problem-solving, creativity, collaboration, belonging, well-being, and purpose (37). Furthermore, when managers show that they genuinely care for their team members, this boosts morale and motivation (38). Leaders' caring and supportive conversations enhance trust and relationships (16), which are known contributors to employee engagement and retention (39). How managers demonstrate that they care for employees varies across cultures, and appears more common in countries with a collectivist orientation (40). However, during the pandemic there was a positive response in many countries when employees felt that their managers cared about them, consistent with previous research (41).

Since the pandemic, managers have continued to experiment with ways of showing their care, including supporting work-life balance (42). Hill (43) recommends organising opportunities for relationship-building, such as periodic on-site activities for all team members to help build a sense of connection and belonging. Understanding what is truly important to employees helps organisations co-design an environment with the flexibility people value and where people actually want to work (1).

Given that so many workers want to adopt a hybrid model, it seems inevitable that organisations who want to attract and retain the best workers will offer this flexibility. Therefore, organisational leaders and managers need the skills to lead effectively regardless of the workplace. Most managers, however, have not been trained in virtual or hybrid leadership skills. This book seeks to address that gap, drawing on research that illustrates the coaching mindset required of successful leaders in our complex global world and the coaching skillset that enables managers to enact leadership successfully regardless of the location of their team members.

RENEWED FOCUS ON WELL-BEING

Mental health issues spiralled during the enforced remote working in the early 2020s. The reasons varied but were often a combination of lack of human contact, inability to see loved ones, inability to socialise, stress due to uncertainty and constant changes, home schooling, and many more disruptions to people's lives.

We have emerged from the pandemic with a much stronger understanding of the importance of mental health and well-being and a renewed focus on well-being. Staff who are stressed or distressed are less engaged, less productive, more likely to take sick leave, and may end up leaving the organisation. Even from a purely economic perspective, it makes sense to support employee well-being. And, of course, from a human point of view it is non-negotiable.

During the pandemic, people had to learn how to relate to others online. Rather than reducing meaningful contact, online collaboration led to richer relationships for some teams. For example, seeing people's children, pets or homes allowed participants to relate to each other as human beings, where previously people might only have seen the 'work' side of a co-worker. In the post-pandemic workplace, we need to take advantage of the opportunities provided by technology, keeping human relationships centre stage. Some online options may in fact enrich our interactions.

Managerial coaching contributes towards healthy workplaces by encouraging positive relationships and supportive conversations. Both internal and external coaching can help employees cope with stress and with the uncertainty created by organisational changes (44, 45). When coaching managers listen to their employees, they can also help their organisations invest their resources in services valued by employees. For example, giving employees a choice of benefits – rather than, say, simply providing gym membership to all employees – has been increasing along with the growth in diversity in the workplace (46).

Leaders need to take care of their own well-being in order to be able to support their employees and their organisation, showing self-compassion as well as empathy (47). Self-care for managers enables managers to continue to function optimally, rather than falling victim to stress and burnout (48). In simple terms, this is like following the advice on airplanes to put on your own oxygen mask first before you help others. The demands on leaders to care for their staff and not merely 'command and control' can lead to exhaustion and vicarious trauma, particularly if leaders are high on empathy but have not yet learned to regulate their emotional response. On the positive side, research has found that when leaders have coaching skills and the ability to manage their own and their followers' emotions effectively, they contribute to 'increased leader effectiveness, a healthier organizational climate, and positive organizational job outcomes' (49, p. 298). Research has also found that leader self-care translates into staff care and that there can be a trickle-down effect when executives and supervisors communicate the importance of taking care of one's health (50, 51). People notice what managers do, more than what they say. If managers do not prioritise their own well-being, for example responding to non-critical emails when taking their annual leave entitlements, employees may feel under pressure to follow suit.

Stress, anxiety, and depression are among the most common work-related health problems, with contributory factors including ineffective communication, poorly managed organisational change, and lack of support from management and colleagues (52). Managing workplace mental health and stress makes good business sense and is in fact a legal requirement in Europe under European Union Framework Directive 89/391/EEC. There are several dimensions to looking after our health, from healthy eating and sleeping to exercise, time with others, and time spent in nature. This requires self-awareness of what works well for us as individuals. For example, we do not all require the same number of hours sleep per day, but we do all need some sleep. Lack of sleep has been associated not only with physical tiredness and irritability but also with emotional exhaustion and reduced creativity (53).

A vigorous work-out in a hotel gym may be the best start in the day for one person, while another might relish a walk by the sea or in a city park. Some people may find it relaxing to listen to music or prefer the stimulus of a podcast while walking or exercising. Research has found that looking at pictures of nature stimulates the same brain waves as being in nature. Hence, if we cannot go outdoors into a natural environment, choosing our video-conferencing background or screensaver can help our well-being (54). If organisations insist on using corporate backgrounds, they could include options with images of nature.

IN CLOSING

Many aspects of coaching have been researched over the past 20 years, with coaching by managers proven to be a powerful way of leading 21st-century organisations. This book explores the skills that managers employ when coaching individuals and teams as well as in different contexts such as coaching in large multinational organisations. The book concludes with a look at the future including how Artificial Intelligence (AI) can be used to support coaching managers as well as how managers can continue to improve their coaching skills. We hope you enjoy reading the book and find some ideas to take away and apply in your world.

NOTE

1 See https://crannimpact.ie/for further information.

REFERENCES

1. Panneerselvam S, Balaraman K. Employee experience: the new employee value proposition. *Strategic HR Review*. 2022;21(6): 201–7.
2. AHRI. Hybrid & flexible working practices in Australian workplaces in 2023. Australian HR Institute. October 2023. https://www.ahri.com.au/resources/hr-research

3. Irvine J. Slacking off working from home? The productivity tsar doesn't think so. *Sydney Morning Herald*. 12 July 2021.

4. Hall K, Hall A. *Leading remote and virtual teams: managing yourself and others in remote and hybrid teams or when working from home*. Crowthorne, Berks.: Global Integration; 2021.

5. World Economic Forum. The future of jobs. World Economic Forum, Cologny, Switzerland. 30 April 2023. https://www.weforum.org/publications/the-future-of-jobs-report-2023/

6. Schwantes M. 4 big reasons why your CEO Is not executing as a leader. Inc Australia. 20 Dec 2023. https://www.inc-aus.com/marcel-schwantes/4-big-reasons-why-your-ceo-is-not-executing-as-a-leader.html

7. Swan D. Companies will regret return-to-office mandates: Atlassian. *Sydney Morning Herald*. 18 Jan 2024.

8. Harjanto R, Suhariadi F, Yulianti P, Nugroho MA, Damayanti N. The importance of trust in cultivating employee loyalty and productivity in a remote work environment. *International Journal of Professional Business Review*. 2023;8(6): e02159-e.

9. Burroughes L, Grant C. Managerial coaching as the foundation for building felt-trust and motivation among employees working remotely. *International Coaching Psychology Review*. 2023;18(1): 45–57.

10. Gaudiino M, Di Stefano G. To detach or not to detach? The role of psychological detachment on the relationship between heavy work investment and well-being: a latent profile analysis. *Current Psychology*. 2023;42(8): 6667–81.

11. Campbell TT. The four-day work week: a chronological, systematic review of the academic literature. *Management Review Quarterly*. 2023;74: 1791–1807.

12. Foulkes L, Andrews JL. Are mental health awareness efforts contributing to the rise in reported mental health problems? A call to test the prevalence inflation hypothesis. *New Ideas in Psychology*. 2023;69: 101010.

13. Petrilli S, Galuppo L, Ripamonti SC. Digital onboarding: facilitators and barriers to improve worker experience. *Sustainability*. 2022;14(9): 5684.

14. Huston T. Giving critical feedback is even harder remotely. *Harvard Business Review*. 26 Jan 2021. https://hbr.org/2021/01/giving-critical-feedback-is-even-harder-remotely

15. Turner C, McCarthy G. Coachable moments: identifying factors that influence managers to take advantage of coachable moments in day-to-day management. *International Journal of Evidence-Based Coaching and Mentoring*. 2015;13(1): 1–13.

16. Lee Y, Kim J. How family-supportive leadership communication enhances the creativity of work-from-home employees during the COVID-19 pandemic. *Management Communication Quarterly*. 2023;37(3): 599–628.

17. Christian A. The diminishing returns of in-office mandates. BBC Worklife. 12 June 2024. https://www.bbc.com/worklife/article/20240612-the-diminishing-returns-of-in-office-mandates

18. Bloom N, Han R, Liang J. How working from home works out. National Bureau of Economic Research Working Paper Series. 2022, July (30292). https://www.nber.org/papers/w30292

19. Lambert P, editor. Measuring remote work using a Large Language Model (LLM). EconPol Forum; 2023. Munich: CESifo GmbH.

20. Thompson P. Forcing workers back to the office is 'dinosaur management' and companies risk losing out. *Business Insider*. 2 Feb 2024. https://www.businessinsider.com/forcing-workers-back-office-risks-talent-exodus-dell-amazon-2024-2

21. Robinson PD. Shadow policies: the controversial 2024 hybrid work trend. *Forbes.* 8 Feb 2024. https://www.forbes.com/sites/bryanrobinson/2024/02/08/shadow-policies-the-controversial-2024-hybrid-work-trend/

22. Tsipursky G. The myth that remote work stifles innovation and creativity is gaining ground – but the same evidence shows that it was only true in the pre-2010s workplace. *Fortune.* 3 Jan 2024. https://fortune.com/2024/01/03/myth-remote-work-stifles-innovation-creativity-evidence-true-workplace-careers-gleb-tsipursky/

23. Tsipursky G. Remote work and innovation: myths and realities. *Psychology Today.* 3 Jan 2023. https://www.psychologytoday.com/intl/blog/intentional-insights/202303/remote-work-and-innovation-myths-and-realities

24. Jarvis M. Analysis of email traffic suggests remote work may stifle innovation. MIT News. 1 Sept 2022. https://news.mit.edu/2022/remote-work-may-innovation-0901.

25. Xu T, Sarkar A, Rintel S. Is a return to office a return to creativity? Requiring fixed time In office to enable brainstorms and watercooler talk may not foster research creativity. CHIWORK 2023: Annual Symposium on Human-Computer Interaction for Work 2023; June 2023; Oldenburg, Germany. ACM. 20 Sept 2023. https://doi.org/10.1145/3596671.3598569

26. Bloom N, Han R, Liang J. Hybrid working from home improves retention without damaging performance. *Nature.* 2024;630: 920–25.

27. Thiel J. CEOs will finally admit next year that return-to-office mandates didn't move the productivity needle, future of work experts predict. *Fortune.* 27 Dec 2023. https://fortune.com/2023/12/26/return-to-office-mandates-no-productivity-impact-experts-predict/

28. Black E. Office mandates offer no financial benefit and staff hate them. *Australian Financial Review* 4 Feb 2024. https://www.afr.com/work-and-careers/workplace/office-mandates-offer-and-no-financial-benefit-and-staff-hate-them-study-20240202-p5f1xt

29. Dexter P. Bosses demanding a return to the office should stop and listen to women. *Sydney Morning Herald.* 3 May 2024. https://www.smh.com.au/business/workplace/bosses-demanding-a-return-to-the-office-should-stop-and-listen-to-women-20240502-p5fofm.html

30. Pendell R. Employee engagement strategies: fixing the world's $8.8 trillion problem. Gallup; Workplace. 14 June 2022. https://www.gallup.com/workplace/393497/world-trillion-workplace-problem.aspx

31. Lipman V. Companies want workers to return to the office. *Psychology Today.* 7 Feb 2024. https://www.psychologytoday.com/au/blog/mind-of-the-manager/202402/companies-want-workers-to-return-to-the-office?eml

32. Ladyshewsky R, Taplin R. Employee perceptions of managerial coaching and work engagement using the measurement model of coaching skills and the Utrecht work engagement scale. *International Journal of Evidence-Based Coaching and Mentoring.* 2017;15(2): 25–42.

33. Carrell WS, Ellinger AD, Nimon KF, Kim S. Examining the relationships among managerial coaching, perceived organizational support, and job engagement in the US higher education context. *European Journal of Training and Development.* 2021;46(5/6): 563–4.

34. Chung H, Booker C. Flexible working and the division of housework and childcare: examining divisions across arrangement and occupational lines. *Work, Employment and Society.* 2023;37(1): 236–56.

35. Robinson B. Remote workers' careers may be on the chopping block, according to recent report. *Forbes.* 7 Feb 2024. https://www.forbes.com/sites/bryanrobinson/2024/02/07/remote-workers-careers-may-be-on-the-chopping-block-according-to-recent-report/

36. Moorman C, Hinkfuss K. Managing the cultural pitfalls of hybrid work. *MIT Sloan Management Review.* 2023;64(3): 1–5.

37. Williams T. Bosses are having a big problem measuring performance because traditional productivity metrics aren't cutting it. *Fortune.* 8 Feb 2024. https://fortune.com/2024/02/08/productivity-insufficient-measuring-performance-deloitte-study-human-sustainability/

38. Arnold DG, Ross RL. Care in management: a review and justification of an organizational value. *Business Ethics Quarterly.* 2023;33(4): 617–54.

39. Amah OE, Ogah M. Qualitative study on the future of leadership as seen by leaders, practitioners, and employees. In: *Leadership and organisational effectiveness post-COVID-19: exploring the new normal.* E-book edition: Springer; 2023. p. 107–23.

40. Helfrich H. Working world. In: Helfrich H, editor. *Cross-cultural psychology.* Berlin, Heidelberg Germany: Springer; 2024. p. 157–72.

41. Eisenberger R, Rhoades Shanock L, Wen X. Perceived organizational support: why caring about employees counts. *Annual Review of Organizational Psychology and Organizational Behavior.* 2020;7: 101–24.

42. Marzec M, Szczudlińska-Kanoś A, Freund B, Miceikienė A. Innovative work-life balance after COVID-19. *International Journal of Contemporary Management.* 2023;59(3): 32–64.

43. Hill NS. Leadership strategies for the hybrid workforce. *MIT Sloan Management Review.* 2023;64(3):1–4.

44. Ebrahimi Z. Work-related stress and uncertainty amid change: can workplace coaching make a difference? *Cambridge Open Engage.* 2023. https://www.cambridge.org/engage/coe/article-details/6585188b9138d231613bb4fa

45. Song J, Li Y. Managerial coaching and subordinates' psychological distress: a cross-level moderated mediation study. *Current Psychology.* 2024;43: 15725–36.

46. White G. Diversity in workplace causes rise in unique employee benefits and changes in cafeteria plans. *Journal of Management and Marketing Research.* 2009;2: 1.

47. Zaki J. How to sustain your empathy in difficult times. *Harvard Business Review.* Jan–Feb 2024 https://hbr.org/2024/01/how-to-sustain-your-empathy-in-difficult-times.

48. Ghossoub Z, Nadler R, El-Aswad N. Emotional intelligence, resilience, self-care, and self-leadership in healthcare workers burnout: a qualitative study in coaching. *Universal Journal of Public Health.* 2020;8(5): 155–62.

49. Haver A, Akerjordet K, Furunes T. Emotion regulation and its implications for leadership: an integrative review and future research agenda. *Journal of Leadership & Organizational Studies.* 2013;20(3): 287–303.

50. Klug K, Felfe J, Krick A. Does self-care make you a better leader? A multisource study linking leader self-care to health-oriented leadership, employee self-care, and health. *International Journal of Environmental Research and Public Health.* 2022;19(11): 6733.

51. Chen F, Wu QL. Health-oriented leadership communication matters: a trickle-down model to enhance employees' health and well-being during turbulent times. *Corporate Communications: An International Journal.* 2023;29(3): 384–404.

52. Van den Broek K, Hupke M, Kuasz F. Psychosocial risks and workers health. European Agency for Safety and Health at Work 2024. https://osha.europa.eu/en/themes/psychosocial-risks-and-mental-health

53. Opoku MA, Kang S-W, Kim N. Sleep-deprived and emotionally exhausted: depleted resources as inhibitors of creativity at work. *Personnel Review*. 2023;52(5): 1437–61.

54. Valtchanov D, Barton KR, Ellard C. Restorative effects of virtual nature settings. *Cyberpsychology, Behavior, and Social Networking*. 2010;13(5): 503–12.

One

INTRODUCTION

Great leaders coach their team members. Despite the many and varied calls on their time, they make time to coach. They do so regardless of whether they are meeting their team members face to face, online, or switching between the two. Put simply, coaching works. We define coaching as a conversation with a purpose, where the coach helps one or more people to learn and to achieve their potential. Managerial coaching is best understood as a form of leadership rather than seen as a variation on executive coaching (1).

Coaching leaders act with good intent. They aim for positive outcomes for employees and their organisation. By balancing the needs of both, they fulfil their role as managers and their role as leaders who develop their people. They are authentic in their interactions and human-centred in their approach.

Coaching is a practical and powerful way to enact leadership (2), applying the sometimes abstract concepts of leadership theory in real-world contexts. We focus in this book on specific coaching skills which can be used by managers every day, namely observation, listening, questioning, goal-setting, feedback, and reflection. These skills can be used in formal coaching sessions as well as in daily conversations between managers and employees. They can be used to motivate and recognise, to challenge and confront. Much of a manager's work is facilitated and enhanced by adopting a coaching approach, even if the manager rarely if ever holds formal coaching sessions. Formal coaching sessions can be used for career development purposes, goal-setting, or problem-solving. At other times the manager's ability simply to listen is enough. The ability to observe, listen, and ask insightful questions forms the basis for accurate feedback. Adopting a goal-setting approach in meetings ensures that actions are agreed. Reflection is a powerful way to

DOI: 10.4324/9781003239826-1

make sure that managers learn from experience and improve their leadership capabilities. Collectively these skills form a sound foundation for successful leadership at all levels of an organisation. Based on previous research findings and our real-world experience, we provide practical recommendations.

In this book, we look specifically at leaders as coaches, in other words, managers who use coaching skills as part of their everyday role. We draw upon research relating to coaching of managers and teams, where those insights may be helpful to managers enacting coaching with their own employees and teams. We also incorporate findings and insights from research in leadership and other disciplines which shed light on the challenges of managing people in today's complex hybrid and virtual workplaces.

As Google's research established, being a good coach is one of the most important attributes of a successful manager today (3). Any manager who wants to be an effective leader will benefit from enhancing their coaching skills, no matter if their employees are in the same office where they themselves work, in a different office (and possibly in a different country), working at home, or a blend of all of these.

This chapter first examines the leadership mindset required of managers in the increasingly complex and demanding workplace of today. We then introduce coaching by managers. The chapter concludes with an outline of later chapters.

A LEADERSHIP MINDSET FOR THE NEW NORMAL

The numerous challenges facing the world today, such as climate change, war, and a stream of corporate scandals, have heightened community expectations for companies and their leaders to behave responsibly and ethically. This goes beyond compliance with legal requirements. Acting responsibly towards a broad range of stakeholders including society and the planet is emerging as a new business standard (4). Responsible leadership includes ethics and values, systems thinking, and a willingness to aim for positive impact both within and beyond one's own organisation (4, 5).

Companies with a reputation for being ethical find it easier to attract and retain good staff, particularly the younger generation (6, 7). At both individual and team levels, people want to work with ethical managers, which is all the more important because the biggest influence on employees deciding to stay or leave an organisation is their immediate supervisor (8–10). Retaining good staff has several advantages as those staff have accumulated corporate, technical, process, and systems knowledge as well as relationships with stakeholders which will take time for new hires to acquire; in addition there is the time and cost of recruiting new staff.

In the changing world of work today, the role of the manager is also changing. Even pre-COVID-19, organisations were grappling with more varied conditions than at any other time in recent history, a context that has been described as Volatile, Uncertain, Complex, and Ambiguous (VUCA) (11, 12). The challenges identified in the VUCA model were exacerbated by the global pandemic which disrupted working patterns, supply chains, and social connections around the world.

The VUCA context has clear implications for managers, emphasising the need for a learning mindset, creative problem-solving, systems thinking, ethics and transparency, resilience, and rapid evidence-based decision-making and action. These requirements lead to a need for empathy, clear communication, shared understanding, positive relationships, strategic alignment, and empowerment. To cope with a VUCA world, researchers suggest that an adaptive and authentic leadership mindset is required, with a focus on continuing leadership development (11, 13, 14). This aligns closely with a coaching mindset. The importance of leaders being authentic, self-aware, and emotionally intelligent has been confirmed by research in many countries, with there being a strong link between authentic leaders and trust (15, 16). This is significant at a time when trust has declined in many organisations (17). Furthermore, 'authentic leadership enhances the level of workplace inclusion, engagement, and creativity among employees' (18).

VUCA is primarily concerned with the external context and how managers and organisations can succeed in such an environment. A traditional approach to strategy cannot keep pace with the rapid technological progress we see today where strategy needs to be dynamic, agile, adaptive, and real time (19). A more recent alternative to VUCA is RUPT (Rapid, Unpredictable, Paradoxical, Tangled), which considers patterns and connections that impact on the effectiveness of organisations (20). The impacts of a VUCA environment on human beings, such as the rise in anxiety experienced by workers, are reflected in another alternative, BANI (Brittle, Anxious, Nonlinear, and Incomprehensible) (21, 22). This human-centred approach aligns closely with a coaching approach to leadership (23).

Brassey and her co-authors (24) advocate that leaders in a volatile world cultivate what they call 'dual awareness', being aware of both our external environment and our own thoughts and feelings, allowing us to choose our responses rather than simply react to situations. This is consistent with research into what worked well during the pandemic and what leaders should do going forward to achieve healthy workplaces:

> effective leaders support each other and grow in their role(s) by: building personal resilience; practicing compassionate leadership; modelling effective interpersonal leadership behaviour; ensuring frequent and authentic communication; participating in networks and communities of practice; balancing short- and long-term commitments; applying systems thinking; and contributing to collaborative, national strategy. (25, p. 216)

In addition to the shift in leadership resulting from working in a VUCA environment, advances in technology have also contributed to a shift from traditional command and control leadership to agile and adaptive leadership (26). Table 1.1 shows some of the changes in leadership that researchers have identified.

Table 1.1 Traditional Leadership Models vs Agile and Adaptive Leadership Style

Traditional Leadership Models	Agile and Adaptive Leadership Styles
Hierarchical structures	Flat and decentralised structures
Leader-centric approach	Team-centric approach
Command and control	Empowerment and autonomy
Rigid top-down decision-making	Collaborative and participative decision-making
Limited delegation of authority	Delegation and distributed leadership
Slow decision-making processes	Agile and fast decision-making
One-way communication	Open and transparent communication
Strict adherence to rules	Flexibility and agility
Focus on stability and predictability	Emphasis on innovation and change
Resistance to change	Embracing and leading through change
Reliance on past success	Willingness to take calculated risks
Limited feedback and input from team members	Feedback and diverse perspectives encouraged
Emphasis on rank and titles	Focus on skills and expertise

Source: adapted from Pawar and Dhumal (26)

As highlighted in Table 1.1, an agile and adaptive leadership style is about embracing and leading through change, rather than managing resistance to change which is the more traditional approach. Given the rapid changes in the world of work, any leadership approach that increases employee engagement and readiness for change is worthwhile (27, 28). Leaders today also need to be adept at using technology and information in collaboration, creativity, creativity, and problem-solving in both face-to-face and virtual contexts (29).

Adaptive leadership links to complexity leadership, emphasising the need for adaptability and flexibility in response to a complex and changing world (30, 31). Like coaches, adaptive leaders encourage collaboration, learning, and innovation. Complexity makes it difficult for people to grasp the whole picture. Systems thinking, as discussed in Chapter Five, enables managers to see their organisation as a whole and how it interacts with its stakeholders and within its context, thus enabling managers to develop insights into complex situations. A systems coaching approach helps managers to ask questions and listen to the answers from different perspectives, to arrive at a holistic understanding, and to foresee potential consequences. This helps amplify the benefits of coaching beyond individuals and teams.

Adding complexity is that workplaces today are both multi-cultural and multi-generational. Leadership is not a universal constant that looks the same in every country or culture or in every organisation. Leadership is context-dependent (32). This insight into leadership suggests that what leadership means in practice will vary in different roles, as well as in different cultural and organisational contexts. This in turn implies that when people take up a new role or move to a different country or organisation, they need to learn what is required of a leader in their new context and not assume that their previous leadership practices will still be effective. There is further discussion of cross-cultural influences on coaching in Chapter Five.

Multi-generational workforces also add complexity (33). In some organisations, for the first time ever, there are five generations in the workplace simultaneously. Not all generations have the same expectations or ways of working. Gen Z or millennials have ambitious life goals and continue their learning in order to achieve them (34). They have a strong preference for autonomy, for connection, and for feedback. Ljungquist and Lund (35) suggest that a transformational leadership style is best suited to meet the challenges posed by Gen Z. Previous research revealed a strong correlation between managerial coaching and transformational leadership (36), although this is not a complete match (2).

There are many theories that underpin effective leadership in today's complex workplaces. Unfortunately there has been little research into how managers can integrate and apply this wide range of theories (14). The underlying assumption of this book is that coaching is leadership in practice. The notion of leadership has evolved over time. For example, the 'great man' theory, where a heroic leader led their country or company into battle is less common than it once was (37). Command and control style leadership has had to give way to coaching leadership to address the complexity and rapid pace of change in today's global workplace, to meet the expectations of multiple generations of employees, and to lead remote, hybrid and face-to-face workers effectively, ethically, and responsibly.

The numerous references cited in this book enable those with the time and motivation to follow up and read more about the theories that resonate with them. As Lewin (38) once said, there is nothing as practical as a good theory. Leadership is a lifelong journey, and we can always benefit from new insights, whether from theory or practice.

Leadership in Remote and Hybrid Contexts

Working remotely or in hybrid mode can be difficult for managers and team leaders. Previously, managers could see their employees every day. They could note when they were working hard, and observe if they appeared highly motivated or might be having issues. They could bring people together easily for team updates or brainstorming, have an informal quiet word with a colleague to resolve an issue, or praise a colleague for a job well done. The world is moving too quickly for the old 'command and control' style of leadership to be effective. Instead, as Buys (39) highlights, we need to empower people and create a culture of responsibility and initiative. This is even more important in the hybrid and remote world of work, where managers cannot see what their employees are doing and have to find other ways to ensure that goals are met.

Working in the 'new normal', managers have to focus on outputs rather than inputs; for example, has an employee produced the requested report by the agreed date and to the specification agreed? Managers have to be crystal clear in their explanation of what is needed, as they cannot casually observe if a job is being done well or badly. Huber (40, p. 67) suggests that 'Regular check-ins, progress updates, and feedback sessions can be useful strategies to keep everyone accountable and on track'. Clear work guidelines give employees clarity and direction, leading to a sense that their work is manageable (41).

The balance between keeping in touch with people working remotely and not micro-managing or imposing too many meetings is difficult to achieve. Providing explicit details of what is required while allowing employees freedom to determine when and how the work will be performed works well in non-customer-facing roles. For some roles, the 'when' may be determined by customer expectations but the 'where' can be determined by the employee – someone whose work is by telephone or email might work from home. The shift to online and hybrid workplaces is actually helpful for all employees as it forces managers to be more explicit about their expectations.

When employees are clear on what needs to be done, they may interpret negatively any further attempts by their managers to clarify requirements (42). While managers may believe they will motivate employees by regularly touching base, in fact, micromanagement leads to disengagement, demotivation, stress, and anxiety, and is a management approach that is particularly disliked by millennials (43). Without supportive leadership, remote working can lead to a drop in employee engagement and performance (44). Thus it is important for managers to understand how they can help support and motivate workers whether they work in the office, at home, or in some combination of the two. The intergenerational differences mentioned above have a heightened impact when working remotely, increasing the need for autonomy, human relationships, and development opportunities (35).

Despite the concern of some managers that remote working may damage workplace relationships, research has found that this is not necessarily the case (45). Nor does remote or hybrid working necessarily have a negative impact on employee engagement, although it can reduce employee engagement where employees already have moderate or high levels of loneliness (46). Well-being programs targeted at increasing hope and reducing loneliness can lessen the potential negative impacts of remote or hybrid work. It has also been found that employees who feel lonely at work are less likely to share their knowledge with their colleagues (47). Hence, there is a solid business case for well-being programs, apart from our duty of care and our desire to help our employees thrive.

Consciously prioritising well-being and making time for activities that support well-being help both managers and employees to stay well. Hall and Hall (48) suggest a range of strategies that managers can use to look after their well-being when working remotely. These include making exercise habitual, adopting 'tiny habits' (e.g. doing a couple of press ups when pausing for a tea or coffee break), ensuring that desks and chairs are ergonomic, and maintaining social connections. Other options are to take a short walk, or making time for meditation or reflection. It is important for managers to lead by example, to look after their own health and well-being and to encourage others to do likewise. Managers can sometimes feel overloaded and organisational support is needed to help them flourish (49). Fortunately research has shown that coaching managers experience less burnout than others (50). A positive leadership approach encourages optimism and a focus on strengths (51).

Online on-boarding of new employees is difficult, particularly in a fully online work context. The social cues people might observe in the physical workplace are less obvious in an online environment. Virtual presence software which allows people to interact with each other via avatars on a screen are now beginning to be used for on-boarding. For example, Gather[1] allows individuals to interact with one or more people at the same time as well as being part of a plenary session, much in the same way as people might have side conversations before or after a meeting or during breaks. Some platforms can be customised with the colour and visual identity of the organisation and include video clips of people in the organisation, its customers, and the physical workplace. Used together, these features can help create a sense of identity and belonging.

Some technology options may be familiar to managers for other purposes. For example, Bryson (52) suggests that specific groups can be set up in online discussion forums which the organisation already uses for other communications, for example Webex or Slack. Document file-sharing software such as Dropbox, Google Drive, and Microsoft OneDrive can facilitate input to strategy development. The authors provide a list of specialised software designed to enable collaboration in developing and mapping strategy (52). Combining collaboration tools with project management software allows managers to keep track of complex projects as well as nurturing a sense of collegiality and shared ownership of outcomes (26).

There is huge potential for the application of new technology to support leaders in decision-making, collaboration and engagement.

Researchers recommend striking a balance between the efficiencies that can be gained through technology and the on-going need for human connection. In this way, researchers argue, leaders will inspire their teams, nurture innovation, and achieve organisational excellence (26). Combining coaching skills with collaboration technology helps managers to establish positive relationships regardless of where employees are based and also allows employees to maintain relationships with each other. As we discuss in Chapter Three, generative Artificial Intelligence (GenAI) can be used to generate prompts for reflection and thus act as an aid to leadership development. It is increasingly important for managers to be both authentic and technologically competent (53).

With growing numbers of employees working from home for at least part of their working week, managers need the skills to have many different types of conversations online, from simple check-ins and catch-ups to collaborative brainstorming, goal-setting, feedback, and resolving conflict. Such conversations are an important part of keeping employees connected, motivated, and aligned. We can and should work at enhancing our leadership skills, role-modelling our on-going learning and encouraging our team members to do likewise.

COACHING – A LEADERSHIP APPROACH FOR TODAY'S COMPLEX WORLD

The contemporary leader is a coach. A study of managers, employees, and human resource development professionals in the UK, US, and the Netherlands found that many spoke about how managers coach their employees, although the interviewers did not ask any specific questions about coaching (54). Adopting a coaching approach to leadership helps managers meet the expectations of their employees as well as their organisations. There is ample research that demonstrates the efficacy of managers coaching their own employees. For example, Ellinger and Ellinger (55, p. 344) found that 'managerial coaching has considerable promise for improving and enhancing multiple work-related performance outcomes at various levels, and for promoting "human flourishing"'. Given the potential for managerial coaching to have such positive outcomes, it is important that we strive to improve our coaching skillset in order to enhance our leadership capabilities.

Coaching is nowadays commonly described as a developmental activity or conversations with a purpose, whether that activity is conducted by a full-time external coach or by a manager using coaching skills with their own direct reports. It is not about 'fixing' employees with a problem.

Rather the focus is primarily on developmental aspects (54). As careers have become more flexible, coaching helps employees to think about their personal and professional goals, and to take responsibility for their own professional development (56).

Coaching helps raise the performance of all employees. Far from being a 'soft and fluffy' approach, it is a positive way to motivate employees and hold them to account for meeting performance expectations and behaving in line with the values of the organisation. Managerial coaching enhances employee motivation without having to rely on managerial control (36). Researchers have found that working remotely requires a higher degree of self-management (57). This relates to autonomy which is one of the three fundamental elements of Self-Determination Theory (SDT), a contemporary theory of motivation (58, 59). Coaching enables autonomy by ensuring a shared understanding of priorities and values so that workers may make many decisions themselves. The other two elements of SDT are competence and social relatedness. Coaching encourages reflection and feedback to develop competence and also helps nurture relationships.

Autonomy requires the participative and empowering leadership behaviours exemplified in managerial coaching (60). Autonomy and empowerment are related, needing clear task instructions and clear communication, which lead to trust and effective remote working (61). Trust is essential for remote working to be effective (62) and is fostered by coaching (63). A coaching approach thus helps achieve the conditions necessary for effective remote and hybrid working.

Competence and social relatedness are also supported by managerial coaching (36). Competence improves not only through training but also through being coached. When managers set goals for a particular skill an employee needs to develop, give feedback, and encourage their team members to reflect, they ensure that learning by doing actually involves learning, rather than simply undertaking a task repeatedly.

Social relatedness is something we have to address intentionally in the online space, as online conversations and meetings can be focused purely on tasks and information, if we do not make time for human interactions. When people work remotely, they can become isolated and more easily upset. Although allowing time for conversations with staff takes time away from completing tasks, such social interactions enhance the manager's well-being as well as that of staff, and ultimately are beneficial for employee engagement, motivation, and performance.

Individual coaching skills (i.e. observation, listening, questioning, goal-setting, feedback, and reflection) are powerful on their own and even more powerful when used together in a coaching conversation. However, it is absolutely critical to adopt a coaching mindset as well as developing coaching skills. When managers have a coaching mindset, they take opportunities for informal coaching conversations on a daily basis, identifying 'coachable moments' and regularly engaging in 'corridor coaching' (64). Even employees who may be reluctant to engage in a formal coaching session may still respond positively to being listened to by their managers, resulting in improved relationships (65). This makes it more likely that employees will take feedback on board.

Used purposefully and with good intent, deploying coaching skills such as listening and asking powerful questions generates multiple benefits, even if the word 'coaching' is never used. As will be discussed in Chapter Five, coaching can lead to a ripple effect where those who have been coached themselves adopt a similar approach with their own direct reports (66), contributing to a coaching culture across the entire organisation.

There is a great deal of evidence for the effectiveness of a coaching approach to leadership not only in English-speaking countries, like the US, UK, and Australia where much of the research underpinning this book was conducted, but across all continents, for example in South America (67), Europe (68), the Middle East (69), Africa (70), China (71), Malaysia (72), Korea (73) and India (74).

The research base for managerial coaching has been growing rapidly over the past 20 years, with early pioneers such as Andrea Ellinger (75) clarifying the link between managerial coaching and learning organisations and confirming the behaviours and beliefs of leaders as coaches from the point of view of employees as well as managers (76). Furthermore, managerial coaching has been found to increase employees' motivation for learning, leading to enhanced talent development (77). Numerous benefits have been identified when managers coach their direct reports (78). These benefits include increased employee engagement, empowerment, and innovation; other benefits are listed in Table 1.2 along with citations of some of the research studies that demonstrated these outcomes, for readers wishing to read the original research.

Coaching approaches to leadership work in many contexts because coaching is fundamentally about effective human working relationships enacted through conversations between two or more people. Being a coaching leader is about more than merely improving our skillset. For coaching to be effective, there needs to be a genuine positive relationship between the coaching manager and the person or people they are coaching. Coaching further enhances that relationship. Recent research

Table 1.2 Benefits of Managerial Coaching

Benefits	Supported by Research
Employee engagement	(79, 80)
Empowerment	(81, 82)
Innovation	(83, 84)
Alignment	(85, 86)
Learning	(55, 81)
Performance	(81, 82, 87–89)
Staff retention	(90, 91)
Productivity	(67, 92)
Readiness for change	(27)

has also found a significant link between managerial coaching and the engagement of new employees (93).

Coaching and mentoring share many of the same skills and result in many of the same benefits. A study of the factors leading to remote employee engagement found that mentoring was the highest contributor whereas results-oriented leadership did not lead to remote employee engagement (94). It has long been known that employee engagement leads to productivity (95), hence, in practice, adopting a coaching or mentoring approach is more likely to achieve the results that those adopting a results-oriented style are striving to achieve.

One of the biggest influences on employees deciding to leave or stay with an organisation is their immediate manager (10, 96). A coaching mindset is a growth mindset, in other words, a mindset which allows for the possibility that others will experience personal growth (97). It is also an attitude of being helpful, motivating, and empowering (98). When leaders have a coaching mindset, opportunities for coaching conversations arise every day. Coaching managers believe in the possibility that employees can change, and they use their feedback skills to help employees to grow, leading to individual, team, and organisational success.

There are numerous applications of coaching in the workplace from casual conversations to longer term career planning – encouraging employees to be self-motivated and to take responsibility for their own professional development, supporting new employees or employees in new roles, and supporting employees who have been in their current roles for a long time and who may have plateaued or even experienced a drop in motivation and performance.

A formal coaching session may take many forms, depending on the purpose of the coaching. It should not run to a script or aim for a pre-planned outcome. That would be to suggest that the manager already knows the answer and has nothing to learn from the conversation. The best outcomes are achieved when the manager approaches the conversation with an open mind and with the best of intentions for both employee and the organisation. By genuinely listening to the employee, the manager's view of a particular situation and of the possible options may change.

Figure 1.1 illustrates how coaching skills combine to enhance performance. When we observe, listen, and ask questions, we may develop ideas for strategy, innovation, or problem-solving. These ideas can feed into goal-setting or action planning, leading to improved performance. Observation, listening, and performance data also give us input for reflection. Listening fosters positive relationships and readiness for feedback. Relationships are critical as they are the foundation for employees trusting their manager and being willing to work with them. Feedback

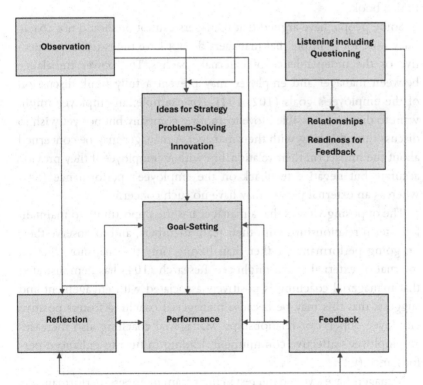

Figure 1.1 Coaching Skills and Performance

also feeds into reflection, goal-setting, and performance. Each of these skills is discussed in more detail in Chapters Two and Three.

One of the principal tasks of leaders is to grow their team members, enabling them to solve problems themselves. Coaching is about learning and development, not about simple information-giving. This does not mean that a coaching manager never gives the answer to a question. If there is a pre-defined answer to a question, then training or a telling approach can sometimes be appropriate (99). The skill of the coaching manager is knowing when to give the answer and when and how to identify and take advantage of 'coachable moments' (64) to help their employees to grow. Research on leadership coaching has found that coaching leads to increases in authentic leadership behaviours and leadership self-efficacy, which lead to change-oriented leadership behaviours, and overall leadership effectiveness (100). Coaching leaders are authentic, self-aware themselves, and help others become self-aware (100, 101).

Table 1.3 summarises how coaching helps with the leadership skills required in a VUCA context and lists where each skill is further discussed in this book.

Some people have argued that managers cannot or should not coach. They note for example that managers do not have the external perspective or the independence of external coaches. The power imbalance between manager and employee may prevent a fully frank discussion of the employee's goals (102, 103). For example, an employee might want to discuss a possible move to another company but not yet wish to discuss their thinking with their manager. A manager may be concerned about the impact on their relationship with an employee if they provide accurate but negative feedback on the employee's performance (64), whereas an external person may have no such concerns.

The opposing view is that a manager has the opportunity to maintain long-term relationships with their team members, and to observe their on-going performance, rather than having only the snapshots that an internal or external coach might see. Research (104) has demonstrated that managerial coaching is positively associated with engagement and suggests that this may be because managerial coaching fosters positive employee–supervisor relationships. Managerial coaching also increases an employee's affective commitment, leading in turn to enhanced performance (92).

Managers have a vested interest in their team members' performance as there are many negative impacts to having to deal with poor performance,

Table 1.3 How Coaching Can Help with the Leadership Skills Required Today

Skill	How Coaching can Help	Chapter
Self-awareness	Coaching helps people to increase their self-awareness, welcome feedback, and prompt reflection on feedback.	3
Innovation and problem-solving	Coaching helps people define a problem (thus avoiding the risk of solving the wrong problem), explore options, and select the best solution.	2 (individual) 3 (team)
Systems thinking	Coaching helps people think about multiple perspectives.	5
Understanding data and patterns	Coaching helps develop people's capacity to ask probing questions.	2
Strategic alignment	Coaching helps by involving people in developing strategy and helps people think through how they can best contribute in their individual or team role.	3 (individual) 4 (team) 5 (organisation)
Decision-making	Coaching helps bring to the surface the relevant criteria for a decision and to agree how these criteria should be weighted, thus allowing for transparent decision-making.	3 (individual) 4 (team) 5 (organisation)
Shared understanding	Coaching helps by listening to people's different perspectives and asking challenging questions to arrive at a shared understanding (e.g. of a specific issue or of the overall company strategy), thereby enabling autonomy, empowerment, and fast decision-making.	3 (individual) 4 (team) 5 (organisation)
Empowerment	The shared understanding and values developed through coaching enables empowerment as team members understand enough to take a decision in line with organisational priorities and values.	2,3 (individual 4 (team)
Positive relationships and supporting staff well-being	Positive relationships are fostered by open and transparent coaching conversations, developing a shared understanding that helps reduce anxiety about the future.	2 (individual) 3 (team)
Communication	Coaching places a strong emphasis on the power of listening, asking powerful questions, and willingly taking feedback.	2,3 (individual) 4 (team) 5 (organisation)
Taking action	By creating a trusting environment where employees are empowered, coaching facilitates action taking, as employees know that mistakes will be treated as learning opportunities rather than a risk of punishment.	2,3 (individual 4 (team)
Learning	Coaching helps people recognise the need to learn and reflect on their learning. Coaching also increases the transfer of what is learned to the workplace.	3 (individual) 4 (team)

including the time and attention it takes, the potential effects on the morale of the individuals directly involved and that of others in the team, and the costs associated with terminating an employee's contract and with recruiting and on-boarding new employees. There is now ample evidence for the effectiveness of leaders as coaches, with some studies suggesting that the impact of internal coaches is stronger than that of external coaches (105). The numerous positive outcomes of managerial coaching listed in Table 1.2 support the case for managers to hone their coaching skills.

Challenges for coaching managers have also been identified by previous research (106, 107). For example, employees may tell coaching managers things they would not normally tell a non-coaching manager, such as their concerns about how well they can perform a task or feelings of being overwhelmed. They do so because coaching helps foster trust and psychological safety. The coaching manager may sometimes experience conflicts of interest between what is in the best interest of the employee and what is in the best interest of the organisation. In such cases, managers may find it beneficial to have a mentor or peer coach. The next section discusses how managers can start coaching their employees.

Coaching as a Leader – Getting Started

The differences between the challenges and expectations of an external coach and a coaching manager mean that training should be tailored to managerial coaching, rather than generic coaching workshops (50). Changing how we behave takes time. Grant (108) found that it took about six months for managers who had been trained in workplace coaching skills to apply those skills habitually. On-going support helps managers persevere until their use of coaching skills comes naturally (109).

It makes sense for a manager who has had little or no exposure to coaching to start with observation, listening, and questioning (as discussed in Chapter Two), as managers use these skills when working with employees on goal-setting and giving feedback (as discussed in Chapter Three). Simply by becoming better listeners, managers develop better relationships with their employees.

Reflection allows us to learn from experience. The manager can use prompts such as:

- What did I learn from today's meeting with X about the customer feedback?

- What was interesting about how X reacted?
- Have I noticed anyone else react like that when I gave them feedback?
- How well was I prepared for the meeting?
- How well did I manage my emotions? Do I need to learn more about emotional intelligence or empathy?
- What other options could I try when I give feedback the next time?
- Where can I learn more about how to give feedback well?

By reflecting regularly, the manager develops their coaching mindset and learns how to be a coaching manager, rather than how to 'do coaching'.

Many managers, particularly when new to coaching, find it useful to have a mental model of the coaching process, as a reminder of where a conversation could go, although each conversation is different. There are many models of coaching. The best known is the GROW (Goals Reality Options Will) model, popularised by the late Sir John Whitmore (102) and often attributed to him. He himself made clear that he did not develop it, but was simply the first to publish it (110). Similar models which add a review or reflection step include CLEAR (Contract Listen Explore Action and Review) (111) and Oscar (Outcomes, Situation, Choices, Action Review) (112). As managers become familiar with what works in their context, they can develop their own model. The important thing is for the manager to be fully present and to be able to weave coaching skills throughout their conversations as needed, rather than slavishly follow any model.

Managers are sometimes concerned about the amount of time coaching might take (113). However, if managers invest time in coaching their employees, they can save time in the long run, as their employees take more decisions and solve many problems themselves (78).

Is Coaching Always the Right Approach?

When coaching is the default mode, this creates a positive trusting relationship that allows a more directive mode to be used when needed. In contexts where coaching cannot be used in the moment, it can be used in retrospect. For example, a more directive approach might be needed in emergency situations or situations where there are tight deadlines to be met, or decisions to be taken quickly and implemented immediately (78). To take an extreme example, the person in charge of an emergency room in a hospital would not stop a life-saving procedure to explore options. Nevertheless, to promote continuous improvement, they could set aside time outside the emergency context for coaching conversations, collective reflection, and exploration of potential improvements for the future. Ibarra and Scoular (37) recommend that managers become adept at situational coaching, knowing when to be directive or non-directive, and when to leave people alone to get on with their work.

There are also times when managers may provide training or mentoring, rather than coaching. The approach adopted in this book is not a purist one that insists that coaching must be used on all occasions. Instead we encourage coaching leaders to draw on the most appropriate means of supporting their individual employees, their teams, and their organisation.

Are All Employees Coachable?

Coachability, defined as a person's willingness to engage in being coached, has been identified as one of the critical success factors for both external and internal coaching (114). Coachability is closely linked with feedback seeking and implementation of feedback, leading to adaptability and performance improvement (115, 116). As managers may not have the luxury of choosing their team members, and coachability is not a common selection criterion even when they do, they may find that some employees are more willing to engage in coaching than others (117). Those who are less willing may nonetheless be resentful if managers give other employees coaching time, perceiving it as favouritism (107). However, even if employees do not wish to take part in coaching, most will value being listened to.

Is Coaching Effective Online?

Despite some managers' fears about the potential difficulty of coaching online, research has demonstrated that coaching can be effective whether conducted face to face, by videoconferencing or by telephone (118, 119), although coaches may express a preference for face to face (119, 120). Researchers have found that managers enacting well-established managerial coaching behaviours can benefit both virtual and traditional on-site employees (121). Indeed, Taylor (122) argues that virtual/digital coaching is actually more effective than face-to-face coaching, and that virtual coaching is now the default choice for leadership coaching. Hunt (123) reported that digital coaching is as effective in terms of behavioural change, self-efficacy, and other outcomes. In fact, some research has shown that text-based and video-based coaching increases people's feelings of anonymity and psychological safety (124). Several authors have reported that digital coaching does not appear to have a negative impact on the relationship with a coach (124). This is important, because effective coaching relies to a large extent on the relationship, with some research suggesting that knowledge of theory and technique only contributes about 15% to successful coaching outcomes (123). Nevertheless, there are still some concerns, with some authors (125) acknowledging that online channels are very effective for information exchange, but querying whether deep human connections can be created online. Concerns have also been expressed that digital coaching can lessen creativity and trust (126). In addition, researchers have found that virtual employees perceived that they were not receiving as much coaching as on-site employees (121). These concerns are likely to diminish as people get used to having coaching conversations in the online space.

In addition to positive relationships, Hunt and Weintraub (127) stress the importance of coaching managers role-modelling the behaviours they wish to see in others; this is particularly the case in the online space as there is less social interaction and hence trust is based on people's observations of what managers do (127). In the virtual and hybrid world, managers strive to ensure a shared understanding of the organisation's mission and purpose, strategy, values, systems, and processes. Involving employees in the process of crafting a shared purpose or mission and strategy not only helps to create a shared understanding but also promotes a commitment to implement (52, 128). This is crucially important in ensuring agile responses in a VUCA world, where organisations can respond much more quickly if employees throughout the organisation can make decisions themselves rather than wait for people in the hierarchy above them to decide. Managers need a coaching mindset and the skills to develop their virtual employees as well as their on-site employees (121).

As remote working becomes business as usual, we also have to equip employees with the tools to manage their own mental and physical health and to equip managers to support remote and hybrid employees. For example, managers need to be sensitive to employees feeling isolated or anxious or having problems separating work and non-work time. A trusting coaching relationship means that employees feel safe talking about the issues they face. If such issues are not discussed, they can result in negative outcomes such as a decline in engagement and productivity, or even depression (129). On the positive side, a review of executive coaching research found that coaching is beneficial for developing psychological capital, self-efficacy, and resilience (130). The physical environment also needs to be considered. For example, if both manager and employee are working from home or from a public place, they need to ensure that confidential conversations are not overheard (131).

HOW TO USE THIS BOOK

This book outlines ways in which leaders can use coaching approaches face to face, online, and in the hybrid work environment. The next two chapters focus on specific coaching skills that are of most relevance to managers, namely observation, listening, and asking questions (Chapter Two), followed by goal setting, feedback, and reflection (Chapter Three). The book then goes on to explore the application of these skills with teams (Chapter Four) and at the organisational level, including in cross-cultural and multinational contexts (Chapter Five). The book concludes with a discussion in Chapter Six of how to evaluate the effectiveness of coaching at the individual, team, and organisational level, how to improve our coaching, and how to tap into artificial intelligence to enhance our coaching.

It is not necessary to read the chapters of this book in any particular order. Perhaps a good starting point is for the reader to ask themselves what attracted them to the book in the first place and what they want to learn about – in other words, to set their own learning goal and reflect on their learning as they read.

Just as training in a workshop is more likely to be transferred to the workplace when it is followed up by coaching (132), so too is the case with learning from reading. Skim reading may spark ideas but the investment in time reading this book is more likely to be repaid if the reader reflects on what they have learned and applies at least some of it in practice. If a team reads sections of the book together, they can define a shared learning goal and reflect together. This enhances the team's ability to support each other.

The suggestions in this book are not proposed as solutions which will work in every context every time. As Harrington pointed out (133) in his research into how organisations tackle improvements, the idea of a universal best practice is a fallacy. Likewise, Thornton (134) warns that she has not yet found a conceptual framework or tool that works for team coaching in every context. Moreover she stresses that the selection and use of a particular tool is only the starting point. It is the ensuing conversation and collaboration that demonstrate if the tool is useful. The coach should not substitute tools for real conversations. It can be easy for an individual or a team to tick boxes and fill in matrices. Unless these tools are accompanied by meaningful conversations, they are a distraction, rather than a genuine aid to effective decision-making and teamwork.

Chapters Two, Three, and Four include vignettes illustrating key points as they may surface in the real world, as well as traps to avoid, and activities related to the topics discussed. All chapters include a list of references to the research underpinning this book for those who would like to read the original research. We hope you enjoy the book and can apply some of what we discuss, whether that be in a physical, online, or hybrid workplace.

NOTE

1 See https://www.gather.town/ for more information.

REFERENCES

1. Digirolamo JA, Tkach JT. An exploration of managers and leaders using coaching skills. *Consulting Psychology Journal: Practice and Research.* 2019;71(3): 195.
2. Milner J, McCarthy G. Managerial coaching: a practical way to apply leadership theory? In: Davis PA, editor. *The psychology of effective coaching and management.* Hauppauge, NY: Nova Science Publishers, Inc.; 2016. p. 353–65.
3. Schwantes M. All great bosses share these 8 traits: yearlong Google study. Inc. Australia. 16 Feb 2024. https://www.inc-aus.com/marcel-schwantes/google-research-says-what-separates-best-managers-from-rest-boils-down-to-8-traits.html#
4. Muff K, Liechti A, Dyllick T. How to apply responsible leadership theory in practice: a competency tool to collaborate on the sustainable development goals. *Corporate Social Responsibility and Environmental Management.* 2020;27(5): 2254–74.
5. Maak T, Pless NM. Responsible leadership in a stakeholder society – a relational perspective. *Journal of Business Ethics.* 2006;66: 99–115.
6. Mishra H, Sharma A. The role of employer branding in the creation of powerful corporate brands. In: Rana G, Agarwal, S. Sjarma, R., editors. *Employer branding for competitive advantage: models and implementation strategies.* CRC Press; 2021. p. 33–50.
7. Chatzopoulou E, de Kiewiet A. Millennials' evaluation of corporate social responsibility: the wants and needs of the largest and most ethical generation. *Journal of Consumer Behaviour.* 2021;20(3): 521–34.
8. Li Y, Soomro MA, Khan AN, Han Y, Xue R. Impact of ethical leadership on employee turnover intentions in the construction industry. *Journal of Construction Engineering and Management.* 2022;148(7): 04022054.
9. Lyons P, Bandura R. Coaching to enhance learning and engagement and reduce turnover. *Journal of Workplace Learning.* 2022;34(3): 295–307.

10. Romão S, Ribeiro N, Gomes DR, Singh S. The impact of leaders' coaching skills on employees' happiness and turnover intention. *Administrative Sciences*. 2022;12(3): 84.

11. Holley D, Coulson K, Buckley C, Corradini E. Wellbeing in the workplace: exploring the VUCA approach. *Journal of Learning Development in Higher Education*. 2022;25: 13.

12. Taskan B, Junça-Silva A, Caetano A. Clarifying the conceptual map of VUCA: a systematic review. *International Journal of Organizational Analysis*. 2022;30(7): 196–217.

13. Murthy V, Murthy A. Adaptive leadership responses: introduction to an emerging classification of Zeitgeist enactments, practices and virtues for a VUCA world. *World Journal of Entrepreneurship, Management and Sustainable Development*. 2014;10(3): 162–76.

14. Hongchai DM, Weber CM, editors. Leadership for technology management in a Volatile, Uncertain, Complex, and Ambiguous (VUCA) world: a review of the literature and a research agenda. 2023 Portland International Conference on Management of Engineering and Technology (PICMET); 23–27 July 2023, Monterrey, Mexico. doi.org/10.23919/PICMET59654.2023.10216793

15. Agote L, Aramburu N, Lines R. Authentic leadership perception, trust in the leader, and followers' emotions in organizational change processes. *The Journal of Applied Behavioral Science*. 2016;52(1): 35–63.

16. Walumbwa FO, Avolio BJ, Gardner WL, Wernsing TS, Peterson SJ. Authentic leadership: development and validation of a theory-based measure. *Journal of Management*. 2008;34(1): 89–126.

17. McLain D, Pendell, R. Why trust in leaders is faltering and how to gain it back. Gallup ; Workplace. 17 April 2023. https://www.gallup.com/workplace/473738/why-trust-leaders-faltering-gain-back.aspx

18. Malodia L, Goyal I. Psychological process that links authentic leadership with followers' creative behaviour. *Metamorphosis*. 2023;22(1): 28–37.

19. Brown S, Conn C, McLean R. Why strategists should embrace imperfection. *McKinsey Quarterly*. 8 April 2024. https://www.mckinsey.com/capabilities/strategy-and-corporate-finance/our-insights/why-strategists-should-embrace-imperfection?cid=eml-web

20. Horth DM. Navigating disruption with RUPT: an alternative to VUCA. CCL. 17 Jul 2019. https ://www.ccl.org/articles/leading-effectively-articles/navigating-disruption-vuca-alternative/

21. Dieffenbacher SF. BANI world: what is it and why we need it? *Digital Leadership*. 3 Sept 2023. https://digitalleadership.com/blog/bani-world/

22. Nataliia H, Olena M. The key administrative competencies of managers required for company development in the Bani world. *Economics*. 2023;11(1): 289–305.

23. Kuusilehto-Awale L, Pulkkinen S, editors. On the relationship between caring and coaching leadership. ENIRDELM Conference, Portoroz, Slovenia; 19–21 Sept 2013.

24. Brassey J, De Smet A, Kruyt M. *Deliberate calm: how to learn and lead in a volatile world.* HarperCollins; 2022.

25. Grimes K, Matlow A, Tholl B, Dickson G, Taylor D, Chan M-K. Leaders supporting leaders: leaders' role in building resilience and psychologically healthy workplaces during the pandemic and beyond. *Healthcare Management Forum*. 2022;35(4): 213–17.

26. Pawar S, Dhumal V. The role of technology in transforming leadership management practices. *Multidisciplinary Reviews*. 2024;7(4): 2024066.

27. McCarthy G, Bird S, Milner J. Change is the new normal – how does managerial coaching relate to engagement and promote readiness for change? Accepted for

the 37th Australian New Zealand Academy of Management (ANZAM) Conference, 2–5 Dec 2024, Wollongong, Australia.

28. Huflejt-Łukasik M, Jędrzejczyk J, Podlaś P. Coaching as a buffer for organisational change. *Frontiers in Psychology*. 2022;13: 841804.

29. Van Laar E, Van Deursen AJ, Van Dijk JA, De Haan J. The relation between 21st-century skills and digital skills: a systematic literature review. *Computers in human behavior*. 2017;72: 577–88.

30. Heifetz RA, Grashow A, Linsky M. *The practice of adaptive leadership: tools and tactics for changing your organization and the world*. Harvard Business Press; 2009.

31. Moore JR, Hanson W. Improving leader effectiveness: impact on employee engagement and retention. *Journal of Management Development*. 2022;41(7/8): 450–68.

32. Oc B. Contextual leadership: a systematic review of how contextual factors shape leadership and its outcomes. *The Leadership Quarterly*. 2018;29(1): 218–35.

33. Mukherjee T, Sivaraman S. Coaching across generations: enabling sense-making in a multigenerational world. *NHRD Network Journal*. 2022;15(2): 189–207.

34. Tarigan J, Cahya J, Valentine A, Hatane S, Jie F. Total reward system, job satisfaction and employee productivity on company financial performance: evidence from Indonesian Generation Z workers. *Journal of Asia Business Studies*. 2022;16(6): 1041–65.

35. Ljungquist S, Lund S. *Gen Z@ work: a changing management situation: a qualitative study of Generation Z in a remote working environment from a management perspective*. PhD thesis. Jönköping University; 2023.

36. Black HT. *Integrating coaching and self-determination theory: the development and validation of the managerial coaching questionnaire*. PhD thesis. The Claremont Graduate University; 2019.

37. Ibarra H, Scoular A. The leader as coach. *Harvard Business Review*. 2019;97(6): 110–19.

38. Lewin K. Psychology and the process of group living. In: Gold ME, editor. *The complete social scientist: a Kurt Lewin reader*. American Psychological Association; 1999. p. 333–45.

39. Buys L. *High-performance coaching for managers*. Randburg, South Africa: Knowres Publishing; 2010.

40. Huber T. *Leading teams: unlocking the power of collaboration*. Amazon; 2023.

41. Jurníčková P, Matulayová N, Olecká I, Šlechtová H, Zatloukal L, Jurníček L. Home-office managers should get ready for the 'new normal'. *Administrative Sciences*. 2024;14(2): 34.

42. Wroblewski D, Scholl A, Ditrich L, Pummerer L, Sassenberg K. Let's stay in touch: frequency (but not mode) of interaction between leaders and followers predicts better leadership outcomes. *PLOS ONE*. 2022;17(12): e0279176.

43. Ryan S, Cross C. Micromanagement and its impact on millennial followership styles. *Leadership & Organization Development Journal*. 2024;45(1): 140–52.

44. Wang H, Xiao Y, Wang H, Zhang H, Chen X. 'Who knows me understands my needs': the effect of home-based telework on work engagement. *Psychology Research and Behavior Management*. 2023;16: 619–35.

45. Gajendran RS, Harrison DA. The good, the bad, and the unknown about telecommuting: meta-analysis of psychological mediators and individual consequences. *Journal of Applied Psychology*. 2007;92(6): 1524.

46. Bareket-Bojmel L, Chernyak-Hai L, Margalit M. Out of sight but not out of mind: the role of loneliness and hope in remote work and in job engagement. *Personality and Individual Differences*. 2023;202: 111955.

47. Cheng J, Sun X, Zhong Y, Li K. Flexible work arrangements and employees' knowledge sharing in post-pandemic era: the roles of workplace loneliness and task interdependence. *Behavioral Sciences*. 2023;13(2): 168.

48. Hall K, Hall A. *Leading remote and virtual teams: managing yourself and others in remote and hybrid teams or when working from home.* Crowthorne, Berks.: Global Integration; 2021.

49. She Z, Li B, Li Q, London M, Yang B. The double-edged sword of coaching: relationships between managers' coaching and their feelings of personal accomplishment and role overload. *Human Resource Development Quarterly*. 2019;30(2): 245–66.

50. Greim EM. *Managerial coaching and manager well-being: exploring the positive and negative outcomes of taking on a coaching role.* PhD thesis. University of Akron; 2018.

51. Cameron K. *Positive leadership: strategies for extraordinary performance.* Berrett-Koehler Publishers; 2012.

52. Bryson JM. *Strategic planning for public and nonprofit organizations: a guide to strengthening and sustaining organizational achievement.* Newark, NJ: John Wiley & Sons, Incorporated; 2018.

53. Musaigwa M, Kalitanyi V. Effective leadership in the digital era: an exploration of change management. *Technology Audit and Production Reserves*. 2024;1(4/75): S. 6 14.

54. Jones J, Lundgren H, Poell R. 'I love and dream of a future where we're all coaches' – an analysis of multiple perspectives on managerial coaching. *European Journal of Training and Development.* Ahead of print. https://doi.org/10.1108/EJTD-11-2023-0181

55. Ellinger AD, Ellinger AE. Providing strategic leadership for learning: optimizing managerial coaching to build learning organizations. *The Learning Organization*. 2020;28(4): 337–51.

56. Pasha N. Diversity, inclusion, and belonging in digital coaching. In: Passmore J, Diller SJ, Isaacson S, Brantl M, editors. *The digital and AI coaches' handbook: the complete guide to the use of online, AI, and technology in coaching.* Abingdon, Oxon.: Routledge; 2024.

57. Höddinghaus M, Nohe C, Hertel G. Leadership in virtual work settings: what we know, what we do not know, and what we need to do. *European Journal of Work and Organizational Psychology*. 2023;33(2): 1–25.

58. Ryan RM, Deci EL. Self-determination theory and the facilitation of intrinsic motivation, social development and well-being. *American Psychologist*. 2000;55(1): 68–78.

59. Gagne M, Deci EL. Self-determination theory and work motivation. *Journal of Organizational Behavior*. 2005;26: 331–62.

60. O'Donoghue D, van der Werff L. Empowering leadership: balancing self-determination and accountability for motivation. *Personnel Review*. 2022;51(4): 1205–20.

61. Gohoungodji P, N'Dri AB, Matos ALB. What makes telework work? Evidence of success factors across two decades of empirical research: a systematic and critical review. *The International Journal of Human Resource Management*. 2023;34(3): 605–49.

62. Blavo Y, Lordan G, Virhia J. Supporting productivity with a 'remote-first' approach. *California Management Review Insights*, 8 May 2023. https://cmr.berkeley.edu/2023/05/supporting-productivity-with-a-remote-first-approach/

63. Ives Y, Cox E. *Goal-focused coaching: theory and practice.* Abingdon, Oxon.: Routledge; 2012.

64. Turner C, McCarthy G. Coachable moments: identifying factors that influence managers to take advantage of coachable moments in day-to-day management. *International Journal of Evidence-Based Coaching and Mentoring*. 2015;13(1): 1–13.

65. Kluger AN, Itzchakov G. The power of listening at work. *Annual Review of Organizational Psychology and Organizational Behavior.* 2022;9: 121–46.

66. O'Connor S, Cavanagh M. The coaching ripple effect: the effects of developmental coaching on wellbeing across organisational networks. *Psychology of Well-Being: Theory, Research and Practice.* 2013;3(1): 1–23.

67. Zuñiga-Collazos A, Castillo-Palacio M, Montaña-Narváez E, Castillo-Arévalo G. Influence of managerial coaching on organisational performance. *Coaching: An International Journal of Theory, Research and Practice.* 2020;13(1): 30–44.

68. Mäkelä L, Kangas H, Korkiakangas E, Laitinen J. Coaching leadership as a link between individual-and team-level strength use at work. *Cogent Business & Management.* 2024;11(1): 2293469.

69. Hajizadeh H, Makvandi F, Amirnejad G. The effective coaching factors in operational managers of Persian gulf petrochemical company in motivation of human resources. *International Journal of Engineering Business Management.* 2022;14: 1–18.

70. Van Wyk R, Odendaal A, Maseko BM. Team coaching in the workplace: critical success factors for implementation. *SA Journal of Human Resource Management.* 2019;17(1): 1–11.

71. Zhao H, Liu W. Managerial coaching and subordinates' workplace well-being: a moderated mediation study. *Human Resource Management Journal.* 2020;30(2): 293–311.

72. Kuan CM, Bakar HA. Managerial coaching to improve on organizational performance: a case study of a multinational company. *Global Business Management Review* [GBMR]. 2023;15(2): 1–19.

73. Kim JS, Park JG, Yoon SW, editors. How does leaders' managerial coaching impact followers' in-role and extra-role behaviors? The mediating roles of intrinsic motivation and self-efficacy. *Evidence-Based HRM: a Global Forum for Empirical Scholarship;* 2023. doi.org/10.1108/EBHRM-05-2023-0107.

74. Rai A, Kim M, Pereira V. How supportive and challenging behaviors of leaders promote employees' thriving at work: an examination of underlying mechanisms. *Journal of Business Research.* 2024;172: 114439.

75. Ellinger AD, Watkins KE, Bostrom RP. Managers as facilitators of learning in learning organizations. *Human Resource Development Quarterly.* 1999;10(2): 105–25.

76. Adele B, Ellinger AD. Managerial coaches' enacted behaviors and the beliefs that guide them: perspectives from managers and their coachees. *Frontiers in Psychology.* 2024;14: 1154593.

77. Mohamad NI, Abd Rahman I, Othman AS, Abdullah S, Ibrahim N. How does managerial coaching affect talent development? The mediating role of subordinates' learning motivation. *Educational Administration:Theory and Practice.* 2024;30(6): 3554–68.

78. McCarthy G, Milner J. Ability, motivation and opportunity: managerial coaching in practice. *Asia Pacific Journal of Human Resources.* 2020;58(1): 149–70.

79. Ladyshewsky R, Taplin R. Employee perceptions of managerial coaching and work engagement using the measurement model of coaching skills and the Utrecht work engagement scale. *International Journal of Evidence-Based Coaching and Mentoring.* 2017;15(2): 25–42.

80. Lyons P, Bandura RP. Manager-as-coach: stimulating engagement via learning orientation. *European Journal of Training and Development.* 2021;45(8/9): 691–705.

81. Ellinger AD. Antecedents and consequences of coaching behavior. *Performance Improvement Quarterly.* 2003;16(1): 5–28.

82. Huang J-T, Hsieh H-H. Supervisors as good coaches: influences of coaching on employees' in-role behaviors and proactive career behaviors. *The International Journal of Human Resource Management*. 2015;26(1): 42–58.

83. Wakkee I, Elfring T, Monaghan S. Creating entrepreneurial employees in traditional service sectors: the role of coaching and self-efficacy. *International Entrepreneurship and Management Journal*. 2010;6: 1–21.

84. Viitala R, Laiho M, Pajuoja M, Henttonen K. Managerial coaching and employees' innovative work behavior: the mediating effect of work engagement. *The International Journal of Entrepreneurship and Innovation*; 2023. https://doi.org/10.1177/20578911187604403: 367-85

85. Wheeler L. How does the adoption of coaching behaviours by line managers contribute to the achievement of organisational goals? *International Journal of Evidence-Based Coaching and Mentoring*. 2011;9(1): 1–15.

86. Lawrence P. Managerial coaching – a literature review. *International Journal of Evidence Based Coaching and Mentoring*. 2017;15(2): 43.

87. Agarwal R, Angst CM, Magni M. The performance effects of coaching: a multilevel analysis using hierarchical linear modeling. *The International Journal of Human Resource Management*. 2009;20(10): 2110–34.

88. Ellinger AD, Ellinger AE, Keller SB. Supervisory coaching behavior, employee satisfaction, and warehouse employee performance: a dyadic perspective in the distribution industry. *Human Resource Development Quarterly*. 2003;14(4): 435–58.

89. Dello Russo S, Miraglia M, Borgogni L. Reducing organizational politics in performance appraisal: the role of coaching leaders for age-diverse employees. *Human Resource Management*. 2017;56(5): 769–83.

90. Ali M, Lodhi SA, Raza B, Ali W. Examining the impact of managerial coaching on employee job performance: mediating role of work engagement, leader-member-exchange quality, job satisfaction, and turnover intentions. *Pakistan Journal of Commerce and Social Sciences [PJCSS]*. 2018;12(1): 253–82.

91. Lee MCC, Idris MA, Tuckey M. Supervisory coaching and performance feedback as mediators of the relationships between leadership styles, work engagement, and turnover intention. *Human Resource Development International*. 2019;22(3): 257–82.

92. Ribeiro N, Nguyen T, Duarte AP, de Oliveira RT, Faustino C. How managerial coaching promotes employees' affective commitment and individual performance. *International Journal of Productivity and Performance Management*. 2020;70(8): 2163–81.

93. Woodard M, Hyatt K. The relationship between coaching behaviors by situational leaders and new employee engagement. *Strategy & Leadership*. 2024;52(2): 6–16.

94. Saurage-Altenloh S, Tate T, Lartey FM, Randall PM. Remote employee engagement and organizational leadership culture, measured by EENDEED, a validated instrument. *International Business Research*. 2023;16(7): 1–31.

95. Saks AM. Antecedents and consequences of employee engagement. *Journal of Managerial Psychology*. 2006;21(7): 600–19.

96. Park S. *Relationships among managerial coaching in organizations and the outcomes of personal learning, organizational commitment, and turnover intention*. PhD thesis. University of Minnesota; 2007.

97. Chase MA. Should coaches believe in innate ability? The importance of leadership mindset. *Quest*. 2010;62(3): 296–307.

98. Koskinen K, Anderson K. Managerial mind-set and behaviours that shape effective relationship building in employee coaching: an integrative literature review. *International Journal of Evidence-Based Coaching & Mentoring.* 2023;21(1): 129–46.

99. Palmer L. *Coaching skills for managers.* Self-published; 2014.

100. Halliwell PR, Mitchell RJ, Boyle B. Leadership effectiveness through coaching: authentic and change-oriented leadership. *PLOS ONE.* 2023;18: e0294953.

101. Kinsler L. Born to be me… who am I again? The development of authentic leadership using evidence-based leadership coaching and mindfulness. *International Coaching Psychology Review.* 2014;9(1): 92–105.

102. Whitmore J. *Coaching for performance.* 4th ed. London: Nicholas Brealey; 2009.

103. Garvey B, Garvey R, Stokes P. *Coaching and mentoring: theory and practice.* Sage; 2021.

104. Carrell WS, Ellinger AD, Nimon KF, Kim S. Examining the relationships among managerial coaching, perceived organizational support, and job engagement in the US higher education context. *European Journal of Training and Development.* 2022;46(5/6): 563–84.

105. Jones RJ, Woods SA, Guillaume YR. The effectiveness of workplace coaching: a meta-analysis of learning and performance outcomes from coaching. *Journal of Occupational and Organizational Psychology.* 2016;89(2): 249–77.

106. McCarthy G, Ahrens J. Managerial coaching: challenges, opportunities & training. *Journal of Management Development.* 2013;32(7): 768–9.

107. Milner J, Milner T, McCarthy G, da Motta Veiga S. Leaders as coaches: towards a code of ethics. *The Journal of Applied Behavioral Science.* 2023;59(3): 448–72.

108. Grant AM. It takes time: a stages of change perspective on the adoption of workplace coaching skills. *Journal of Change Management.* 2010;10(1): 61–77.

109. Milner J, McCarthy G, Milner T. Training for the coaching leader: how organizations can support managers. *Journal of Management Development.* 2018;37(2): 188–200.

110. Whitmore J. Business coaching international. *Coaching: An International Journal of Theory, Research and Practice.* 2009;2(2): 176–9.

111. Hawkins P, Smith N. *Coaching, mentoring and organizational consultancy: supervision and development.* Maidenhead: Open University Press; 2006.

112. Gilbert A, Whittleworth K. *The OSCAR coaching model.* Monmouth: Worth Consulting Ltd; 2009.

113. Ellinger AD, Hamlin RG, Beattie RS. Behavioural indicators of ineffective managerial coaching. *Journal of European Industrial Training.* 2008;32(4): 240.

114. Weiss JA. *An examination of employee coachability and managerial coaching in organizations.* PhD thesis. De Paul University; 2019.

115. Johnson MJ, Kim KH, Colarelli SM, Boyajian M. Coachability and the development of the coachability scale. *Journal of Management Development.* 2021;40(7/8): 585–610.

116. Weiss JA, Merrigan M. Employee coachability: new insights to increase employee adaptability, performance, and promotability in organizations. *International Journal of Evidence Based Coaching & Mentoring.* 2021;19(1): 121–36.

117. Ellam-Dyson V, Palmer S. Leadership coaching? No thanks, I'm not worthy. *Coaching Psychologist.* 2011;7(2): 108–17.

118. Passarelli AM, Trinh MP, Van Oosten EB, Varley A. Communication quality and relational self-expansion: the path to leadership coaching effectiveness. *Human Resource Management.* 2023;62(4): 661–80.

119. Gerrity JP. *A correlational study between managerial coaching approach and communication medium, and coachee curiosity.* PhD thesis. Northcentral University; 2019.

120. Innegraeve M, Passmore J. Flipping to digital: the coach's perspective on the limited adoption of technology in coaching. *International Journal of Evidence-Based Coaching & Mentoring.* 2024;22(1): 35–50.

121. Hammack-Brown B, Nimon KF, Ellinger AD. Examining measurement invariance of a managerial coaching scale across traditional and virtual employee groups: implications for expanding managerial coaching research. *Human Resource Development International.* 2024: 1–26. doi.org/10.1080/13678868.2024.2361181

122. Taylor L. *Coaching in a virtual world.* Independently published; 2021.

123. Hunt P. Keeping up-to-date with technology change. In: Passmore J, Diller SJ, Isaacson S, Brantl M, editors. *The digital and AI coaches' handbook: the complete guide to the use of online, AI, and technology in coaching.* Abingdon, Oxon: Routledge; 2024. p. 49–63.

124. Passmore J, Diller SJ, Isaacson S, Brantl M. Introduction: Coaching in the digital era. In: Passmore J, Diller SJ, Isaacson S, Brantl M, editors. *The digital and AI coaches' handbook: the complete guide to the use of online, AI, and technology in coaching.* Abingdon, Oxon.: Routledge; 2024. p. 1–20.

125. Carvalho C, Kurian PO, Carvalho S, Carvalho FK. Managing managerial coaching: the role of stakeholders. *Industrial and Commercial Training.* 2023;55(2): 295–305.

126. Otte S, Bangerter A, Britsch M, Wüthrich U. Attitudes of coaches towards the use of computer-based technology in coaching. *Consulting Psychology Journal: Practice and Research.* 2014;66(1): 38.

127. Hunt JM, Weintraub JR. *The coaching manager: developing top talent in business.* 3rd ed. Los Angeles: Sage; 2017.

128. McCarthy G. *Coaching and mentoring for business.* London: Sage; 2014.

129. DeRosa D, Citrin JM. *Leading at a distance: practical lessons for virtual success.* John Wiley & Sons; 2021.

130. Nicolau A, Candel OS, Constantin T, Kleingeld A. The effects of executive coaching on behaviors, attitudes, and personal characteristics: a meta-analysis of randomized control trial studies. *Frontiers in Psychology.* 2023;14: 1089797.

131. Hawley R, Turner E, Iordanou I. Managing ethics online. In: Passmore J, Diller SJ, Isaacson S, Brantl M, editors. *The digital and AI coaches' handbook: the complete guide to the use of online, AI and technology in coaching.* Abingdon, Oxon.: Routledge; 2024. p. 212–26.

132. Olivero G, Bane KD, Kopelman RE. Executive coaching as a transfer of training tool: effects on productivity in a public agency. *Public Personnel Management.* 1997;26(4): 461–9.

133. Harrington HJ. The fallacy of universal best practices. *The TQM magazine.* 1997;9(1): 61–75.

134. Thornton C. *Group and team coaching.* London: Routledge; 2016.

Coaching Skills in the Face-to-Face, Hybrid,
and Virtual Environment

Two

Observation, Listening, and Questioning

INTRODUCTION

As illustrated in Figure 2.1, a coaching skillset comprises several individual skills, namely Observation, Listening, Questioning, Goal-setting, Feedback, and Reflection. Each of these skills can be deployed separately or together with other coaching skills, with individuals or with teams, face to face or online. These skills can be used in many different ways such as to challenge or confront an employee, to build rapport, show empathy and support, to help someone think or to help them stay calm, to motivate or to reprimand. In this chapter, we will focus on observation, listening, and questioning, in the individual coaching context. We also explore challenges for managers seeking to deploy these skills in the hybrid workplace, in other words, in both face-to-face and online

Figure 2.1 Coaching Skills

DOI: 10.4324/9781003239826-2

contexts. The chapter includes boxes illustrating skills and activities to help managers improve their skills and potential traps to avoid.

OBSERVATION

Why Is Observation Important?

Observation is an essential skill for leaders, providing first-hand data relating to how an employee is performing and how their actions or non-actions are impacting on customers and colleagues. In a world where leaders are increasingly expected to make evidence-based decisions, having data we can trust is a good foundation for a coaching conversation. Unlike the external coach, the coaching manager has multiple opportunities to observe their team members in their normal everyday work, as well as possibly having additional information from survey or performance data, which can help the manager give specific, meaningful feedback. Feedback is discussed in Chapter Three.

Observation helps us understand when a person is doing well or not so well. When we notice someone doing something well and comment on it, the employee feels seen, which is as important as feeling heard. When we comment on it in public, others see the behaviour being celebrated.

Observations do not tell us why a particular event might be happening. They give us the starting point for a conversation. For example, if we notice that a person who was previously always on time, always dressed professionally, and always completed their work to a high standard, starts to show up late, looking unkempt, and their work starts to slip, the reasons may vary widely (e.g. difficulties at home, mental health issues, or problems in the workplace). The sooner we understand what is happening, the sooner we can provide relevant support to help the person perform at their best again.

Adopting the positive mindset of a coaching leader, we assume that people want to do a good job. If we notice that is not happening, it is our responsibility as leaders to address. Coaching is not a soft option, but rather a leadership approach that helps achieve organisational excellence, just as elite athletes have coaches to help them achieve and maintain peak performance. Failing to address the poor performance of any one individual has a demotivating effect on other employees.

Good Practice in Observation

Observing accurately means noticing what is done, what is said, how it is said, what is not said, body language and tone of voice, and the context in which the incident happens. It provides data and it requires sense-making to turn that data into information.

Observing accurately requires that we not jump to conclusions but rather are aware of the inferences we are making. A useful framework is Argyris's Ladder of Inference (1) popularised by Ross in the *Fifth Discipline Fieldbook* (2). The Ladder of Inference highlights the steps we take when we observe:

1. We choose what to focus on, what to include in our observation, and what to leave out.
2. From our observation, we then select some of the data and try to make sense of it.
3. We make assumptions, draw conclusions, adopt beliefs, and act on those beliefs.

Reflection can help make each of the steps of the Ladder of Inference explicit. As managers, we can choose many different aspects of work to observe, both in the physical workplace and online. If we do this intentionally, we ensure that we have data for all aspects of work, all workers, and all time periods. If we do not approach observation systematically, we may gather more data for some periods than others, or for some employees more than others, without even noticing.

Being intentional in our observation also helps us guard against implicit bias, because, as Kahnemann (3) observes, jumping to conclusions can serve to reinforce our first impression or intuitive beliefs, whereas intervening in this mental process allows us to consider all relevant data before forming a judgement. For example, we might assume that a parent of young children will need more time off and might then conclude that they are less committed to the organisation than others. If we act on that belief without challenging it, we might not give that employee the same opportunities as others. Not only is this unfair and discriminatory to the individual, but it may also mean that we are not developing the employee's potential to contribute to the organisation.

Furthermore, we may observe one instance and mistakenly assume it is a pattern (4). There are many factors that influence the assumptions we make, including our own tiredness, the accuracy of our memories, or other things that are preoccupying us at the time. While we may consciously try to avoid stereotypes and discrimination on grounds such as race, gender, sexual orientation, religion, age, or disability, we may have an unconscious bias in favour of or against an employee based on their previous behaviour, how similar or different they are to us, or what we have been told by others about them.

Hunt and Weintraub note that 'effective feedback is only possible when it is based on accurate observation or other kinds of comparable performance data'. It is therefore imperative that managers take the time to ensure that their observations and the inferences or conclusions they draw are valid. Otherwise, employees can become defensive and unwilling to take any of the feedback on board, even if some of it is accurate.

As discussed in Chapter Three, it is wise to ask employees for their perspective on the observation, particularly if the observation suggests that there is an issue to address and hence a difficult conversation to be had. Box 2.1 highlights how important it is for managers to sense-check before attempting to address the wrong problem or berate an employee for a problem not of their making.

Box 2.1 Observations Are the Starting Point for a Conversation

Scenario 1 — I know what I saw
Tom notices that his team member Mario has arrived late three mornings in a row. Tom challenges Mario on the third morning, accusing him of laziness, having a poor work ethic, and threatening that he is at risk of losing his job.

Mario starts to speak but Tom doesn't want to listen, saying 'I know what I saw. You have been arriving late every day, end of story, either start coming on time, or there will be serious consequences.' Mario tries one more time to speak but then gives up.
Later that day he hands in his resignation.

Scenario 2 — What's happening?
Tom notices that his team member Mario has arrived late three mornings in a row. Tom knows that Mario has been a highly motivated hard-working employee for many years, and this is unusual. He stops to have a chat with Mario on the third morning and asks what's happening. Mario explains that his mother-in-law was taken into hospital with a suspected brain tumour and his wife is staying at her parents' house to look after her father. Mario has been taking the children to school and the school traffic has

been delaying him. He has been working through his lunch-hour to catch up and he has also been doing some work at home once the children are in bed. He is up to date with all his projects. Tom asks Mario if there is anything the company can do to help. Mario appreciates the offer but says he is coping for now. And he promises to keep Tom in touch with what is happening from now on. Mario is grateful for Tim's support and feels safe confiding in him. He is glad he works for a company that values and supports him.

Jumping to conclusions saves time when we jump to the correct conclusion but is risky in unfamiliar situations and when the stakes are high (3). Improving how we conduct observations and use the data we glean from our observations helps us improve the quality of feedback we give and enhances the level of sustained performance our employees achieve, ultimately leading to improved organisational performance.

Observing in the Hybrid and Virtual World

In a hybrid workspace, leaders have the opportunity to observe how people behave both in online and in face-to-face meetings. If a person becomes emotional in a meeting, whether face to face or online, leaders can step in to support that person, offer to spend time with them outside the meeting, and bring the meeting back on track. Similarly if one person is dominating the conversation, interrupting others, being rude or disrespectful, the leader should intervene so that everyone is clear that such behaviour is not tolerated. The conversations that result from these observations outside the meeting will vary depending on what has been observed.

Complicating things in the hybrid space is the fact that a person may find it difficult to speak up in virtual meetings, although they are not otherwise lacking in confidence or competence. For example, cultural patterns may make it more likely that a person will only speak up if called upon (5). Managers can assign ownership of tasks for people to implement outside the meeting and report back on at the next meeting, to build up their team members' competence and confidence. The manager can then work with the individual employee to help them improve their skill at taking part in or chairing hybrid or online meetings, a skill they are likely to need well into the future. It can be more difficult to ensure that all voices are heard, particularly in a hybrid meeting with some people in the room and some online. A manager should observe a few meetings before any discussion with participants, to ensure that what the manager believes is an issue is not just a one-off problem.

Technology exists to monitor keystrokes and online screen activity. However, implementing such technology is likely to result in employee resentment and lessen trust. Bright (6) warns that: 'Behind all of this nonsense are managers who continue to hold views about product-ivity from circa 1900. It is management with a stopwatch and clipboard dressed up in high-tech garb. It was a bad idea then and still is.'

When employees feel they are not trusted, this results in lower prod-uctivity and engagement (7) and increased stress and anxiety (8). Alternatives recommended by researchers include having regular touch points to discuss progress and issues (8).

One of the recommendations often made for remote or hybrid workers is to move away from measuring inputs and activities to a focus on outputs. As Microsoft CEO Satya Nadella points out (9), this requires clear goal-setting and clear communication which enables both managers and employees to have a shared understanding of what is expected and whether it has been achieved. This works well in both face-to-face and online envir-onments. In fact, some of the poor performance experienced in face-to-face settings can be prevented or ameliorated through better goal-setting and communication. In other words, shifting the focus towards outputs is also beneficial for work undertaken in a purely face-to-face environment. What seems like a drawback in remote or hybrid working may turn out to be an advantage if it is the stimulus for managers to move towards a more effective form of leadership – namely, a coaching style of leadership focused on outcomes, clear goal-setting and communication, rather than one that emphasises physical presence and/or micro-managing.

Traps to Avoid

One of the main traps to avoid is jumping to conclusions based on our observation. This leads to resentment on behalf of the person observed who may have a completely different perspective on what was happening.

Some managers value colleagues whom they see more often in the office more highly than those whom they see less often (10). This creates a sense of injustice among other staff who see it as favouritism. Previous research has found that perceptions of injustice negatively impact organ-isational performance (11).

Here are three activities which can help you get better at observation:

1) A good way to check how quickly we jump to conclusions is to observe a real-life meeting or a video of a meeting, with a piece of paper in front of us. On the piece of paper, draw a line down the middle and on one side write 'What I see' and on the other side 'What I infer'. When managers first do this exercise, they often say they see things like apathy or confusion or lack of motivation (depending on the meeting being observed), when in reality none of these things can be observed. We have to ask ourselves what we are seeing that makes us think that we are seeing apathy or confusion or lack of motivation. And once we do that, we realise that there could be different explanations for what we are seeing. We are then better placed for a positive conversation with team members.

2) If we really write down everything we see, it takes far longer than the event we are observing. Try it once and it may raise your awareness of how much detail we usually ignore – do we always notice a person's body language or tone of voice? Do we notice the reactions in the room when a person speaks, or do we focus only on the person speaking? Do we focus only on what is being said or also on how it is being said? Once we are aware of how much we ignore of what we see, we can better guard against bias.

3) We are often not as good at reading body language as we think we are. Explain to your team that you are trying to improve your ability in this area and need their help. Observe a meeting or part of a meeting, and make notes of what you think someone's body language is saying. Then check with them later if you were close to recognising how they felt. This is particularly useful with an online meeting which can be recorded, as the team members themselves may have forgotten how they were feeling in the moment and watching the recording can prompt them to remember.

LISTENING

Why Is Listening Important?

Leaders need a deep commitment to listening intently to others (12). Listening to people shows them that they are valued, respected, and that their ideas matter. Listening leaders are particularly needed in times of crisis (13) such as the world is currently experiencing, as we emerge from the pandemic to face war, climate change, and other global challenges. Unfortunately, being genuinely listened to is a rare experience (14). The benefits of listening to employees are often under-rated. Listening is 'a multi-dimensional practice that requires commitment and constant attention', according to Bryant and Shearer (15), if leaders want to avoid being trapped in a bubble where they only hear good news and are constantly reinforced in their own opinions.

Listening is the single most important skill for coaching leaders. It helps us to understand other people's point of view – but only if we truly listen to understand, and not simply wait our turn to speak and convince the other person of our point of view. Purposeful listening also prevents us from acting immediately on our observations based on untested inferences, a risk highlighted in the earlier discussion of the Ladder of Inference.

Listening helps foster positive relationships (16). This is important as relationships have been identified as one of the critical success factors in coaching, perhaps even the most important (17). Listening is an act of affirmation that 'enables the coach to connect with the speaker and their world' (18). Similarly Cox (14) sees listening as demonstrating care and validation. Listening helps establish trust (19), making employees feel valued as their managers engage with them as human beings, not simply as a pair of hands to get work done. In addition to relationship benefits and helping the team leader understand the team member's perspective, paying attention through quality listening also helps the other person to become clearer in their own thinking and more self-aware (20). Listening, according to Kluger and Itzchakov (21), leads to a temporary state of togetherness between the listener and the person being listened to, which in turn enhances creativity, well-being, and relationships.

Researchers have categorised listening in various ways as summarised in Table 2.1.

All of these models stress the need to go beyond simply listening for information and to move to a more powerful space where the listener connects with the speaker at a deep and meaningful level. Cox (14) draws on previous research to create what she calls an integrative model of listening; this combines active listening and authentic listening with an emphasis on reflexivity (self-reflection) and openness, enabling a coach and coachee to create meaning and a shared understanding.

Citrin (26) suggests that people are 'less likely to be hostile or resistant if they feel that they are being listened to'. Acknowledging people's

Table 2.1 Listening Models

Authors	Description	Features	Source
Rogers	Active Listening	Listening with empathy for total meaning, noting all cues including non-verbal	(22)
Hawkins and Schwenk	Levels of Listening	1. Attending – coach shows that they are listening 2. Accurate – attending plus paraphrasing 3. Empathic – attending, accurate plus using similar metaphors and non-verbal cues 4. Generative empathic – attending, accurate, empathic plus helps the coachee shape their story	(23)
Scharmer	Levels of Listening	1. Downloading – reconfirming what we already know 2. Factual – listening for new information 3. Empathic – emotional connection, seeing through the other person's eyes 4. Generative – connecting to deeper meaning and to an emerging future whole, shift in identity	(24)
Whitworth	Levels of Listening	1. Internal – listening for our own information/ purpose 2. Total focus on the coachee 3. Global – notices energy and emotion	(25)

emotions helps both the manager and the employee. For example, once managers accept that they cannot overcome fear of change with a purely rational explanation and understand that celebrating success not only fosters a sense of belonging but also makes people happy and hence motivated to repeat their success, they are better placed to lead their employees through good times and bad. If a leader can 'hold' the space, and help employees make sense of what is happening, employees can respond better to change and stressful situations (27). Listening is also critically important in mediation and conflict resolution (28), useful skills for managers in many conversations (although they may have had little or any training in conflict management). By addressing conflicts, managers foster harmony and promote positive relationships in the workplace, enabling employees to focus on their work (29).

It can be particularly difficult for managers who are experts in an area not to jump in with their own ideas and offer their solutions (30). If they refrain from doing so, they are more likely to help employees develop their thinking and problem-solving skills. Employees are more likely to devise their own solutions when they find themselves being listened to and their ideas valued (20).

Managers who do not listen to their employees display an arrogance that is to the detriment of their organisation. Organisations with humble leaders have been found to outperform those with less humble leaders (31), with listening found to be an effective way to engage employees (32). Employees who are close to the customer and core processes have a depth of understanding of the current situation that managers may lack, even if they were once in the employee's role. This is not to say that the managers cannot input their own ideas. Nonetheless, by starting with the employee's ideas, employees develop their thinking and managers get a better understanding of the opportunities and constraints. Together they can then build a stronger approach.

Listening is essential for innovation to flourish. Rogers (16) argues that listening lessens the likelihood of one's ideas being criticised, and makes people feel safe putting forward their ideas. As Conn says (33), 'People need to feel listened to. Your people have fantastic ideas, but there's nothing more boring than being told to stay in your lane.' The characteristics of a coaching culture, as described in Chapter 5, are similar to the characteristics of an innovation-friendly organisation (34).

Good Practice in Listening

Perhaps the first and most obvious thing to do when listening is not to speak while the other person is speaking. As Ives and Cox point out, 'If we are talking, we cannot listen properly' (19, p. 144). Nor is it enough not to speak out loud. We should also not be mentally rehearsing what we want to say while the other person is speaking. We need to focus 100% on what they are saying and how they are saying it. The quality of our attention helps the quality of the other person's thinking (20).

While active listening was popularised in the western world by Carl Rogers in the 1950s (16), deep listening has been part of Aboriginal Australian ways of interacting with others for many thousands of years. Dadirri is described as 'a process of listening, reflecting, observing feelings and actions, reflecting and learning; processes which involve re-listening at deeper levels of understanding and knowledge-building' (35). It is used in indigenous trauma healing as well as in more general discussions. This highlights how much we have to learn from First Nations peoples that can help us in the twenty-first century.

Listening is about more than the physical sounds we perceive – that is hearing, not listening. Listening is about being fully present, giving the other person our full attention and making sense of what we hear. Replying on auto pilot with a nod or a 'yeah' is not listening. The presence of the listener is hugely important (18) to achieving the benefits of listening, such as the person who is being listened to feeling valued and heard. Cox (14) discusses the relationship between mindfulness and presence, seeing mindfulness as ensuring that the coach is fully aware of what is happening in the moment, whether in terms of their own thoughts and physical or emotional responses or of the environment around them. Presence includes this awareness but with a focus on the other person. Cox suggests using the term 'being present' rather than 'presence' as a way of emphasising what we do when we are fully present for the other person and sensitive to how the conversation evolves. She warns that whereas mindfulness has proven benefits for the individual, being fully present can be exhausting, creating a need for self-care.

To listen effectively, we should show with our body language that we are paying attention. For example, when someone comes to our office, we might say: 'Let me just save this document ... done ... now let me close that and listen to you properly.' This shows the other person that they have our full attention. It allows us to take note of body language and tone of voice, as well as what is said and how it is said, whereas if we continue to work on our computers while notionally listening to the other person, we are unlikely to perceive anything beyond the words being said, and even some of those may not be heard if we are paying more attention to what is on our screens or to other distractions in the room or in our heads. While curious about what people are telling us, we may also wonder about what they are not telling us, or why they are telling us a particular thing. On the other hand, we should not let our curiosity distract us from a full focus on the speaker (36).

Listening well implies listening non-judgementally. When we are seeking to understand the other person's point of view, we should first focus on making sure we have understood correctly, not on whether we agree or disagree. Carol Wilson (37) provides some advice on what non-judgemental listening means in practice. For example, she suggests not having a default response of 'okay' or 'excellent', which implies either approval or that a topic has now been dealt with. Instead she advocates reflecting back, paraphrasing, or (the option that she identifies as often the best option) remaining silent, keeping eye contact and allowing the person to expand on their own thoughts. Levels of eye contact vary in different cultures and between neurodivergent and neurotypical people, so care needs to be taken that we signal our attention in appropriate ways.

One of the outcomes of being listened to when we have a problem to solve is that we become clear on the issue itself. Einstein once said that if he had an hour to solve a problem, he would spend 55 minutes defining the problem, and then the solution would be easy. We can see this in action when people come to their managers with a problem. If the manager simply solves the problem, that particular issue is resolved but the employee has not learned from it. If, instead, the manager listens to the employee as they explain the issue, the employee will often realise for themselves what needs to be done without the manager telling them. And they become increasingly adept at solving their own problems. One of the benefits to an executive or an entrepreneur of having a coach or mentor is that it gives them a sounding board, a safe place to test out ideas and to get clarity on their thoughts. Managerial coaching makes that benefit available to all employees.

Although silence plays a key role in allowing the person speaking to clarify their thoughts, it is uncomfortable for many people (36). We are used to people taking turns to speak, and often rush in to speak as soon as the other person stops. This is particularly the case in Anglo cultures (5). We may wonder if the other person will judge us if we do not speak – will they think we have nothing to say or perhaps think that we are not very smart and have not understood what they have said? On the other hand, when we hold the space and create a safe place for the person to be silent or to think out aloud, we are giving them the rare gift of attention in a busy world. Indeed it has been said that 'the most valuable listening happens in the silence, when no one is talking' (18). The person we are coaching may be silent before answering one of our questions as they process the question, or they may be silent after their initial answer as they think further about the question. Holding the silence can enhance the quality of their thinking. Allowing silence for reflection can also enhance the outcomes of a negotiation, with both parties benefiting (38).

In the section on observation above, we discussed how bias can affect the data we select or pay attention to. Similarly in listening, we need to be aware of possible filters which may impact our ability to listen non-judgementally and make sense of what we are hearing. These filters include our own cultural background, our age, our gender, our current state of mind, our prior knowledge, our assumptions, the time we have available, and the physical environment (39). Being aware of the possible influences of these filters enables us to hold conversations with maximum effectiveness. We can for example ensure that we take time to free our minds of other concerns before the start of the meeting, have enough time for the meeting so that we do not rush away to another meeting or spend time in one meeting thinking about the next, and check that the room or video-conferencing background is set up appropriately.

Listening in the Hybrid and Virtual World

Just as we should pay full attention to the person who comes into our office by shutting down our monitors and looking at as well as listening to them, so too in the online world we should focus fully on the speaker. Ideally we would leave our cameras on and look at the camera to re-create that sense for the other person of being listened to. By looking at the camera, we establish eye contact with everyone looking at their screen (40). We should not look at other screens or multi-task. The distraction posed by other screens can mean we are less 'present' in the meeting we are supposed to be in, we may lose some of the information being shared, and we are often more tired after such meetings because of the effort of trying to pay attention to multiple tasks (41). Citrin (26) mentions a CEO who has important discussions while walking along the beach, not allowing anything in the office to distract them from the conversation. Parsloe (42) suggests adopting the same body posture in a telephone coaching session as we would in person. We can show through our body language, how we are sitting, and our facial expressions that we are interested in what the other person is saying. Nodding can help create rapport (40). It is helpful sometimes to use an old-fashioned telephone call rather than a video conference as we can all suffer from 'Zoom fatigue'. A telephone call allows us to rest our eyes. Body language is harder to detect in virtual calls, although facial expressions can be very revealing in a video conference. As with any form of observation, we should be wary of forming judgements on the basis of our interpretation of other people's expressions (43).

Listening is particularly important in telephone conversations, as tone of voice is one of the most telling features in telephone conversations and also useful in video calls. Indeed Parsloe says it is amazing how much of a person's body language we can detect when actively listening to someone on the telephone (42). In fact it has been suggested that focusing on the voice rather than on visual cues enhances the quality of deep listening (44).

Emotional intelligence is helpful in noticing the ways that people describe a situation and the tone of voice they use to do so. How fast they speak, how loudly they speak, the pitch at which they speak – all of this helps us get a sense of how the other person is feeling about the conversation. If we have just given some negative feedback, they may react angrily. Even if they say some polite words like 'thank you for the feedback', their tone may suggest that they are feeling anything but grateful. And as we will discuss in Chapter Three, these indicators of a person's emotions on hearing feedback may be our cue to pause the discussion and reconvene when the person has had a chance to absorb what has been said and is ready to move forward. Over time, we also get better at understanding what a particular tone of voice means for a particular employee.

In an online space such as a videoconference or a telephone call, silence can be more awkward than in a face-to-face conversation. People may think the call has dropped or the connection has temporarily frozen. Then both people may speak at once. And yet the benefits of silence are so great that it is worth cultivating our ability to be comfortable with silence in both face-to-face and online meetings. In an online meeting or on a telephone call, we can explicitly introduce a moment of silence, for example by saying something like 'That's an interesting idea, let's think about that for a moment' or 'That's so interesting, don't worry if I don't say anything for a minute or two, I'm reflecting on what you said just now'. This makes sure that the other person knows the silence is intentional and not a technology glitch. If the silence is on the employee's side, the manager can check if the employee wants more time to think or if they'd like to continue with the conversation.

One way to compensate for the lack of body language on an online call is the use of additional chat features, either within the videoconference call itself or on a separate chat platform. The equivalent of a side conversation in a face-to-face meeting, such options allow people to use emojis and react to what is being said on the main call. Emojis can of course be misinterpreted. There is also a risk on some platforms where multiple chats are open at the same time that a person may post a message on one chat that is meant for another. And these days, people also need to be aware that messages posted on company-hosted platforms may be viewed by the People and Culture department or other company representatives at a later date. Caution is therefore advised in using such channels.

Traps to Avoid

Sometimes managers who have learned about the importance of listening try to do so while doing other things or while their mind is on other things. This does not achieve the benefit of truly listening and can make the other person feel that what they are saying does not really matter.

In trying to establish rapport or demonstrate empathy, we might share personal stories. This may interrupt the other person's flow of thought (45). This is something we should usually avoid, although there may be times when it can be helpful, such as establishing credibility in a particular area.

If managers jump in with their own questions and suggestions the employee is not helped to develop their own ability to think and resolve their own problems. It can offer a short-term solution, but the employee is likely to keep coming back to the manager to solve their problems for them. Box 2.2 shows how an employee can develop their own thoughts if a manager simply listens without putting their own ideas forward.

Box 2.2 The Power of Listening

Anne messaged her boss:
'The German team is holding things up again 😠!'
John did not reply immediately.
Anne messaged again:
'I need your support, John. You need to ring them up and get them to sort it out.'
Two minutes later she messaged again.
'Or we should just find some way of doing the work without them.'
When John saw the messages, he could sense Anne's frustration. He messaged back:
'Do you want a quick chat?'
Anne gave a thumbs-up reply and John called her.
'So they're holding things up again,' said John. He said this as a statement, not a question.
'Yes,' said Anne. 'It's just not getting any better.'
'Mmm,' said John and waited in silence.
'I think we should set up a project to figure out what's happening,' said Anne. 'I wonder ...'

She stopped and looked away from her screen.

John maintained silence as he felt that Anne was working things out in her own mind.

'Just wondering, what if, what if we had a joint project group, some of their team and some of ours? We each know our part of the puzzle but if we really want to get to the bottom of this, we need to see both sides.' As she talked, she got more excited.

'You know, I think maybe this could work,' she said. 'I'm sure they're not intentionally holding things up, maybe they just want to be thorough. Or maybe they don't understand our priorities. To be fair, they were only acquired last year. And they're nice people to work with, it's just frustrating when they keep taking so long. So are you okay if I contact their manager and see if they want to give this a go? We can sort out today's problem and start to make a plan. And talk to our own people as well obviously?'

'Sure,' said John. 'Glad you've found a way forward that could be beneficial to both teams. Well done! Let me know how it goes.'

'Will do,' said Ann with a smile as she left the office.

John was pleased that Anne had come up with a way forward herself and he did not need to step in. The project would be a good development opportunity for her and would benefit the company too. He wasn't sure what they and the German team would be able to do to resolve the recurring issues but by working together, they would get to know each other better and that in itself might lead to more collaboration.

Reflecting on their conversation, he was glad they had switched to a video call. Messages were fine for quick information sharing but he found them not as useful for working out more complex issues. It's another decision we have to make these days, he thought. Previously we just walked over to the person we wanted to talk to whereas now we have to decide if we use email or messages, phone call or video call or face to face. But I think I'm starting to work out what works best for different types of conversation, just thinking back on a few of the conversations I've had this week. Might be worth discussing at our next team meeting to see what options other people think are useful for different purposes. He made a note in his calendar to think a bit more on it at the end of the day and then to decide.

Getting Better at Listening

Here are three activities which can help you get better at listening:

1) With a peer or partner, practise listening without asking any questions as they tell you about a workplace challenge. Nod to show that you are listening and encourage the other person to continue speaking, with phrases like 'Can you tell me more about that?'. You can then reflect back or paraphrase what they have said. Continue with this until the other person confirms that you have correctly understood the challenge they face. Many managers initially find this exercise difficult as they are used to jumping in and making suggestions as soon as they think they know what the problem is.

2) Explain to a peer or partner that you want to improve your ability to listen when on the telephone and would like to try to recognise emotions on a telephone call. Pay particular attention to their tone of voice and try to identify their emotions as they speak. Ask them after the call what emotions they were feeling and compare with what you thought you were sensing. By practising on the telephone, you eliminate any visual cues and sharpen your ability to detect under-lying meaning and feeling.

3) In an online meeting, take time periodically to summarise what has been said. This forces you to stay focused throughout the meeting, listening carefully to what is said so that you can summarise it accurately (people will speak up if they feel their point has been misrepresented). It is useful for everyone in the meeting as it helps to ensure a shared understanding of what has been said. It validates the contributions of the participants. And as most people's attention wanders at some point, it ensures that key points are noted by all participants. You can compare the points you listed with the points recorded by AI-enabled meeting platforms.

QUESTIONS

Why Are Questions Important?

The answers to a coach's questions provide a wide range of information, not only factual information, but also information about how the other person thinks and feels. Questions help the other person clarify their thinking and prompt them to action. Questions can help develop rapport, generate options, and generate commitment. When coaching managers ask questions, it is with a genuine desire to help the employee, not simply to satisfy their own curiosity which could de-rail the other person's thinking, prompting them to think along the lines we are thinking. We should focus instead on questions that will help the speaker. Servant leadership which emphasises the role of the leader in supporting others (46–48) has much in common with coaching as both approaches to leadership share the skills of listening and asking questions (49).

People often have favourite questions that they fall back on as they find them useful (50). It is nonetheless useful from time to time to sit back to think about how we ask questions and to expand our repertoire of questions for different contexts, using some of the many resources in books, on the Internet, or questions suggested by generative Artificial Intelligence (GenAI). The type of question we ask varies with the purpose and with the complexity of the situation. In the moment, however, it can be equally effective simply to nod and encourage the other person to continue speaking, rather than to try to come up with a clever question.

How we respond to other people's questions is also important. Making the questioner feel stupid will discourage them from asking again (51) and the organisation will lose the possibilities that those questions may have led to, whether in novel solutions, highlighting risks, or the deep thought that results from pondering insightful questions.

Good Practice in Asking Questions

Questions need to be used carefully, to avoid a conversation becoming an interrogation. As mentioned, we might simply encourage the other person to continue speaking, either explicitly or by nodding and waiting. Another alternative is to reflect the speaker's own words back to them. While this can feel odd initially, sometimes simply hearing their own words spoken out loud helps people to clarify whether what they said was indeed what they meant, whether they can expand on it or whether in fact they can rephrase it to represent their thoughts more accurately. Hearing their own words spoken out loud can also help the person feel validated in the insight they have just articulated (37). A third alternative is to paraphrase what they have said. This helps ensure the coach has correctly understood what is being said. If not, the employee will usually put them right very quickly.

The quality of questions depends on the quality of the manager's listening (18). Someone who listens deeply and attentively to the other person has a good understanding not only of what the other person is saying but of how they feel about it. Three people could use the same words to describe a sequence of events, but one might be defensive about their own role in the incident and perhaps fearful about repercussions, another might feel guilty about their role and not want to delve too deeply into what has happened, while another might accept their role in what has happened and be keen to help come up with a better way of doing things in future. The manager may need to address people's fears and doubts before moving onto problem-solving. And it is by listening and observing that the manager can best assess when the other person is ready to hear feedback.

Questions for Information and Clarification

Questions can help confirm whether our observations are accurate and if we have the full picture. If we are trying to establish the facts, we might ask some open-ended questions starting with 'What', such as 'Can you tell me what happened?'. We might also ask how something happened. If we are trying to work out patterns, we might ask about when or where something happened, who was doing what, and what else was happening at the time. This set of questions 'who', 'what', 'where', 'when', and 'how' helps us to understand the situation. It should be made clear that asking 'who' is not about assigning blame, but shows a genuine interest in understanding what has happened. Such information gathering is often what people think of when asked about the purpose of questions. In a conversation using the GROW (Goal, Reality, Options, and Will – what the person will do next) model (52), such questions help the person being asked the question to describe the current reality as they see it. Being aware of the focus of the conversation at a particular point in time helps us choose appropriate questions (19). For example, we can use open questions in exploring options and closed questions to tie down the detail of what to do next.

In coaching, we rarely use 'why' when asking about something that has not gone well. Although 'why' is used in root cause analysis (53), most if not all of the relevant information can be obtained by using other questions about how something happened. Asking someone why they did something can make them defensive about their own actions. They can become ever more convinced of why that was a good way to do it, as they explain their rationale by saying something like 'I did it this way because ...' (34). There is also research showing that asking questions focused on solutions helps build self-efficacy and is more effective in helping people move towards goals compared with problem-focused questions (54). Interestingly Eurich (55) found that 'why' is an ineffective question for prompting self-awareness, as either it can lead to unproductive negative thoughts or people can jump quickly to a wrong conclusion. Asking open questions about what is happening leads to more actionable insights.

In contrast, Cox (14) argues that 'why' questions can be used to help the coachee and that the concern about 'why' questions is less relevant in goal-focused coaching, where 'why' can help understand the underlying motive for a goal (19). The guiding principle in coaching is about helping the employee succeed in the organisation where they and their manager work. If the coaching manager sees a benefit to the coachee in asking the 'why' question, they should do so without worrying about theoretical guidelines. Guidelines, after all, are just that, rules of thumb that are often helpful, but which can be ignored when appropriate.

Asking clarifying questions helps employees to articulate their thoughts and helps the manager to understand. It is important that a clarifying question does not sound like the manager does not believe the person or that they in some way disagree with what has been said. In the early part of a conversation, the focus is on ensuring that the employee knows that they have been heard and that their manager understands their position. A clarifying question can be as simple as asking a person to explain their idea in a different way. Or it can take the form of a summary with the request that the other person confirm or amend. For example, if the manager summarises a conversation by saying 'So am I correct if I say that the key issue for you is …', the employee might agree or might say 'no', 'not quite', or even 'no, I know that's what I said, but it's not really what I meant'. This then allows the employee to explain things more clearly, provided that they feel safe in disagreeing.

Questions for Generating Options

Simple questions can be used to generate options. Asking general questions like 'Anything else?' or 'What else might be possible?' often triggers further ideas when ideas start to dry up in a brainstorming session. Wilson (37) suggests a range of ways to word questions to prompt ideas, including asking the person to think about what someone else might do in the same situation and imagining they have already achieved their goal, then to look back at their journey and describe how they got there.

Employees sometimes get stuck in their thinking because of the assumptions they are making. These assumptions may be about the person themselves and what they can do, or about the organisation in which they work, about what customers may or may not accept, and many other topics. These assumptions may hold the person back as they do not even consider some options possible. Questions can be used to identify and challenge such self-limiting assumptions, those beliefs that we sometimes unknowingly hold and that constrain our imagination. Coaching questions help bring these tacit assumptions to the surface where they can be considered, and their validity questioned. For example, when looking for solutions to long-standing problems, a manager might explicitly ask: 'What assumptions are we making here?' The individual or team can review those assumptions, keep any that are valid, and brainstorm solutions without making some or all of those assumptions.

A coaching approach encourages innovative thinking (34). Some questions have been shown to boost creativity prior to a brainstorming sessions (34). These questions may have nothing to do with the topic at hand but are used in the same way as warm-up exercises prior to a physical activity, to get the brain thinking creatively and getting people used to building on each other's ideas. One example is to ask people to think of solutions to a different problem but with each proposed solution starting with a different letter of the alphabet. For example, if the set problem is to stop birds flying into jet engines, ideas might include:

Artificial birds to scare away real birds from planes,
Buzzing noises to deter birds,
Covers for jet engines not in use

and so on. Pushing people to come up with ideas that start with different letters forces people to search harder for ideas. Another activity is to ask people to think of alternative uses for a particular item, such as disused offshore oil platforms or fax machines. Again the idea is just to get people coming up with ideas, freewheeling from one idea to the next, without caring how sensible or silly an idea may be.

There are structured approaches to generating ideas such as TRIZ and SCAMPER (34) with a set range of prompt questions which ask about possible substitutes, combinations, adaptations, additional uses, and even whether the idea is needed at all. These approaches are useful because they encourage us to keep searching for ideas. When we have a bigger set of ideas, we are more likely to find some good ones or some which can be combined to form a good idea. These structured approaches also help combat groupthink which can encourage group members to alight quickly on a solution, albeit one which may be sub-optimal.

Design thinking questions ask people to think about the perspective of a potential user of the solution, to explore the pain points they experience, and potential ways of lessening their pain (56) in order to come up with better solutions than whatever the user currently employs. Empathy with users can however lead to people focusing too much on a problem whereas focusing on solutions can lead to generating more ideas (54). For example, a team working for a railway company might consider alternatives to rail transport for passengers wishing to get from A to B, such as buses, taxis, or flying. The manager might prompt the team to think about what is good about how the alternatives serve passengers, for example frequency of service (buses), convenience of being picked up from home (taxis), or speed of service (air). The team might then come up with ideas for combining an on-demand bus service to bring people to the railway station or a long-term plan for a high-speed rail network to compete with airlines. Research has found that design thinking generates a much bigger number of possible solutions (56) compared with jumping quickly to a solution.

Adopting a user perspective and improving the user experience is increasingly seen as routine in the private sector. It is also becoming more common in the public sector, for example, in designing accessible footpaths for people with disabilities and designing playgrounds for all ages and abilities. This approach is not a substitute for interacting directly with customers and users but can help the team generate ideas to test. Co-designing solutions is the next step, working with users to develop what works best for them. A team might alternate between initial conversations with users to understand their concerns, before bringing in other expertise and experience, testing ideas and piloting products with users, and gathering feedback on the product in use. Questions can be adapted for different groups, from getting input from primary school children into the design of playgrounds through to asking for input from retirees about potential new financial products and services. The ability to help people think through a situation from different perspectives is useful not only in generating new or improved products or services but in resolving conflict as outlined below.

Appreciative Inquiry is another option that enables a broader view of a problem, allowing more options to surface before narrowing the selection. For example, instead of brainstorming ways to improve a specific product such as an electric car, an Appreciative Inquiry approach might ask about what would make the ideal electric car if there were no constraints. Freeing people up from the constraints they usually self-impose without even thinking about it (e.g. costs, resources, time) allows some ideas to emerge that may not be feasible in their present form, but which may form the nucleus of a more innovative idea than would otherwise be proposed.

It is also worth remembering that simple prompts such as 'What else?' can help a person or a team to keep coming up with more ideas. Such questions are valuable as they do not impose the manager's thoughts but rather encourage others in their creative thinking. The original question can be repeated many times as long as new ideas keep emerging (20).

Questions for Visualisation and Commitment

Another way to help a person think about solutions or goals is to ask what is sometimes called the 'miracle question'. This question first came to public attention in the solution-focused approach to therapy (57). Variations which may be more appropriate for a business context than a question about a miracle or a magic wand include simply asking what things would look like if the problem had already been solved. This can help the person visualise the solution and then work out the steps needed to achieve it. Similarly, asking people to imagine what it will feel like when they have succeeded, and how their friends or families will react, can establish an emotional connection to the solution, helping to affirm commitment.

Questions for Decision-Making

Once ideas have been generated, questions can be used to help people prioritise and shortlist ideas for further investigation. Questions can also help identify the criteria that really matter to the person or the organisation and whether some of these criteria are more important than others. This needs to be done objectively and in advance of shortlisting, to avoid the criteria being weighted to justify a choice that was in fact made intuitively or for other reasons.

At the right time, questions can be used to prompt the person to define precise actions and timelines, such as who will do what by when. These questions ensure that responsibility for the actions to be undertaken is clearly assigned. Posing these questions too early can shut down exploration around ideas to pilot and result in a sub-optimal solution. Hence, it is better to ensure that as many ideas as possible have been generated, before selecting ideas to take forward. However, once ideas have been selected, it is important to decide the next steps.

A goal-setting coaching conversation may include questions about the importance of a particular goal to the person, and only later should we ask questions that tie a goal down to a specific and measurable aim. The attention we pay in listening carefully can help us detect through the other person's tone of voice or body language if they have reservations about the goal being discussed. We can then ask questions to bring these concerns to the surface and address them.

Scaling questions (58) can be used to help a person or team decide how to move forward. For example, the manager might ask if achieving the goal is a ten, where does the person believe they are now? Different words and numbers can be used depending on the individual or scenario. The manager might then ask what actions could move them up one or two points on the scale. This seems more achievable than moving from zero to ten and often results in practical next steps. Scaling questions work well even when people are feeling stuck or hopeless about achieving a goal.

Questions can also be used to help someone think through the possible consequences of their choices. Such questions might include 'How would X react if …?' and 'What do you think might happen next?'. The manager can then pose questions that help generate options as the person thinks through possible scenarios. This is particularly useful with employees who are prone to acting without thinking ahead and helps them think more carefully about the potential impact of their proposed actions on others.

Questions for Rapport and Relationships

As mentioned in Chapter One, coaching helps foster relationships. One way we do this is through questions that show that we are interested in the other person. For example, if at the start of a conversation we want to establish rapport, we might ask if the other person has seen a recent sporting event or news story, in other words, something where we think we may be able to establish shared ground. Unlike external coaches, managers can build up awareness of employees' interests over time and how best to connect with them.

Joining online or hybrid meetings early allows time for conversation with those who also arrive early. As Hawkins (59) reminds us, virtual meetings can be impersonal. Going online early and welcoming people in a warm and engaging way helps create a sense of connection. In a meeting of a new team or a large group who may not all know each other, people can be asked to write something in the chat box such as where they are located or what the weather like is where they are – simple chit chat that nonetheless takes the meeting from being a pure information session to something more interactive and personal. Hawkins also stresses the importance of virtual presence, of thinking about what is behind us or the virtual backgrounds we use. This ensures that the picture we present is consistent with the message we want to convey.

Managers sometimes have to resolve conflict between colleagues (28). Just as observation and listening are useful in this context, so too are respectful questions that allow each person to articulate their thoughts and their feelings. This may initially occur in separate meetings with the warring parties. Asking each person about their desired outcome can help identify ways forward. Some conflicts arise because of misperceptions. Addressing these misperceptions helps form the basis for a positive relationship. However, other conflicts are more to do with personalities who do not get on with each other. Where this is the case, arriving at an agreement of how these colleagues can nonetheless work together may be the best outcome in a meeting of all the parties involved.

Questions to Challenge and Confront

In challenging and confronting poor behaviour, questions can be used to help the manager understand the context from the employee's perspective and to prompt the employee to consider the perspective of colleagues or clients. Then the manager and employee can use questions to generate options and agree on actions, as discussed in Chapter Three on feedback.

Sometimes people think that their experience is universal, saying things like 'Everyone does this' or 'this always happens' or 'that never happens'. A manager can challenge such generalisations in different ways depending on their relationship with the employee and how they think they can best provide a circuit-breaker to the employee's way of thinking. For example, a manager might refer to something that shows that the generalisation does not apply universally: 'I'm not sure if that's really the case, let's think about that for a minute. What about when …?' Another manager might be more forthright in disputing the statement, stating that what the employee has just said is not always the case and explaining their reasoning. Box 2.3 illustrates some ways that a manager might challenge assumptions and help an employee clarify their thoughts.

Box 2.3   Questions that Challenge Assumptions and Help Clarify Thinking

David was feeling stuck as he tried to work out how to deal with a tricky situation. A valued customer had contacted him, frustrated at the delays and errors in his recent orders. David knew that his colleagues in manufacturing had had problems with their supply chain as well as some staff on sick leave. He wasn't sure how honest to be with the customer. He called his manager Juanita to talk through the situation.

'So what's the issue, David?' asked Juanita.

'It's Pierre Lamont, Juanita,' David replied. 'I'm afraid he's going to move his account.'

'Oh, what makes you think that?' asked Juanita.

'He's rung up 3 times in the last few days and he's not happy.'

'Hmm.'

'And if he moves his account, it will be a disaster,' said David seriously.

'Has he said anything that suggests he is thinking of moving his account?' asked Juanita.

'Mm, well no, he hasn't, but if he does, we'll be way down on sales, we'll miss our targets. I just don't know what to do. I can't tell him about our internal problems,' said David.

'What do you think we could do, David?' asked Juanita.

'Er well, I've already sorted out his current orders so that's okay. I suppose I could talk to Ops. Maybe we need a customer prioritisation list so that if we can't meet all the orders on time, we know who to prioritise,' replied David.

'And is there anything else you think we should be doing?' asked Juanita.

'Well maybe I should be proactive in reaching out to the customers who are impacted by our delays, so they don't just walk away and give us a bad reputation. Come to think of it, the fact that Pierre has contacted us three times, maybe that means he wants to stay with us if he can. I was thinking it meant that he would probably move his account but now we've talked it through, I think it's the opposite. As long as we can deliver, he wants to stay with us.'

'You mentioned not being able to tell Pierre about our internal problems. What makes you think that?' asked Juanita.

'Well I can't, can I?' said David. 'We'd look so incompetent, he'd definitely move his account.'

'You feel Pierre would move his account because we have supply chain issues and staff who are sick,' said Juanita.

'Well, maybe not,' said David thoughtfully. 'He's been with us for a long time and there are supply chain issues across the sector. I'm sure if I shared where some of the delays are happening, he would be understanding, up to a certain point anyway. And he's a nice guy, I don't think he would hold people being off sick against us. The main thing would be to be clear about when he'll receive his orders and keep in touch with him about any future delays. I think I'll ask him about how often he'd like an update and I can do the same for our other big customers. And maybe because I'm talking to them more often, and being honest with them, and showing we understand the problems our delays cause for them, maybe we'll end up with our customers being more loyal than ever. Thanks Juanita, I think I just got wrapped up in thinking about what would happen if Pierre moved his account, and how it would affect me personally, not meeting targets, when we need the money with the baby on the way. You've helped me be more realistic about what is likely to happen and to think through what I can do to make sure that the worst-case scenario doesn't happen. Thanks Juanita!'

Juanita was glad that David had had the self-awareness to realise how he had jumped in his thinking to a catastrophe situation and in a short conversation had been able to come up with some things they could do not only to avert the catastrophe, but that would also be good for customer relationships and sales. Without those actions, Pierre might indeed have moved his account and David's worst-case scenario would have eventuated. She decided to check in with David in a few days' time to see how things were turning out.

Managers use their judgement as to which approach to use with particular employees, depending partly on the manager and partly on the person they are challenging and the relationship between the two. The coaching manager should avoid labelling the employee as a liar. It is the statement that is being challenged, not the person. Once a common frame of reference has been established, the manager and employee can discuss what needs be done to improve the situation. It may be that it is the perception rather than the reality that is an issue. If so, the perception needs to be addressed.

There are times when we ask questions to help the other person reflect more deeply. This may relate to their own professional development or to a work-related situation. Reflection is a powerful aid to professional development, allowing us to learn from experience rather than simply repeat our experience. When prompting in relation to a work-related situation, we can ask questions about what else was happening at the time of a particular incident, whether other similar incidents have happened before (and if so, how the person dealt with them), and help the person to think beyond a simple description of the events. Once the incident has been fully explored, we may then want to shift to problem-solving or goal-setting mode, or to switch from one on one to a group session. The aim is to extract maximum learning from the event. If the event was a negative one, then the problem-solving response should aim not only to address the particular issue but also to address any underlying or systemic issues with the intent of preventing a recurrence. Adopting a reflective approach may also identify areas for professional development for individuals or teams. Reflection is discussed further in Chapter Three and team coaching in Chapter Four.

Just as we need to minimise bias in our observations and our listening, we also need to reduce bias in the way we ask questions. While certain questions should not be asked, such as those that are discriminatory and illegal in many countries (e.g. questions relating to ethnicity, gender, age, or other forms of discrimination), Hart et al. (60) found that people generally overestimated how sensitive other people would be to sensitive questions and the potential impact on their relationship if the other person reacted negatively. This was the case regardless of whether conversations took place online or face to face. Some biases are quite obvious, such as if a coaching manager only coaches people below a certain age because they believe that older people do not have the potential to grow. Bias may reveal itself in subtle ways, such as paying more attention to some aspects of what the client is saying than others. The coaching manager needs to reflect on their coaching conversations to identify where they may be displaying bias.

By thinking in advance about the person or people we are going to coach, we can have a range of questions ready in our toolkit which we can tailor during the meeting depending on how the conversation is going. In other words, being prepared does not mean having a script which we read out regardless of what the other person says or how they react. Rather, it means that in the moment we can be fully present with the other person, and able to draw effortlessly on our repertoire of possible questions to help them move forward. As mentioned earlier, there are many effective alternatives to asking questions, such as paraphrasing or simply encouraging the speaker to continue. The coaching manager should not get so concerned with asking the next clever question that they stop focusing on what the employee is saying.

Questions in the Hybrid and Virtual World

Working from home blurs the divide between one's work life and one's home life, for example allowing people to see their colleagues' homes, children, or pets on a videoconference. Managers in the hybrid workspace should make an effort to relate to the whole person, posing some questions about their employees' life outside work as a way of demonstrating that they care. How they do this will vary in different cultures, as discussed in Chapter Five.

Some questions can seem more abrupt online than face to face. Tone of voice and body language can soften the effect, as can alternating questions with paraphrasing and encouragement to the speaker to continue. The Centre for Creative Leadership suggests that leaders think about a time when they have previously experienced the emotion they wish to project in an upcoming meeting so that they are drawing on an authentic experience (43). Just as people lean in towards a table in a face-to-face meeting, so too they can lean into the camera for a virtual meeting. Varying pace and intonation and speaking with enthusiasm work in both face-to-face and online settings.

Email can make communication and conflict worse, with emails which are perceived as neutral by the sender sometimes perceived as negative by recipients (26). Leaders therefore should pause before initiating or replying to an email, before deciding whether to communicate by email, in person, online, or by telephone. The choice might depend on some practical aspects, such as the location of the recipient, and on criteria such as the nature of the topic to be discussed. For example, a complex topic likely to arouse an emotional response is best discussed face to face or by video conference, to allow managers to observe body language and to adapt their message depending on how the conversation evolves.

Summarising and paraphrasing are particularly important in the virtual world as the lack of visual cues can increase the risk of misunderstandings (26). To compensate for the less personal nature of the interaction, the manager can include some of the emotional aspect of the message in their paraphrasing. Metaphors can be useful in sense-making (61). For example, if a person describes feeling like they are drowning in paperwork, the manager might explore what might make a good lifebuoy, life vest, or lifeboat, and might also explore if there are things that might help the person swim better, or ways of lowering the water levels (i.e. volume of paperwork) so that the person does not drown. By using the same metaphor as the team member, they demonstrate that they are on the same wavelength and relate to their scenario.

Brainstorming ideas is perfectly possible in the online world, and can be facilitated with a wide range of tools (62), from the use of Artificial Intelligence prompts to spark ideas to collaboration software and mind-mapping tools included on platforms like Microsoft Teams and Webex. It is worthwhile experimenting with these tools in advance in order to make the most of the time when the team is together. The use of these tools has allowed innovation to flourish online in recent years, whereas previously co-location had advantages for innovation compared with working remotely (63).

Traps to Avoid

Using a pre-prepared list of questions. As Cox (14) points out, questions are contextual, depending on the task at hand and the people involved. It can be helpful to develop a selection of questions we find useful, but not with the intent of always asking specific questions, regardless of what direction the conversation takes.

Spending too much time thinking up clever questions is counter-productive. It is more important to be fully present and listen to the other person.

Asking too many questions one after the other can be intimidating and not conducive to the employee coming up with their own ideas. Alternating questions with silence or with affirming statements and body language to show we are listening can encourage the other person to continue to think out loud.

Avoid asking leading questions which are really suggestions in disguise. Because the manager is the boss, their questions may be taken as a recommendation for the other person to act upon. This does not help the employee to develop their own thinking. Rather than ask 'Have you thought about x?', ask an open question such as 'What ideas do you have?' so that the employee genuinely gets the opportunity to put their idea forward.

Getting Better at Asking Questions

Here are three activities which can help you get better at asking questions:

1. Practise with two peers who also want to improve. One person acts as the manager listening to an employee, and asking some questions as they talk about a workplace challenge. Another peer observes. Each person shares their reflection and feedback after each role play. Each person takes a turn at being the manager, the employee and the observer.

   Try varying the ratio of how many questions you ask compared to how many summarising or paraphrasing statements you make. If your natural inclination is to pepper the other person with questions, try listening without asking questions or asking only one question at a time and listen intently to the answer before deciding how to follow up.
2. Ask questions that help the coachee to think. If, for example, they have an idea for improving a bottleneck situation, ask them how the solution might work for all the stakeholders, to help them think about different perspectives, foresee possible impacts, and improve the design of their solution.
3. Use a generative AI tool as a learning tool to suggest questions to keep from getting stale. As noted above, this is not to use the same set of questions to ask regardless of what an employee might say, but rather to have a range of questions which may prove useful in some contexts. For example, if you ask Microsoft Copilot for questions that a coaching manager might use to help an employee to think more deeply, Copilot instantly suggests several options including:

What assumptions are you making about this situation? Encourages employees to examine their underlying beliefs and biases.

What is the root cause of the challenge you're facing? Explores the fundamental reasons behind the issue.

How does this align with your core values? Prompts reflection on personal values and ethical considerations.

What alternative perspectives could you consider? Encourages openness to diverse viewpoints.

IN CLOSING

The coaching manager's ability to observe, to listen, and to ask questions helps establish a positive relationship between manager and employee. Observation provides data that can be the basis for feedback and reflection, leading to growth and development. Listening is one of the most powerful and yet often underestimated actions to ensure that the manager truly understands the perspective of others. Coupled with a coaching mindset, observation, listening, and questioning provide a sound foundation for meaningful goal-setting, effective feedback, and learning through reflection. These latter coaching skills will be explored in the next chapter.

REFERENCES

1. Argyris C. The executive mind and double-loop learning. *Organizational Dynamics.* 1982;11(2): 5–22.
2. Ross R, The ladder of inference. In: Senge PM et al, editors. *The fifth discipline fieldbook.* Doubleday: New York; 1994. p. 242–52.
3. Kahneman D. *Thinking, fast and slow.* New York: Macmillan; 2011.
4. Hunt JM, Weintraub JR. *The coaching manager: developing top talent in business.* 3rd ed. Los Angeles: Sage; 2017.
5. Meyer E. *The culture map.* New York: Public Affairs; 2015.
6. Bright J. Why 'green-dot' obsessed managers are ruining remote work. *Sydney Morning Herald.* 23 May 2024. https://www.smh.com.au/business/workplace/why-green-dot-obsessed-managers-are-ruining-remote-work-20240523-p5jg36.html
7. Spataro J. Microsoft: 'Using technology to spy on people at work is not the answer'. *Fortune.* 22 Sept 2022. https://fortune.com/2022/09/22/microsoft-technology-surveillance-employee-work-jared-spataro/
8. Chan XW et al. Work, life and COVID-19: a rapid review and practical recommendations for the post-pandemic workplace. *Asia Pacific Journal of Human Resources.* 2023;61(2): 257–76.
9. Thier J. Microsoft's remote-work-friendly CEO puts his finger on the big problem with working from home. *Fortune.* 18 Oct 2022. https://fortune.com/2022/10/17/microsoft-ceo-satya-nadella-remote-work-problem-productivity-paranoia/amp/
10. Hill NS. Leadership strategies for the hybrid workforce. *MIT Sloan Management Review.* 24 April 2023. https://sloanreview.mit.edu/article/leadership-strategies-for-the-hybrid-workforce/
11. Sarwar A, Muhammad L. Impact of employee perceptions of mistreatment on organizational performance in the hotel industry. *International Journal of Contemporary Hospitality Management.* 2020;32(1): 230–248.
12. Spears LC. Character and servant leadership: ten characteristics of effective, caring leaders. *The Journal of Virtues & Leadership.* 2010;1(1): 25–30.
13. Durning SJ, Cervero RM, Roberts LW. The need for listening leaders. *Academic Medicine.* 2022;97(2): 165–6.
14. Cox E. *Coaching understood.* London: Sage; 2013.

15. Leavy B. Bryant and Sharer: seven challenges most likely to make-or-break leaders. *Strategy & Leadership*. 2021;49(2): 22–28.

16. Rogers CR, Farson R. Active listening. In: Newman RG, Danziger MA, CohenM, editors. *Communication in business today*. Heath and Company: Washington, DC; 1957.

17. Bluckert P. Critical factors in executive coaching – the coaching relationship. *Industrial and Commercial Training*. 2005;37(6/7): 336.

18. Burt S. *The art of listening in coaching and mentoring*. Abingdon, Oxon.: Routledge; 2019.

19. Ives Y, Cox E. *Goal-focused coaching: theory and practice*. Abingdon, Oxon.: Routledge; 2012.

20. Kline N. *Time to think, listening to ignite the human mind*. London: Ward, Lock, Cassell; 1999.

21. Kluger AN, Itzchakov G. The power of listening at work. *Annual Review of Organizational Psychology and Organizational Behavior*. 2022;9: 121–46.

22. Rogers CR. The necessary and sufficient conditions of therapeutic personality change. *Journal of Consulting Psychology*. 1957; 21(2): 95.

23. Hawkins P, Schwenk G. The interpersonal relationship in the training and supervision of coaches. In: Palmer S, McDowall A, editors. *The coaching relationship*. Abingdon, Oxon.: Routledge; 2010. p. 221–39.

24. Scharmer O. *Theory U: leading from the future as it emerges*. Cambridge, MA: Society for Organizational Learning; 2007.

25. Whitworth L, Kinsey-House H, Sandahl P. *Coactive Coaching*. Palo Alto: Davies Black Publishing; 2007.

26. DeRosa D, Citrin JM, *Leading at a distance: practical lessons for virtual success*. Hoboken; John Wiley & Sons; 2021.

27. Petriglieri G. The psychology behind effective crisis leadership. *Harvard Business Review* 22 Apr 2020. https://hbr.org/2020/04/the-psychology-behind-effective-crisis-leadership.

28. Kline N. *More time to think*. Pool-in-Wharfedale: Fisher King; 2009.

29. Mohamad NI et al. How does managerial coaching affect talent development? The mediating role of subordinates' learning motivation. *Educational Administration: Theory and Practice*. 2024;30(6): 3554–68.

30. Milner J. The motivational micromanager. *Organizational Dynamics*. 2024; 53(3): 101054.

31. Ou AY, Waldman DA, Peterson SJ. Do humble CEOs matter? An examination of CEO humility and firm outcomes. *Journal of Management*. 2018;44(3): 1147–73.

32. Owens BP, Johnson MD, Mitchell TR. Expressed humility in organizations: implications for performance, teams, and leadership. *Organization Science*. 2013;24(5): 1517–38.

33. Brown S, Conn C, McLean R. Why strategists should embrace imperfection. *McKinsey Quarterly*. 8 April 2024. https://www.mckinsey.com/capabilities/strategy-and-corporate-finance/our-insights/why-strategists-should-embrace-imperfection?cid=eml-web

34. McCarthy G. *Coaching and mentoring for business*. London: Sage; 2014.

35. Burgess C, Grice C, Wood J. Leading by listening: why Aboriginal voices matter in creating a world worth living in. In: Reimer KE, Kaukko M, Windsor S, Mahon K, Kemmis S, editors. *Living well in a world worth living in for all*, volume 1: *Current practices of social justice, sustainability and wellbeing*. Singapore: Springer Nature; 2023. p. 115–36.

36. Franklin M. *The HeART of laser-focused coaching: a revolutionary approach to masterful coaching*. Thomas Noble Books; 2019.

37. Wilson C. *Performance coaching: a complete guide to best practice coaching and training*. London: Kogan Page Publishers; 2020.

38. Bareket-Bojmel L, Chernyak-Hai L, Margalit M. Out of sight but not out of mind: the role of loneliness and hope in remote work and in job engagement. *Personality and Individual Differences.* 2023;202: 111955.

39. Thompson K et al. *Learning to listen, listening to learn.* Milwaukee, MD: Alverno College Institute; 2007.

40. Hall K, Hall A. *Leading remote and virtual teams: Managing yourself and others in remote and hybrid teams or when working from home.* Crowthorne, Berks.: Global Integration; 2021.

41. Cao H et al. Large scale analysis of multitasking behavior during remote meetings. Proceedings of the 2021 CHI Conference on Human Factors in Computing Systems. Yokohama, 8–13 May 2021. Association for Computing Machinery.

42. Parsloe E, Leedham M. *Coaching and mentoring, practical conversations to improve learning.* 2nd ed. London: Kogan Page; 2009.

43. Center for Creative Leadership. How to improve your virtual communication: tips for leaders. CCL, 14 Jan 2023. https://www.ccl.org/articles/leading-effectively-articles/how-to-craft-your-persona-for-effective-virtual-communication/

44. Tawadros T. Video-mediated coaching. In: Passmore J et al., editors. *The digital and AI coaches' handbook: the complete guide to the use of online, AI, and technology in coaching.* Abingdon, Oxon.: Routledge; 2024. p. 89–100.

45. Minehart K, Symon BB, Rock LK. What's your listening style? *Harvard Business Review.* 31 May 2022. https://hbr.org/2022/05/whats-your-listening-style

46. Pawar A et al. Organizational servant leadership. *International Journal of Educational Administration, Management, and Leadership.* 2020;1(2): 63–76.

47. Winston BE. Relationship of servant leadership, perceived organizational support, and work-family conflict with employee well-being. *Servant Leadership: Theory & Practice.* 2022;9(1): 2.

48. Winston BE. *Servant leadership and employees' well-being: a workplace of passionate, peaceful, and productive people.* In: Dhiman SK and Robert GE, editors. *The Palgrave Handbook of Servant Leadership.* Switzerland: Springer; 2023. p. 93–115.

49. Blanchard K. Coaching and servant leadership go hand in hand. 2021 https://www.linkedin.com/pulse/coaching-servant-leadership-go-hand-ken-blanchard/.

50. Rostron SS. *Business coaching international.* London: Karnac; 2009.

51. McLean R, Conn C. *The imperfectionists: strategic mindsets for uncertain times.* Hoboken, NJ: Wiley; 2023.

52. Whitmore J. *Coaching for performance.* 4th ed. London: Nicholas Brealey; 2009.

53. Gangidi P. A systematic approach to root cause analysis using 3× 5 why's technique. *International Journal of Lean Six Sigma.* 2018;10(1): 295–310.

54. Grant AM, O'Connor SA. The differential effects of solution-focused and problem-focused coaching questions: a pilot study with implications for practice. *Industrial and Commercial Training.* 2010;42(2): 102–11.

55. Eurich T. What self-awareness really is (and how to cultivate it). *Harvard Business Review.* 4 Jan 2018. https://hbr.org/2018/01/what-self-awareness-really-is-and-how-to-cultivate-it

56. Carlgren L, Rauth I, Elmquist M. Framing design thinking: the concept in idea and enactment. *Creativity and Innovation Management.* 2016;25(1): 38–57.

57. Stark MD, Kim JS, Lehmann P. Solution-focused brief therapy training: what's useful when training is brief? *Journal of Systemic Therapies.* 2018;37(2): 44–63.

58. Visser CF. The origin of the solution-focused approach. *International Journal of Solution-Focused Practices.* 2013;1(1): 10–17.

59. Hawkins P. *Leadership team coaching: developing collective transformational leadership.* E-book ed. : Kogan Page; 2021.

60. Hart E, VanEpps EM, Schweitzer ME. The (better than expected) consequences of asking sensitive questions. *Organizational Behavior and Human Decision Processes.* 2021;162: 136–54.

61. Thompson R. Coaching and mentoring with metaphor. *International Journal of Evidence Based Coaching and Mentoring.* 2021(S15): 212–28.

62. Cooperrider DL, Fry R. Appreciative inquiry in a pandemic: an improbable pairing. *The Journal of Applied Behavioral Science.* 2020;56(3): 266–71.

63. Tsipursky G. The myth that remote work stifles innovation and creativity is gaining ground–but the same evidence shows that it was only true in the pre-2010s workplace. *Fortune.* 3 Jan 2024 https://fortune.com/2024/01/03/myth-remote-work-stifles-innovation-creativity-evidence-true-workplace-careers-gleb-tsipursky/

Three

Goal-Setting, Feedback, and Reflection

Figure 3.1 Coaching Skills

INTRODUCTION

A coaching skillset, as introduced in Chapter Two, comprises several individual coaching skills. Following the introduction of observation, listening, and questioning in the last chapter, we now go on to discuss the remaining three critical coaching skills for managers, namely goal-setting, feedback, and reflection. We will discuss each of these in the individual coaching context. Team coaching will be discussed in Chapter Four. Individual alignment with organisational goals is discussed in this chapter while organisational goal-setting is discussed in Chapter Five.

Goal-setting is a long-established requirement in many organisations, although there have been criticisms of how a strict focus on objectives

DOI: 10.4324/9781003239826-3

can lead to unethical behaviour or to people 'gaming the system' (1). Nonetheless there is general support for goals at both individual and organisational levels. Goal-setting can be a highly motivational process when managers adopt a coaching mindset and consider the interest of the employees as well as the organisation, seeking the best for both. Agreed goals provide a baseline for feedback on how an employee makes progress towards their goals and creates a shared understanding of whether or not goals have been achieved. Regular conversations on progress towards goals helps maintain focus on their achievement and avoids surprises when the final deadline arrives.

Where a coaching relationship exists, it is easy for managers to give and to receive feedback. Feedback skills can be used to address performance issues as well as to give recognition. Even when a conversation is difficult, the trust established through coaching allows that feedback to be given in a positive way, making it more likely that the feedback will be accepted.

Following a discussion of goals and feedback in the virtual as well as the face-to-face environment, this chapter reviews reflection, as a way to learn from experience, feedback, and other data points, in order to continue to improve. The chapter also includes boxes illustrating skills, practical activities, and potential traps to avoid.

GOAL-SETTING

Why Is Goal-Setting Important?

The true power of goal-setting lies in identifying how individuals and teams can contribute to the overall strategy and goals of the organisation as well as to an individual employee's motivation. This alignment, when achieved with genuine consideration of the goals of the individual, accelerates the organisation's progress towards execution of its strategy. Goal setting is a common feature of coaching (2), helping people to recognise the gap between where they are now and where they want to be, and to identify options for how to get there. The skill of the leader as coach is to prompt employees to think further ahead than they might otherwise do, to challenge them to consider alternative paths to their goals, and only to tie goals down to specifics when meaningful goals have been identified. Coaching has been shown to increase the likelihood of achieving goals (3). This makes it all the more important to ensure that the goals chosen are meaningful.

Coaching goal-setting sessions help employees feel seen, heard, and valued. Managers learn what is important to employees and how the employees see themselves. Employees become clearer on what is important to them and on how they contribute to the organisation. Research has found that when workers understand the importance of what they do, their motivation and performance improves, particularly when they understand the impact of what they do on others (4). Agreed goals are more powerful than imposed goals and more likely to be achieved when there is a shared understanding.

A goal which is important to the individual provides intrinsic motivation, which is associated with personal growth and well-being (5, p. 223). There is ample evidence that goal-setting can motivate people to work harder and to use discretionary effort to achieve their goals. This effect can also be seen outside the workplace, for example, when people walk extra steps to achieve their daily target or spend longer on a computer game in order to attain the next level. Latham and Locke (6) found that specific goals that were neither too difficult nor too easy were most likely to motivate people to achieve a higher level of performance. If goals are seen as too difficult, employees may not even try to achieve them, whereas if they are too easy, employees may not use the discretionary effort they are capable of.

Several types of goals are relevant in the workplace. All are important and, if done well, they contribute to the success of both the organisation and the individual. Ives and Cox (2) suggest that there is a hierarchy of goals, at the top of which are abstract goals which drive intermediate goals which in turn drive concrete goals. An example of an abstract goal might relate to climate action or helping to create a better world, the importance of which the person feels deeply. As more organisations seek to address the UN Sustainable Development Goals (SDGs) and Environment Social and Governance (ESG) obligations, it is easier for individuals and organisations to align their goals with these broader society goals. Perceptions of social impact increase motivation and lead to improved performance (4). Explicitly addressing ESG encourages potential employees to see the organisation as a desirable place to work and improves staff retention (7).

Within an organisation, there are overall organisational goals, team or unit goals, and individual goals as shown in Figure 3.2. Meaningful personal goals are long term while teams and organisations with a short-term perspective set short-term goals. Some cultures have a long-term orientation which would place their goal-setting in the top right quadrant of Figure 3.2.

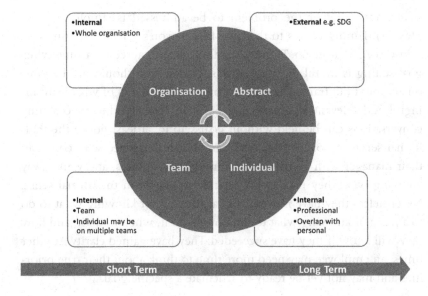

Figure 3.2 Types of Goals

For all these types of goals, there is a need to define clear expectations and to create a shared vision of what success looks like. The more that goals are aligned, the less stress there will be for employees trying to achieve all of them. Conflicting priorities such as between different business units or between a central headquarters and a business unit waste people's time and reduce their motivation.

Goal-setting conversations should make explicit the need to discuss issues along the way rather than wait for an employee to reach the deadline without having achieved the goal. This lessens the temptation for managers to micro-manage and constantly check in, as they know they will receive progress updates at agreed intervals. The coaching manager also makes sure that the employee knows it will be seen as a positive if they ask questions about things that are slowing their progress as issues arise, rather than wait for the next check-in or due date. It is important that a sense of psychological safety is created, ensuring that seeking guidance is not seen as a sign of weakness, so that employees feel supported, even when aiming for challenging goals or stretch targets.

Good Practice in Goal Setting

In goal-setting, both context and timing are important. Context includes, for example, whether the environment is rapidly changing or relatively stable, and whether the problem to be addressed is simple or complex (5). Timing relates to the time in a person's career – starting out, mid-career, or later on. Timing can also relate to agreeing a time when goal-setting is useful. In other words, goal-setting should not be done on autopilot but framed as part of a broader discussion of what is meaningful and relevant at a particular point in time. Productive coaching conversations can be held without goal-setting, at least not in the traditional sense of goal-setting. For example, an employee who comes to their manager with an issue, talks through the options, and walks away knowing what they plan to do has not set a goal in the formal sense. Nevertheless they have moved from a place of not knowing what to do to a place of knowing what to do, how to do it, when to do it, and how they will know if they have succeeded. They have gained clarity. At other times, an employee may need more time to think about their true priorities and may not yet be ready to articulate a specific goal.

Alignment with Organisational Goals

Most individuals have little direct input into the formulation of organisational goals. However, they can and should have input into how the actions they take individually or in their teams will help address the organisation's goals. I once visited a factory where each manufacturing cell had a one-page document in their area that in simple terms explained how their work contributed to the company's strategic goals. Each of the workers could explain their contribution as regards the quality and quantity of what they produced and why that was important to customers. They also spoke about health and safety and why that was important to them and their families. Everything they did was aligned with the strategy. They understood that everyone in the company was aligned and that they all shared a common purpose. There was a sense of pride in their work. Some companies have a 'goal share' scheme where it is not only individual salespeople or executives who get a bonus. Everyone gets a bonus when shared goals are achieved.

One of the main roles of a middle manager is to operationalise the organisation's vision and translate organisational strategy into action (8). When organisational goals are cascaded to teams and individuals, coaching managers help employees to understand how they contribute to the organisational goals and how their goals and the organisation's goals are aligned. Such alignment contributes to employee satisfaction, engagement, and their sense of meaning and purpose at work (9). In fact, Latham and Locke (10) found that assigned goals could motivate to the same level as goals that are set participatively, provided that the rationale for the goals is made clear.

Goals can also be set for completing projects or tasks, so that everyone understands what needs to be done. This ensures that the employee knows what is needed and the manager knows when to expect the task to be completed. As managers move from monitoring employees to monitoring outputs, this form of goal-setting helps establish a shared understanding of performance expectations. As discussed below, this is particularly useful in a hybrid or virtual work environment.

Goal-setting also has a role in structured problem-solving and in addressing feedback. Imagine that an issue has been identified in an employee's area of responsibility. The employee is well placed to understand the issue in depth and may come up with good ideas to resolve it. The manager may have experience from a range of different contexts that may help the employee to strengthen their idea. Together they can agree on the best way forward and then tie down the action plan. This collaborative approach draws on the expertise of both employees and managers, avoids blame and defensive reactions, and instead focuses on how to make progress moving forward. Researchers suggest that for tasks requiring creativity, long-term goals and encouraging autonomous learning and exploration are useful (11).

Professional and Career Goals

One of a leader's principal responsibilities is fostering the growth and development of those working with them. A coaching approach is a highly effective way to address this responsibility. It is an opportunity for the manager to spend time with an employee exploring what is important to them. Individual goals can be long-term aspirational goals, such as what someone would eventually like to be known or remembered for, as well as shorter- or medium-term career goals, which can include priorities for learning and development activities which take the person towards their long-term goals.

For example, an employee might say that their goal is to get promoted and that they need that promotion to increase their salary. A coaching manager might encourage the employee to think about why the promotion matters to them and what it is about the next level of responsibility that interests them. This encourages self-awareness and heightens motivation as it draws on intrinsic motivation. Although people soon get used to a higher salary, intrinsic motivation is longer lasting. By thinking further ahead in their career, the employee can also see that there may be various routes to get there. Scaling questions can be useful in discussing what the ideal scenario would look like. This can help the person gain clarity about their goal. And this clarity helps them articulate how they will know when they have achieved their goal.

Using Ives and Cox's terminology, an abstract goal for an employee might be to be acknowledged as a leader in their field. The intermediate goal might be promotion as it can help the person advance towards their abstract goal. The intermediate goal of promotion may drive concrete goals such as gaining certification in a particular area of expertise or making a presentation at a national conference. In other words, the hierarchy of goals helps position the intermediate goal in terms of a longer-term goal that matters to the employee and helps identify short-term goals that will help achieve both intermediate and longer-term goals. A similar proposition is put forward by Höchli (12), arguing that people are more successful in achieving their long-term or superordinate goals if they aim to achieve both long- and short-term goals than if they pursue either long-term or short-term (subordinate) goals alone.

This is not to deny the benefit to an employee of having career conversations with a mentor or coach who is not their line manager. A mentor or external coach does not have the same priorities as the line manager and can be totally focused on the employee, whereas the line manager also considers organisational priorities and other team members. A coaching manager who genuinely considers the interests of the employee is likely to be more effective in enhancing employee engagement which will result in more benefits for the organisation than one who is self-interested and concerned primarily about their own Key Performance Indicators (KPIs). Research into effective leaders with 6,000 CEOs and senior executives in 24 countries found that self-centred behaviours were far more common among less effective leaders than among effective leaders (13).

Many people are familiar with SMART (Specific Measurable Attainable Relevant and Time Bound) goal-setting, which has its place in tying down an agreed goal into specific measurable details. The danger in jumping to SMART goal-setting too soon is that the goal may not be one that really matters to the employee. They may simply go through the motions to keep their manager happy (14). Bright (15) suggests that attempting to reduce complexity to simple goals or rules is likely to fail because both human beings and the world we live in are more complex and open. On the other hand, Gilson et al. (16) suggest that it is difficult for people to continue with goal-directed behaviour if outcomes are ambiguous or uncertain or if path-goal dependencies are complex. What is needed is to define goals that are meaningful and then to specify the details. Tick-box goal-setting will not achieve the motivational power of conversations about the real goals to which the employee is truly committed.

A popular approach to goal-setting used in successful companies like Google and Atlassian is OKR, Objectives and Key Results (17). In this approach, employees choose the objectives they will target which are in line with the organisation's priorities and the employees decide how to measure them. Achieving OKRs relies on intrinsic motivation rather than financial rewards. Employees are encouraged to aim for stretch targets. Organisations that use the OKR process do not expect people to achieve all of their objectives. In fact, not achieving the OKRs but making good progress on them is deemed success (18). OKRs have been shown to relate to autonomy, competence, and relatedness, the elements of Self-Determination Theory (19). Managers have on-going conversations with their employees throughout the year rather than a one-off discussion about goals and whether they have been achieved.

Wilson (20) proposes an alternative to SMART which she argues is more appropriate for coaching conversations: the EXACT model (Explicit, eXciting, Assessable, Challenging, and Timing). Wilson suggests that SMART is still useful for organisational goals set by others, whereas EXACT is more useful for challenging people to aim higher with a meaningful goal that excites them. In a similar vein, a BHAG (Big Hairy Audacious Goal) (21) has been suggested as an alternative to SMART, or at least as a precursor to SMART, where people first articulate an ambitious goal and then use SMART goals or project management tools to plan the detail of how they will achieve it.

Differences in attitudes towards goal-setting have been observed in different generations (22). Younger generations are perceived to attach value to idealistic values, to meaningful and satisfying work, to want frequent feedback and opportunities for growth. Desjardins (22) proposes an alternative to SMART goal-setting for Gen Y (or millennials) which he terms SAVE: Specific, Attainable, Valuable, and Elevated. 'Specific' and 'attainable' are common to SMART goal-setting. 'Valuable' in Desjardins's terms relates to a sense of purpose, and 'Elevated' relates to setting challenging goals. The latter two fit with research into human motivation and are likely to apply to other generations also.

As flatter organisational structures have become more common, it can take some creative thinking to identify aspirational yet attainable goals. As Latham and Locke (10) reported, goals which are perceived as impossible can be demotivating. On the other hand, a goal that is too easy does not motivate people either. People who have had negative experiences of going through the motions of goal-setting policy may be cynical about what value, if any, goal-setting can bring, as illustrated in Box 3.1.

Box 3.1 A Pre-Goal-Setting Meeting

John got himself a strong coffee before heading into a conversation about goal-setting with Peter. John had joined BlackCo about six months earlier and hadn't yet had a goal-setting conversation with Peter. He had heard that Peter was unlikely to be open to any form of coaching conversation. However, since John had been appointed as team leader, he and Peter had developed a reasonable relationship and he felt there was some chance of getting to a reasonable outcome.

John: Morning Peter, how's it going?

Peter: Okay up to now – I suppose we have to go through this goal-setting stuff?

John: Yes we do, but how about we see if we can come up with something that makes sense?

Peter: Well that would be new … what were you thinking?

John: Well you heard at the Town Hall Meeting last week that we're trying to do better at holding on to the new employees that we take on. We spend a lot of time and money recruiting and training people, and it's all wasted if they don't stay. Plus it's not a good look when we have to tell our customers every couple of months that they'll have a new contact. Some of our new employees haven't been staying very long.

Peter: I'm not surprised, some of them come in thinking they know everything and not wanting to buckle down and learn.

John: You seem to be getting on well with Osama though?

Peter: Well, Osama is different, he wants to do things right. And we came up with a way where I show him something new every week, so he's not overwhelmed, and he comes to me in between if there's something he's not sure about.

John: That sounds like a good way to go about it. Is the same happening for our other new starters?

Peter: I don't know to be honest, I doubt it really. People tend to get on with their own jobs and forget what it was like when they started out. I know I'm cynical a lot of the time, but I actually do care about the young ones.

John: Sounds to me like you could help us get better at keeping our new employees if you're willing to share what you're doing with the rest of the team?

Peter: Oh okay, but how does that relate to a goal?

John: Well you can see that it would be good for our team anyway but there is also an overall company goal that feeds down to each department and team, so if we can show that we're doing well, that gives us some goodwill that we can call on when we need to. What do you think?

Peter: Definitely sounds better than some of the meaningless goals we've had to write up previously that were just to keep HR happy. But how do we make this into a goal?

John: Last year, we had ten new starters and five of them left within three months. What do you think would be a reasonable target for this year?

Peter: Maybe keep eight of the ten who started this year? And maybe go back to the five who started last year and see how they're getting on? John: That sounds great, Peter. Can you have a think about how we might get our colleagues on-board to see how important this is and how you might share what you're doing with Osama?

Peter: Well okay, but it mightn't work, you know.

John: You're right, it mightn't. But what you're doing now is working and it would be great if we can get more people to try what you do.

Peter: Okay, I'll give it a shot. Maybe Osama and I can do something together.

John: Wonderful. When you've had a think, we can catch up again and formalise a goal – one that makes sense this time.

Peter: Sure, as long as you do the wordsmithing bit.

Both left the meeting with a smile.

At different levels of an employee's career, different goals may become relevant. For someone early in their career, goals may revolve around responsibilities in which they gain experience, possibly involving lateral moves rather than promotion. A good time to have career discussions is soon after a promotion, so that instead of 'resting on their laurels', employees can see both how they will succeed in their new role and what further opportunities for professional growth may lie ahead. Mid-career, an employee might be keen to move up a specific professional or functional ladder, to demonstrate their expertise in a particular area or to broaden their areas of expertise. In the latter part of someone's career, they might think about the legacy they want to leave behind, succession planning for those coming after them, and thinking forward to how they could use their skills in not-for-profit organisations or other post-retirement options. Meaningful conversations that are truly about what matters to the employee can deepen the relationship between manager and employee.

Visualising Success

Questions that tap into feelings and other senses as well as rational thought help enhance commitment and motivation and hence increase the likelihood of goal attainment, for example 'What does that feel like?', 'What are people saying to you about your success?', 'How are you celebrating?', 'Who is celebrating with you?'. In Box 3.1, John was able to tap into the fact that Peter genuinely cared about the younger employees in the team.

Visualising ourselves achieving our goals creates neural pathways similar to those that would be created if we actually did the action in real life (20). This works in three ways. Firstly the part of our brain called the Reticular Activating System (RAS) filters out much of the irrelevant noise in the world around us and presents us with relevant data. If, for example, we are enjoying a pleasant walk along a country lane, surrounded by birdsong, humming bees, and occasional lowing cows or bleating sheep, we might be 'miles away' in our thoughts. But if our brains detect a fast-approaching car, they will put us on alert to make sure we are not in danger. The relevance for goal-setting is that we can prime our RAS to focus on what is relevant to achieving our goals through visualising ourselves achieving those goals.

Second, we know from self-efficacy research that it is easier to do something again than when we do something for the first time (23).

Visualising ourselves having achieved a goal creates the same effect. We can imagine ourselves having already completed a task successfully and so we know that we can do it again.

Third, when we celebrate success, we release dopamine, which is associated with feelings of pleasure. Our brains then associate achieving goals with feeling happy and we continue to strive to achieve other goals. This results in a virtuous circle of striving, achievement, and celebration of attaining both organisational and individual goals. Some coaches ask visualisation questions about the future, such as 'How will you celebrate?. Wilson (20) recommends framing visualisation questions in the present tense to create energy, and notes that the more senses are involved in the visualisation, the deeper the neural networks become embedded and the easier for people to access their ability to achieve their goals. Goal-setting then is not only an intellectual exercise but also draws on positive emotions to fuel our motivation.

Implementation and Follow-up

When goals are meaningful, they are intrinsically motivating and enhance people's well-being. This in turn leads to people spending time and energy on achieving their goals. In contrast, if the goals are not genuinely important to the person owning the goals, then the effort is meaningless (24). Any effort spent on tracking progress is of little use, apart from demonstrating progress towards something meaningless. The attraction of specific goals is that they give an illusion of control and lend themselves to demonstrating the effectiveness of coaching or other support that helps in achieving those goals (14). Specific goals can be used to generate beautiful charts and spreadsheets to show that targets have been met. Clutterbuck and Spence (5, p. 225) warn that focusing on specific narrow goals can lead to 'inattentional blindness', where we fail to see some important things because we are focusing closely on something else.

Once we have identified truly meaningful goals and are motivated to achieve them, then it is important to tie down the details and this is where SMART goals prove useful. Simple questions such as Who? What? Where? When? and How? make goals explicit. This allows progress indicators to be identified. Rather than spending inordinate amounts of time trying to measure everything, indicators that progress is being made towards the agreed goals are enough to allow managers and employees to focus on what matters.

It is important that managers follow up with employees on the progress they are making. Change, particularly behavioural change, is difficult, and if no one is interested, it can be easy to revert to previous practice. Grant suggests that it can take about six months for behavioural change to become habitual (25). Coaching managers have a significant advantage over external coaches as they have the opportunity not only to define meaningful goals aligned with organisational priorities but also to follow up on implementation.

Goal-Setting in the Hybrid and Virtual World

The motivational impact of goal setting is primarily cognitive (10) and hence relatively straightforward to undertake in the online space. Where there is an emotional component such as may arise in visualising success, this tends to be positive emotions which are unlikely to cause difficulties in an online conversation.

Indeed, some online goal-setting software platforms may make it easier to have a conversation on goals online than face to face, offering screensharing and providing prompts for things to consider, a shared record of what has been agreed, and automatic reminders. Some goal-setting apps link with online calendars and prompt for action as deadlines approach. They allow the user to define how much each action contributes to the overall goal and show how near to the goal the person has moved as a result of the actions completed. The advantage of such apps is that they are always available, and they are free or at least cheap, compared to paying for an external coach.

Recent studies comparing goal attainment by people interacting with a human coach and people interacting with a virtual coach have found similar results (26, 27). Terblanche (26) suggests that some of the success of the app in their trial may be due to the fact that the app in their research was developed based on goal theory, whereas the human coaches may not have been as familiar with the theory. Furthermore, when they are busy, humans can forget things like following up on progress, whereas the app does not forget. Goal-setting apps are available for both individual and team goals.

Some apps include journals and visualisation tools such as mind maps to help the user see how all the actions fit together, a vision board with visual representations of what is meaningful about the goal for the individual, or visual dashboards to represent progress. Online programs are

increasingly being used to track progress towards goals, such as Motivational Coach Bot.[1]

Advances in Artificial Intelligence (AI) make it easier to track performance data and reduce human error in assessing performance (28).
As managers learn to focus more on outputs than on seeing workers
in the office, software can help by indicating if a goal or task is on
track and by providing early warning if not. Apps can provide advice
and affirmations as well as action plans for achieving goals, incorporating users' preferences in terms of gentle reminders or more assertive
approaches.

Progress tracking can be made visible to both an individual and their
manager so that there are no surprises and no secret surveillance. Of
course software is not a substitute for a meaningful conversation about
goals. And people should be wary of spending more time updating their
progress on their goal-setting app than in doing the work needed to
achieve their goal.

Traps to Avoid

Setting goals and targets requires careful consideration. Concerns have
been expressed about the possibility of motivating risky or unethical
behaviours (29), particularly when people are rewarded for achieving
goals, such as through a bonus system. Organisations need to take care
to reward the behaviours they want to see and avoid perverse incentives
or unintended consequences. For example, if sales performance is seen
as the only or most important criterion for bonuses, sales representatives
may indulge in unethical behaviour to achieve those goals or factory
managers may pay less attention to quality or safety.

In multi-site companies, overarching company goals should be
tailored for each location. A company might decide to set stretch goals
of doubling (where the target is increasing) or halving (where the target
is decreasing) the previous year's performance. While fine as a general
rule, imagine if a company has a goal of zero workplace fatalities but
unfortunately two people died the previous year. Halving that would
mean setting a goal of one fatality the next year. Obviously workplace
fatalities should never have a target above zero.

Setting vague goals can lead to disagreement between manager and
employee about whether or not a goal has been achieved (and consequently whether any associated reward should be given).

Focusing only on short-term goals without any consideration of how they relate to long-term goals means that progress may not be made towards long term goals. Instead goal-setting conversations should consider how each short-term goal helps progress towards a longer-term goal.

Getting Better at Goal-Setting

Here are three activities which can help you get better at goal-setting:

1. Practise setting goals with your team for fictional team members such as the Easter Bunny. By practising in a non-threatening environment with no personal implications, team members can raise questions about how goals are set and understand the importance of being explicit.
2. For each goal you identify, think about potential risks or challenges which might prevent someone from achieving a goal. Then brainstorm ways of overcoming those challenges.
3. Practise setting goals in a role play with a peer, observed by another peer. Each person takes a turn at being the manager, the employee, and the observer. Each person shares their reflection and feedback after each role play. We do not usually have someone observing us when we coach so having feedback as you actually engage in goal-setting gives you useful data to consider. This is an activity worth repeating periodically as we can develop a habitual way of framing how we help people set goals. An observer or the person being coached will flag if they feel we are on autopilot rather than being present in the moment.

FEEDBACK

Why Is Feedback Important?

Feedback is important so that employees know that they are performing effectively, contributing to the organisation and acting in line with the organisation's values. If there is poor performance, this needs to be addressed. Employees may be totally unaware of any issues and have a misleading impression of their own performance, either overestimating or underestimating their ability in what has been termed the Dunning-Kruger effect (30). Regular conversations between managers and employees establish a shared understanding of expectations, calibration of what 'good' performance means, and regular realignment with organisation/team values and goals, as well as nurturing positive relationships. Freedman suggests that feedback from managers, peers, coaches, or mentors is helpful in developing a more realistic self-image and lessening the risk of the Dunning-Kruger effect mentioned above (30). A coaching mindset ensures that these conversations are held with the positive intention of supporting employees. Done well, feedback is not only about performance but also encourages autonomy and innovation (31).

As mentioned in Chapter 2, research has shown that firms led by humble CEOs outperform firms whose CEOs are less humble (32, 33), with listening found to be an effective way to engage employees (34). Their top teams are also more likely to collaborate and jointly make decisions. Humility implies that leaders are not so arrogant as to think they know everything or know best. The higher leaders go in an organisation, the less likely it is that they will get honest feedback from others. As feedback is a vital component in improving our performance, leaders actively solicit feedback and may call on external coaches or mentors to hold them to account.

Feedback is also linked to learning. Adult learning theories underpin all coaching (35), underscoring the need for learning to be relevant and self-directed. Applying this to feedback suggests that feedback should be given when relevant, not in a once-a-year performance review. To tap into the motivating powers of autonomy, employees should have the freedom where possible to choose how best to address the feedback they receive. Feedback and reflection can lead to transformative learning experiences (36).

What we do at work matters more than what we say. Hence, managers should role-model the behaviours they would like to see. It is critically important to address promptly any issues or behaviour that are not in line with organisational values and not keep them for an annual or other periodic review. If people notice that such behaviour continues, they begin to regard such behaviour as acceptable, regardless of an organisation's stated values or code of conduct. As David Hurley, former Governor of New South Wales, once said, 'The standard you walk past is the standard you accept' (37). If poor performance or behaviour which is not in line with company values is not addressed, this creates resentment among others and a sense of injustice which can impact on staff well-being, lead to lower morale, and lessen employee engagement and people's willingness to put in discretionary effort. This can lead to lower performance more generally and higher staff turnover (38). Furthermore, tackling behavioural issues at an early stage prevents their escalation into major issues or conflict.

Many employees say that they do not receive enough feedback. Managers have often not been trained in how to give feedback effectively, particularly in the online space. They may be afraid of upsetting an employee with whom they have an on-going relationship and/or fear an emotional response from the employee. Yet we know that employees are thirsty for feedback. Indeed, millennials are particularly keen to receive feedback (39).

Some research has suggested that when employees seek feedback on their performance, it may be more about 'impression management' than about improving their performance (40), but that even when this is the case, there is a benefit, as these feedback conversations enhance the relationship between manager and employee and increase trust, as well as leading to improvements in performance.

Good Practice in Feedback

Articulating clear expectations is important so that employees are not surprised to receive feedback on something they had not realised was an expectation. Once the feedback has been understood, careful listening and powerful questions help people come up with innovative solutions. The manager can then switch to goal-setting to lock in the changes to behaviour or performance. The manager then continues to use observation, listening, questioning, and reflection as they monitor the changes and give further feedback, hopefully attesting to the improvements made.

A simple guide to providing face-to-face or online feedback is provided below.

Effective Feedback Guide

1. Preparation is the key to successful feedback, whether online or in person. Choose a time that will work for the employee; for example, if the employee collects their children from school each day, do not organise the meeting during that time. Make sure you are clear on the facts but also be aware that the employee may have a different perception. Refresh your understanding of relevant organisational policies or procedures.
2. If a face-to-face meeting is not possible, hold a videoconference meeting in preference to a telephone call, so that you can at least see

facial reactions and some body language. Make sure that your technology is working, that your camera is level with your eyes, and that your microphone carries your sound clearly.

3. In the meeting, outline your observation carefully and accurately, explaining what you saw or heard, and the impact of what you saw or heard. Stick to one topic. Do not confuse the issue by providing feedback on other issues at the same time. Use your own words. Using a script makes managers seem inauthentic and lessens trust (41). If the feedback is part of a formal disciplinary procedure, make sure you follow the procedure and that you know what you can and cannot say.

4. Allow silence as the person processes what they have been told and tries to reconcile it with their memory of the event. Many people find silence awkward and on an online call may even wonder if the technology has frozen. To avoid this, when you have finished outlining the issue say something like 'Let's pause there and when you're ready, I'm really interested in your view of what was happening'.

5. If the employee gets upset, reconvene at a later time when they have had a chance to process.

6. When the employee is ready to explain their understanding of what happened, listen without judging. Really try to understand their perspective.

7. Focus on body language and tone of voice as well as the words, to gain a true understanding of how the employee feels as well as how they think. Body language is less obvious on a videoconference and not visible on a telephone call. However, tone of voice can be very telling.

8. Have a break so that the employee has a chance to think about what has been said. Having conversations online means no travel time is required, so there is no extra cost to splitting the meeting into two or even three parts. This allows the employee to get over any initial upset at the feedback they have received and more likely to shift later to a creative mindset.

9. When you reconvene, move to a shared problem-solving approach. Bring in other team members if useful at this stage – not to revisit what has happened but to co-design the solution. Then use SMART goal setting to ensure that both you and the employee(s) are clear on what needs to be done.

10. Use collaborative tools like Slack or chat platforms like Webex or Teams to keep in touch with employees regardless of where they work so that you can provide whatever type of support they need on an on-going basis. Trust your employees and encourage them to complete the agreed actions. Checking in regularly shows that you are interested in their progress, but do not micro-manage the fine details.
11. Acknowledge improvements and explore the issue further if more needs to be done.

Regular, frequent feedback helps employees keep on track and helps managers to see where and how they can support employees in their work (42). Making feedback specific shows that it is genuine, and that the person is seen and valued. Expectations of how often people need to check in and what form of interim reports are required help to ensure that managers are not simply waiting for a finished output. At the same time, an agreed check-in process avoids the demoralising effects of micro-managing, which often occurs when managers are concerned that they are not seeing progress or anxious that a particular output may not be delivered on time. Regular feedback and two-way communication increase employee engagement which in turn leads to increases in productivity (43, 44).

Coaching managers notice people's strengths and when people are doing things well. Recognising good behaviour in line with the organisation's values and contributing to the organisation's or team's goals and strategy reminds every one of the behaviours that are valued. Focusing on people's strengths is motivating and more likely to lead to improvements than a focus on their perceived weaknesses (45). If we only give feedback when something is not being done well, then subconsciously the employee may feel that we are not being fair, as we have not appreciated all the good work they do.

It has been suggested that the ratio of positive feedback to negative needs to be about three to one or higher for people to flourish (46). There is little if any actual evidence for such a ratio (47), although positive feedback contributes to positive morale and so it intuitively makes sense to give positive feedback frequently. It is also recommended that praise or positive feedback is given in public and negative or constructive feedback given in private (48). A benefit of giving feedback in public is that it signals to others which behaviours are valued. Recognition may be explicitly framed as examples of what the organisation's values look like in practice. On-going reinforcement of the values through individual and group feedback helps bring the values to life.

Before providing feedback to employees on issues concerning their work or behaviour, it is important to ensure that the other person is ready to hear it. This may seem odd to a manager who wants to deal with issues promptly, yet this approach helps ensure that the feedback will be acted upon. Otherwise, the feedback will likely fall on deaf ears or lead only to a short-term improvement before the issue recurs and possibly worsens. There is a wide variation in how receptive people are to feedback (49). An individualised approach helps craft an approach suitable for each individual (38).

The purpose of feedback is to lead to or sustain improvements. In other words, feedback should be actionable. Even if we have evidence of poor performance, understanding the context can help us identify how best to address the issue. A person who is abrupt with customers may be so for various reasons, for example a sleepless night due to a young baby at home, stress due to excessive workload and inability to meet targets, or a reaction to a meeting that went badly just before the customer interaction. Understanding what is contributing to the issue can help the manager work with the employee on strategies to prevent a recurrence. The manager can also identify if a pattern is forming, and if so, how any negative patterns may be disrupted. Focusing on the relationship and on learning helps create optimal conditions for feedback (50, 51). Listening to the other person's experience of the incident in question shows respect and a willingness to work together, which forms a sound basis for agreeing how to address the feedback.

There is usually a difference between the way we see ourselves and the way others see us. This was highlighted in the 18th century by the Scottish poet Robert Burns when he wrote:

> Oh, would some Power the gift to give us
> To see ourselves as others see us! (52) [modern English version]

In giving feedback, the coaching manager can not only help the employee improve their performance but can also help the employee develop their self-awareness and ability to see things from different perspectives (53).

Pronin (54) reviews research relating to the difference between how we see ourselves and how others see us, making the point that we judge others by their actions but ourselves by our intentions. Put differently, if we know we intend to do something, we make allowances for that, even if we have not done it yet. However, with other people we see only that they have not yet completed the action in question. Bearing this in mind, if we are working on something ourselves it is wise to let our teams know what we are doing, especially if it is a project or an issue that is going to take time. Otherwise, they may believe that we are not doing anything about it.

Before giving feedback, we should check the assumptions we are making about what is behind people's behaviour, such as if we think the employee is lazy, slow, or overworked. These assumptions may be coloured by our experience with this particular employee in the past, by our experience with other people, or by stereotypes or biases we can counter once we are aware of them.

The difference between how we see ourselves and how others see us can mean that negative feedback is a huge blow to the person receiving the feedback. People may have a totally inaccurate perception of their performance (30). Confronted with other people's perceptions, people may react emotionally, rejecting the feedback without even considering it, and/or criticising the manager providing the feedback.

If the data underpinning the feedback is inaccurate or incomplete, the defensive reaction can be very strong, with feelings of injustice running high. By ensuring the employee has the opportunity to explain what has happened from their perspective, there is a better chance of the manager understanding the situation correctly and there is also less chance of a negative emotional response when the employee feels that they have been heard.

Feedback can, but does not necessarily have to, be enacted differently by executive coaches and coaching managers, particularly in relation to the way forward. An executive coach is generally non-directive and focused on the process of enabling the coachee to identify ways to address the feedback provided. The coaching manager may use feedforward, where the focus is on improvements that can be made in the future, identifying and building on people's strengths (55). This is consistent with the growth mindset of coaching leaders and positive ways of giving feedback (56–59). Feedforward can be particularly useful when helping people achieve their goals (60). The coaching manager can help employees to visualise what the changes might look like, just as we do when visualising achieving our goals. This helps employees commit to implementing the changes agreed.

Preparing for Feedback

Depending on the nature of the feedback, feedback may be given formally or informally. Once the manager has decided which is appropriate in a given context, simple things like picking a mutually agreeable time and a suitable location show respect for participants and can avoid the conversation getting off to a bad start. Feedback conversations do not have to be across a desk or even a table – these physical positions can appear adversarial. Some potentially difficult conversations can be held over a coffee or during a walking meeting, allowing participants time to reflect on the feedback provided. The manager needs to be well prepared, familiar with the details about the issue or perceived issue, as well as with any relevant policies and procedures, and what to do if records of the meeting or further steps are needed.

Diversity and Feedback

In our diverse workplaces, using coaching skills allows managers to work effectively with people regardless of gender, age, or other forms of diversity. For example, although previous generations may have accepted that they might not get much or indeed any feedback from their managers and assumed that they were doing well unless told otherwise, Gen Y/millennials and later generations actively seek feedback (61–65). This does not mean that managers need to treat different generations differently. Rather, managers can use a coaching approach to give feedback to all their employees, regardless of age, adopting an individualised leadership approach to tap into the motivation of each employee. Feedback is the foundation for learning (66), prompting us to consider where and how we might enhance our knowledge or skills. As such, it is a critical attribute of learning organisations, enabling organisations to stay current and succeed in a rapidly changing VUCA world.

As noted above, age may play a role in how open people are to seeking or receiving feedback. Cultural considerations also play a role. For example, in some cultures fear of losing face makes it extremely important that any negative feedback is given in private. Cultural preferences may also affect how directly or indirectly the feedback is phrased (67). If feedback is given indirectly to an employee used to direct feedback, the employee may not realise the importance of that feedback. On the other hand, if feedback is given directly to an employee used to more indirect feedback, the employee may be offended. Cultural differences are explored further in Chapter Five.

After Feedback

People are more likely to stick with changes if their line manager shows an interest and follows up, as already mentioned. Otherwise, it is easy to go back to previous ways of working (25). An effective way to ensure that feedback is acted upon is to articulate a goal relating to the feedback and follow up as we would on other goals.

Feedback in the Hybrid and Virtual World

It is easy for managers and employees to avoid feedback conversations when either or both are working remotely. A manager might for example notice that one team member is particularly good at setting others at ease in the few minutes before the start of a formal online meeting. They could then appreciate the colleague for their contribution to a positive workplace. Or they might specifically comment on the way an employee delivers a regular report on time and to a high standard.

In hybrid workplaces, managers can choose which meetings to hold virtually and which in person. A face-to-face conversation is preferred by some managers for difficult conversations. On the other hand, a manager who fears an emotional response might prefer an online conversation as may an employee who might temporarily turn off their camera while they consider the feedback and regain their composure.

Giving or receiving negative feedback online can feel more awkward than in person (68). We are unable to see body language as well as we can when face to face. Telephone conversations have to rely on tone of voice. It is nevertheless amazing how much can be gleaned about a person's emotions from their tone of voice. For instance, we can usually tell if people are angry or happy, excited or impatient.

As with visual observations, what we think we are seeing may not actually be accurate and we need to check our interpretations of body language. With some people, we can do this by asking them about how they are feeling; with others we might label the emotion we think we are hearing and ask if we are correct. If a person is very upset, it may be best to suggest a break and resume at a later time or date. An interesting recent study found that self-views in a video conference can negatively affect a person's own self-evaluation and confidence, and their evaluation of the person they are speaking with (69). The authors recommend disabling the self-view option when individuals anticipate a difficult conversation.

While minor issues can be dealt with in informal conversations in the office, this is more difficult in the online space as we need to agree a specific meeting time, select the technology for the meeting, and deal with any technical issues; all of this creates more of a hurdle than casually meeting someone in the corridor and asking for a quiet word. Advising the employee of the general topic helps avoid the employee getting anxious every time their manager organises a time for a conversation. Some of those conversations may be about operational matters or future planning, but if a manager simply requests a time for a catch-up, the employee has no way of knowing if there is something to be worried about. Stoeckli et al. (70) found that online feedback using a dedicated feedback app worked well for simple operational-level feedback and enabled feedback to be collated easily. However, they recommended sensitive or controversial topics be discussed in person. Nowadays this is not always possible. Hence, it is important to create trusting relationships which allow for these conversations to be held online.

Psychological safety needs to be in place before trust can be built (71). According to the Center for Creative Leadership (CCL), psychological safety is 'the belief that you won't be punished or humiliated for speaking up with ideas, questions, concerns, or mistakes' (72). Edmondson suggests that uncertainty has increased in the workplace post-pandemic and that where psychological safety is missing, preventable failures are likely as well as less innovation (73). The importance of psychological safety is emphasised by Peters and Carr (74, p. 95), who say it is the factor that underpins all coaching.

Box 3.2 Finding a Way Forward

Anna ended the phone call with a client and knew she was going to have to talk to Maria, one of her hybrid employees who worked Tuesday–Thursday in the office and Monday and Friday from home. Trouble was, Maria tended to get emotional whenever anyone said anything that implied she was less than perfect. And she was very good at most of her job. But now an important client was saying that Maria was never available on Friday afternoons. And Anna knew that Maria wasn't on leave, so she should be around.

Anna messaged Maria to ask if she were available for an online call. Maria responded quickly to say she would be in five minutes. Anna started the call by asking how things were going. Maria said things were fine. Anna then asked if there were any issues she should know about. Maria said not as far as she was aware. Anna said there was some concern from clients about it being hard to contact the company on Friday afternoons.

Maria was silent for a moment, and then said they should just leave a message, and someone would get back to them. Anna challenged this, saying that was not acceptable as the company has a policy of being available 9am–5pm Monday–Friday. Maria then started to get upset, saying that lots of people aren't available on Friday afternoon. Anna waited for Maria to calm down and then asked her to tell her about a typical Friday afternoon. Maria started with a clear description of the early afternoon but then stumbled to a halt.

'What happens then?' asked Anna. 'I pick up my children from school,' said Maria, in a low voice. 'My mother is in hospital, she normally does it, but she can't now.' 'I'm so sorry to hear about your mother, that must be very worrying for you,' said Anna. 'Now that I know, we can get someone to cover for you.'

'I thought it was just a few minutes and no one would notice,' said Maria.

'It's important for our company's reputation that we live up to our promises and are available when we say we will be,' said Anna.

'I understand that,' said Maria. 'I wasn't thinking straight, it was all so sudden and so stressful, I was just trying to do everything.'

'Okay,' said Anna. 'Let's figure out how we can make sure that you can collect your children and our clients still have someone available all Friday afternoon. What do you think?'

'Well, Jenna is used to covering for me during the school holidays. Maybe she could do that, and I can cover some of her work early in the morning or later in the evening when the children are in bed. And Anna, I am sorry I've let you down and the company down. I was afraid to say anything in case you thought I was being unreliable and now that's exactly what you think. And I thought you might say I had to take Friday afternoons off, and I can't afford to take less pay,' said Maria tearfully. 'Look, I'll speak to Jenna and come back to you to confirm, and that's our short-term solution,' said Anna. 'When things have settled down for you, we'll have a chat about what to do if something like this happens again, so the clients aren't left unsupported, and neither are you. And in the meantime, if anything else crops up, just let me know and we'll figure something out.'

Anna closed the call, feeling she needed to do some reflection on how to create a sense of psychological safety so that employees would come to her if they had problems, before those problems started to affect their work and their customer relations. She decided to talk to her own mentor and see if there was a short course she could take that would give her some ideas.

A key enabler for effective feedback is psychological safety, the belief that there is no risk to the employee in asking questions, raising issues, or obtaining feedback (75). Psychological safety is associated with employee engagement, learning, commitment, and performance. Asking for help in an online forum can be difficult for new members of a team until they feel a sense of safety (76). Assigning buddies or mentors to new employees can help in the early days. Although working remotely can make it more difficult to establish psychological safety (76), doing so is particularly important if a team is to thrive when working in remote or hybrid mode.

Traps to Avoid

Providing no feedback or only vague or ill-defined feedback is unhelpful, as the person will not know how to improve their performance. Feedback needs to be specific, not simply saying 'Hey, you're doing a great job, well done', but commenting on a specific thing done well (or poorly).

Managers who only give negative feedback miss the opportunity to motivate employees who have performed well and to signal to others the behaviours and performance that are valued in the organisation.

Some managers ask employees how they like to receive feedback. An employee might, for example, say they prefer feedback to be given 'straight, not sugar-coated'. Despite saying this, sometimes these employees do actually get upset by blunt feedback. The coaching manager needs emotional intelligence to work out how best to communicate feedback that may be difficult to hear, allowing the employee time to manage their emotions and consider the feedback calmly.

A common practice is what is called the 'feedback sandwich', where a manager first says something positive with the intent of creating a positive environment for what they really want to say. They then provide the negative feedback and follow this up with a positive message so that the employee leaves the meeting feeling positive. Unfortunately this practice can have negative effects. Some employees totally miss the constructive feedback in the middle, focusing only on the positive messages that the meeting begins and ends with. Others become so used to the fact that after any praise, there will be criticism, that they dread being praised and discount any positive feedback, When asked for their views of direct and sandwiched feedback, participants in a recent study unanimously preferred direct feedback (77).

In other words, separating positive and negative feedback is often a better option than diluting the message in a 'feedback sandwich'. There can be a meeting specifically to focus on the need for improvement, with, at other times, managers providing ample positive feedback on what the person is doing well, so that they know they are appreciated, and more inclined to listen to feedback when improvements are needed. One way to ensure that feedback is received and understood is to switch to goal-setting relating to the change that needs to happen and following up the meeting with a written record.

Getting Better at Feedback

Here are three activities which can help you get better at feedback:

1. Think of a negative incident caused by a member of your team. Consider how feedback and feedforward might be framed to get the best outcome going forward. Which would you use in real life? What makes that a better choice?
2. Reflect on times when you have been given feedback in a way that you found effective. What did the other person do that worked for you? Think about other times when you were given feedback that made you feel demotivated or frustrated. What was it about those times that made the feedback have that effect? Reflecting on your own experiences can help you develop your approach to feedback, but remember that not everyone will respond the same way so keep developing your range of approaches to giving feedback.
3. Practise giving feedback online in a role play with a peer, observed by another peer. Each person takes a turn at being the manager, the employee, and the observer. Each person shares their reflection and feedback after each role play. As with goal-setting, this is an activity worth

repeating over time and with different people as we can always learn from seeing how others give feedback as well as receiving feedback on how we give feedback. This also allows us to practise positive ways of receiving feedback which we can use with our own teams, giving them the assurance that if they give us feedback, we will take it well.

REFLECTION: WHY IS REFLECTION IMPORTANT?

Reflection is how we learn from experience. In today's complex and rapidly changing world, continuous learning is important – who wishes to have worked for 20 years in an organisation which seems like one year's experience repeated 20 times? According to the World Economic Forum, there is an increased emphasis in businesses on 'the importance of resilient and reflective workers embracing a culture of lifelong learning as the lifecycle of their skills decreases' (78). Rather than ruminating endlessly on something that happened in the past, reflection helps us to learn from experience, problem-solve, and move forward (79).

Reflection helps us to make sense of events and to articulate what has happened or is happening, which then allows us to share and compare our understanding with others. Du Toit argues that coaching processes support and enhance sense-making (80). Kolb's experiential learning cycle (81) includes reflection on something someone has experienced, generalising from that experience, and experimenting with alternative ways of doing things. Coaching managers help their employees to reflect and also take time to reflect themselves. Reflection allows us to disentangle different observations and experiences, consider our beliefs and possible interpretations, clarify our thinking, and create meaning from chaos. This forms the basis for on-going learning (82).

Reflection helps us become more self-aware, aware of our impact on others, accept feedback, and become more aware of our own strengths and areas for improvement (83, 84). Muff's Responsible Leadership Competence Framework identifies self-awareness as the central element in Responsible Leadership (85). Self-awareness also allows us to self-regulate; that is, when we are aware of our own emotions and responses, we are better able to manage them (86). Eurich (87) claims that despite most people believing they are self-aware, very few people actually are. This discrepancy is higher in senior leaders, according to the authors, perhaps because senior leaders are less likely to hear critical feedback and so their positive self-image goes unchallenged. Jones (88) distinguishes between reflection which helps us challenge our self-limiting beliefs and consider our latent strengths, and rumination which tends to focus on negative thoughts in a way that does not help us move forward.

The conscious competence model is a useful way of tracking our progress in developing our skillset (89). In this model, people progress from being an unconscious incompetent, where they are not even aware of their lack of ability, through to being a conscious incompetent, where they are aware of what they are doing wrong and where they need to improve. As they develop their skills they become a conscious competent. Finally, in the original model, they become an unconscious competent, where the new skills are applied effortlessly. This fourth stage can sometimes lead to complacency, with people working on auto-pilot or believing that they are now 'good enough', leading some researchers to suggest a fifth stage, reflective competence or reflective practitioners (90), where they continue to reflect and improve.

Another useful tool for reflection is the Johari Window (91). It highlights that there are aspects of ourselves that we are aware of and so are others, aspects which we are aware of but keep hidden from others, aspects others are aware of but we ourselves are not (our blind spots), and aspects neither we nor others are aware of but which we can be sure exist. The author argues that it takes effort to hide parts of ourselves from others and that there is more likely to be sharing of ourselves where there is trust. Freedman (92) suggests that we can use a version of the Johari Window to move from being an unconscious incompetent to become a conscious incompetent and then a conscious competent.

Commitment to improvement is a key aspect of reflection and requires people to be willing to make changes. As Eurich (87) says, no matter how much progress we make, there is always more to learn. The added benefit is that when we role-model reflective practice, being open to and acting on feedback, we encourage our team members to do the same.

Good Practice in Reflection

Schön (93) distinguishes between two types of reflection: reflection in action and reflection on action. When we are in a goal-setting meeting with a colleague, for example, we may have time to reflect quickly and adjust the questions we had in mind if we realise that the colleague has a major issue at home or if we realise that the colleague lacks some fundamental training we think necessary for them to do their work effectively. The more attentively we listen to the other person, the more likely it is that we will reflect and adapt our part of the conversation. Coachbots or coaching apps can provide insights during a coaching session or between coaching sessions (94).

Reflection on action takes place after the event. Rather than rely on our memories, especially when we work in a busy environment, it is useful to keep notes on events that we will later look back on. Good questions to ask oneself regularly are 'What can I learn from this?' and 'What will I do differently next time?'. This applies whether an experience has been positive or negative, an isolated or a recurring event. Periodically managers benefit from reviewing a longer period of time to see if they can identify patterns in their reflections and arrive at a deeper level of understanding of themselves and of their teams.

Jenny Moon (95) gives examples of different levels of reflection. At the most basic level is a factual description of an event. The same event could be written about with a reflection from one point of view. Further levels of reflection could consider multiple perspectives, analyse different possible causes, take emotions and prior thinking into account, and include self-questioning. Just as managers pose questions to employees to prompt them to reflect, so too managers can ask themselves questions to develop their reflection into a more in-depth review. The more honest the reflection, the more likely that it will lay the foundation for positive change.

In their book *Deliberate Calm* (96), authors Brassey, De Smet, and Kruyt also describe different levels of reflection. At the first level is a manager who works mostly on autopilot and is only aware of their own perspective. The second level is a manager who is able to reflect after an event but not during the event. At the third level is a manager who is aware during an event but not able to respond in the moment. At the fourth level, managers are aware and able to respond after a short pause or time out. Pausing can help managers choose a thoughtful response. At the fifth level, managers are aware and can adapt their behaviour as needed. Reaching the fifth level is challenging, requiring managers to be honest with themselves and to seek feedback from others.

Deeper levels of reflection allow people to identify patterns and triggers in the events on which they are reflecting which can then prompt them to decide what to do differently. Exactly how that new behaviour will be enacted takes further investigation. It is useful to have a sounding board when making sense of reflections and in deciding what to change. The sounding board can be a manager or a peer. These days it might even be an app, with the app recording the reflection non-judgementally and posing questions to prompt deeper reflection.

To give ourselves accurate feedback, we need to be alert to the signals in our environment, reflecting on what is working well or not so well, aware of the impact or consequences of our decisions, actions or inaction, willing to try to understand the situation and willing to try something new. The Ladder of Inference mentioned in Chapter Two suggests that the way we select and make inferences from data is prone to bias. In undertaking reflection, we need to be careful in how we select the events upon which to reflect and the data we examine in support of our reflection. Reflection helps us make the steps explicit between selecting data and taking action, prompting us to consider the assumptions we are making, the conclusions we are drawing, and the beliefs we are adopting. Reflecting with other people can also help guard against bias.

Box 3.3 Reflection: Something Happened in That Meeting

Well, that went well, thought Tom as he rushed off to his next meeting, mentally preparing for the topic to be discussed. But something was niggling him about the last meeting. Something happened in that meeting, he thought, something different.

He mentally replayed the meeting. It was a normal team meeting where they collectively reviewed an issue that had come up with a customer and brainstormed possible solutions. Even though they did this on a regular basis, he always reminded people at the start about the rules of brainstorming. No criticism of ideas in the first phase, no matter how bizarre they might seem. Go for quantity not quality. Build on each other's ideas and so on. Then he realised what was different. Fang had spoken up. Fang never spoke up in meetings. Whether it was cultural or gender or a combination of the two, he didn't know and Tom had not wanted to push it. He decided to think about it later. Whenever possible, he kept 15 minutes free at the end of the working day so that he could think back over the meetings and other events during the day. It helped him make sense of things and decide how to move forward. Having identified what was niggling him, he focused fully on his next meeting.

At the end of the day, he thought again about the brainstorming session. What was different this time? Was it something he had said or done or something one of the team had? There was one new team member, Li. That was it, Tom realised. When they had come up with a few ideas (none of which were too exciting, if he was honest about it), he had asked 'What else?', as he usually did when they paused, until no more ideas emerged. He had learned that in a workshop and it did sometimes result in more ideas coming out. Li had spoken quietly but clearly, commenting that since she had joined the company, Fang had been exceptionally helpful and maybe her knowledge and expertise could help the group. Fang had nodded – it was almost a bow, he thought in retrospect – and then Fang voiced an idea that everyone jumped on enthusiastically, adding some suggestions, but it was still recognisably Fang's idea that they decided to implement.

I need to understand this better, thought Tom. I don't want to push Fang to do something she isn't comfortable with, but she clearly has good ideas which the team would benefit from. He decided to learn more about cultural norms and perspectives.

Tom also decided that he would thank Fang for her contribution to the meeting and ask her directly about what had made a difference for her. He also decided to ask Li for her perspective and thank her for encouraging Fang to speak up. He would ask both of them if they would be comfortable discussing the issue at a team meeting, so that the team could collectively reflect on what they could each do to ensure everyone felt safe speaking up. Just voicing the rules at the start wasn't enough. If just one person could make a difference, imagine what the whole team could do, he thought excitedly.

Tom felt some of the weight of being a leader lift off his shoulder as he realised that everyone in the team could encourage each other, it wasn't just something that he alone had to do. And he was sure that this would lead to more ideas emerging in their brainstorming sessions as well as more respect for each other's expertise. And maybe when they discussed the brainstorming sessions as a team, they might come up with other ideas for improving their team performance too. I almost missed this opportunity, thought Tom, when I was rushing between meetings, but capturing the odd moment here or there where things work differently and then reflecting on them can lead to real improvements.

Reflection Prompts

We can reflect on our own or with others, whether that is with teams that we lead or teams we are members of, or with mentors or coaches. Generative Artificial Intelligence (GenAI) can be helpful in suggesting prompts for reflection, particularly if we give these apps prompts specific to our context, for example our role, industry sector, size and location of our work, and whether hybrid, virtual, or face to face. This helps avoid continually using the same questions to prompt reflection.

Table 3.1 shows examples of reflection questions generated by five Generative AI apps for a coaching manager. The full responses were far longer, with extracts included here to give a flavour of what the apps provide. The apps used were Gemini (Google), ChatGPT (OpenAI), Claude (Anthropic), Copilot (Microsoft Bing), and Perplexity.

Although coaching apps may seem superficial, they are non-judgemental in their responses. This gives users a feeling of safety in reflecting honestly

Table 3.1 Examples of Reflection Prompts for Managers Generated by AI Apps

Write questions for a coaching manager to prompt reflection				
Gemini (Bard)	ChatGPT	Claude	Copilot	Perplexity
Describe a recent coaching session that didn't go as smoothly as you'd hoped. What did you learn from it? What are the biggest challenges your coachees are facing right now in achieving their goals?	Are there instances when you could improve your listening skills to better understand your team members? Are there situations where you could improve the depth and impact of your questioning?	How equitably do I distribute opportunities or challenging assignments on my team? What would help ensure I recognise all potential? How can I foster deeper trust, respect, and commitment between myself and each employee?	What would I do more of, less of, or differently moving forward? How is my energy during coaching sessions, and what does that tell me? Where did I feel constriction or judgement, and what triggered it? Are there any past patterns I need to consider for myself or my clients?	What do you think went well? What are some of the go-to questions in your coaching toolbox? Why do you use those questions? How do you know when a question is effective? How will you plan to improve?

on their experience. In a research study, this in turn helped people to be more receptive to feedback from their supervisors and enhanced their resilience (97).

Another way in which technology can enhance our coaching is by using a video of coaching sessions (with the participant's permission), with software such as Ovida which provides data analysis of recorded conversations (98). The data provided can include how many questions there were, how many open questions, how much of the time the coach is speaking, and how many times the coach interrupts. This can be used as the basis for reflection, increasing self-awareness and contributing to self-development, particularly once managers get used to the technology and to being recorded.

Self-coaching is the application of coaching skills to our own situation, asking ourselves questions as a coach would do, setting and following up on goals, and reflecting on our experience (99, 100). When this is our default way of being, we are constantly learning and adjusting our leadership approach.

Reflection in the Hybrid and Virtual World

As managers we can help individual team members deepen the quality of their reflections by prompting them to go beyond a simple description of an event and a description of a single event. These conversations can be held online or face to face. An advantage of online discussions is that it is easy to add notes in the chat and to keep a record of what is discussed.

Coaching apps incorporating AI such as journalling apps can help with self-coaching (101). While AI does not (yet) have the agility and wisdom of a human coach, it can help by posing questions. Such apps vary from unstructured, where the user can capture any thoughts or images they like, to highly structured templates with a series of reflection prompts. Some apps have been developed based on positive psychology and related fields and include a daily meditation with a focus on gratitude, stress, or mental health. Trying a different app periodically can help users avoid settling into routine responses to the same prompts.

To facilitate reflection in a face-to-face or online meeting, a short time-out can be useful. Short time-outs are usually welcomed by participants in online meetings as an opportunity to rest their eyes or stretch their legs as well as to clarify their thinking about something that is proving challenging. For managers who take a little longer to decide on the way forward, such time-outs are invaluable.

Managers who have not yet tried reflection may not realise the power that it has to help us improve what we do and help us to help others improve. Those who write off reflection as a superficial description of events lose an opportunity for sense-making and for personal growth.

Crafting a narrative of how we want to be perceived underestimates the power of an honest in-depth reflection. Managers who have begun to realise the power of story-telling may consciously or unconsciously adopt the same approach in their reflection, usually with themselves as the hero of the story, reducing their opportunity for insight.

Reflection without action can be an interesting way to pass the time but adds little value to the manager's own development, or to their team or organisation. Reflection should lead to action as Drucker (102) advocated 70 years ago: 'Follow effective action with quiet reflection. From the quiet reflection will come even more effective action.'

Getting Better at Reflection

Here are three activities to help you get better at reflection:

1. Some managers find a daily or weekly journal useful, while others prefer to reflect when there has been a specific event that has not gone well or where they feel they could do better. Some prefer to record their thoughts on their phone when in the car or walking. Others exchange ideas with an AI app (more on AI apps in Chapter Six). Find what works for you and make it a habit.

2. Allowing time between meetings, or at the end of the day or the week, allows managers to process what has happened, think about what has worked well, and consider where they might improve or need some professional development. When we walk between meetings, there is a natural break. With online meetings, we have to guard against going from one meeting to the next without any pause (103). Allowing a few minutes between meetings is helpful in reflecting on the previous meeting and preparing for the next.

3. Find your blind spot either using a self-assessment instrument or a tool like the Johari Window and seeking feedback from others. We all have blind spots. The critical thing is to be honest and not to waste time in fooling ourselves. The purpose is not to present a perfect façade to ourselves or anyone else but to use the outcome as a prompt for reflection and to identify ways to grow. If we identify and address one area to improve, that is a positive outcome. A few months later or the following

year, we might address another area. We cannot address all our opportunities for improvement at the same time, but we should try to address one or two, make progress, get more feedback, and continue to grow.

IN CLOSING

The individual coaching skills of observation, listening, and asking questions discussed in Chapter Two, and the skills of goal-setting, feedback, and reflection discussed in this chapter, combine to provide a powerful way of enacting leadership in the workplace. Observation and listening (including questioning) form the basis for feedback, for ideas for strategy, for problem-solving, and for innovation. Goal-setting helps implement these ideas and address feedback or insights from reflection which in turn leads to performance improvements. Listening also helps foster positive relationships which is motivating in itself and also makes it more likely that feedback will be accepted. All these skills could be used in one coaching session with an employee; for example, a manager might:

- Ask questions to establish rapport and readiness for feedback
- Share feedback
- Listen to employee perspective
- Ask questions to clarify
- Reflect together
- Observe and decide whether to continue or to re-convene

If continuing:

- Agree a goal for the future
- Ask questions to generate options and commitment to chosen option

Managers might also use just one of these skills, such as listening to a colleague talking through an issue they are facing. When leaders act as coaches, they have the choice to adopt a formal or informal approach, use one coaching skill or combine a number of coaching skills, and use their skills face to face or online.

The focus for a coaching manager is on helping their team members perform at their best, leading to improved outcomes for the individual, as well as for the team (as discussed in Chapter Four) and for the organisation (as discussed in Chapter Five). Coaching managers continuously seek feedback and reflect, so that they improve their own performance as leaders and have a positive impact on their teams and their organisations.

NOTES

1 See https://zapier.com/templates/motivational-coach-bot for more information.

REFERENCES

1. Cardona P, Rey C, Cardona P, Rey C. *Management by missions: connecting people to strategy through purpose*. Switzerland: Palgrave Macmillan; 2022.

2. Ives Y, Cox E. *Goal-focused coaching: theory and practice*. Abingdon, Oxon.: Routledge; 2012.

3. Spence G. GAS powered coaching: goal attainment scaling and its use in coaching research and practice. *International Coaching Psychology Review*. 2007;2(2): 155–67.

4. Grant AM. The significance of task significance: job performance effects, relational mechanisms, and boundary conditions. *Journal of Applied Psychology*. 2008;93(1): 108.

5. Clutterbuck D, Spence G. Working with goals in coaching. In: Bachkirova T, Spence G, Drake DB, editors. *The Sage handbook of coaching*. London: Sage; 2017. p. 218–37.

6. Latham GP, Locke EA. Enhancing the benefits and overcoming the pitfalls of goal setting. *Organizational Dynamics*. 2006;35(4): 332–40.

7. Narayanan S. Employee engagement and motivation for ESG at workplace. In: Singh SKA, Haldar, P., editors. *Digital disruption and environmental, social & governance*. India: Bazooka Publications; 2022. p. 139.

8. Kieran S, MacMahon J, MacCurtain S. Strategic change and sensemaking practice: enabling the role of the middle manager. *Baltic Journal of Management*. 2020;15(4): 493–514.

9. Nicolau A, Candel OS, Constantin T, Kleingeld A. The effects of executive coaching on behaviors, attitudes, and personal characteristics: a meta-analysis of randomized control trial studies. *Frontiers in Psychology*. 2023;14: 1089797.

10. Locke EA, Latham GP. The development of goal setting theory: a half century retrospective. *Motivation Science*. 2019;5(2): 93.

11. Liu W, Zhang B, Sun R, Li S. Busting the blackbox between managerial coaching behaviors and employee outcomes from a perspective of discrete emotional process mechanism. *Leadership & Organization Development Journal*. 2024;45(6): 954–75.

12. Höchli B, Brügger A, Messner C. How focusing on superordinate goals motivates broad, long-term goal pursuit: a theoretical perspective. *Frontiers in Psychology*. 2018;9: 1879. doi: 10.3389/fpsyg.2018.01879

13. House RJ, Dorfman PW, Javidan M, Hanges PJ, De Luque MFS. *Strategic leadership across cultures: GLOBE study of CEO leadership behavior and effectiveness in 24 countries*. Sage Publications; 2013.

14. Garvey B, Garvey R, Stokes P. Coaching and mentoring: theory and practice: Sage; 2021.

15. Bright JE, Pryor RG. The chaos theory of careers. *Journal of Employment Counseling*. 2011;48(4): 163–6.

16. Gilson LL, Davis WD. *Managing in an age of complexity and uncertainty*. SAGE Publications: Los Angeles; 2019. p. 243–6.

17. Doerr J. *Measure what matters: the simple idea that drives 10x growth*. London: Penguin; 2018.

18. Sparks R. https://www.atlassian.com/agile/agile-at-scale/okr: Atlassian. 2023.

19. Rompho N. Do objectives and key results solve organizational performance measurement issues? *Benchmarking: An International Journal*. 2024;31(3): 669–82.

20. Wilson C. *Performance coaching: a complete guide to best practice coaching and training.* Kogan Page Publishers; 2020.

21. Collins J, Porras J. *Built to last.* Harper Collins; 1994.

22. Desjardins C. Don't be too SMART, but SAVE your goals: proposal for a renewed goal-setting formula for Generation Y. *Journal of Applied Leadership and Management.* 2021;9: 73–87.

23. Bandura A. Self-efficacy: towards a unifying theory of behavioral change. *Psychological Review.* 1977;84(2): 191–215.

24. Francis S, Zarecky A. Working with strengths in coaching. In: Bachkirova T, Spence G, Clutterbuck D, editors. *The SAGE handbook of coaching.* London: Sage; 2017. p. 363–80.

25. Grant AM. It takes time: a stages of change perspective on the adoption of workplace coaching skills. *Journal of Change Management.* 2010;10(1): 61–77.

26. Terblanche N, Molyn J, de Haan E, Nilsson VO. Comparing artificial intelligence and human coaching goal attainment efficacy. *Plos one.* 2022;17(6): e0270255.

27. Diller SJ. Ethics in digital and AI coaching. *Human Resource Development International.* 2024;27(4): 584–96.

28. Stroet HP. *AI in performance management: what are the effects for line managers?* PhD thesis. University of Twente; 2020.

29. Ordonez LD, Schweitzer ME, Galinsky AD, Bazerman MH. Goals gone wild: how goals systematically harm individuals and organizations. *Academy of Management Perspectives for Managers.* 2009;23(1): 6–12.

30. Dunning D. The Dunning–Kruger effect: on being ignorant of one's own ignorance. *Advances in Experimental Social Psychology.* 2011;44: 247–96.

31. Lee WR, Choi SB, Kang S-W. How leaders' positive feedback influences employees' innovative behavior: the mediating role of voice behavior and job autonomy. *Sustainability.* 2021;13(4): 1901.

32. House R, Javidan, M. Lessons from project GLOBE. *Organizational Dynamics.* 2001;29(4): 289–305.

33. Ou AY, Waldman DA, Peterson SJ. Do humble CEOs matter? An examination of CEO humility and firm outcomes. *Journal of Management.* 2018;44(3): 1147–73.

34. Owens BP, Johnson MD, Mitchell TR. Expressed humility in organizations: implications for performance, teams, and leadership. *Organization Science.* 2013;24(5): 1517–38.

35. Cox E, Bachkirova T, Clutterbuck D, editors. *The complete handbook of coaching.* London: Sage; 2010.

36. McCarthy G. *Coaching and mentoring for business.* London: Sage; 2014.

37. Baxendale R. Q&A: David Morrison 'stole' best line from David Hurley. *The Australian.* 2 Feb 2016.

38. Brown M, Kulik CT, Lim V. Managerial tactics for communicating negative performance feedback. *Personnel Review.* 2016;45(5): 969–87.

39. Magni F, Manzoni B. Generational differences in workers' expectations: millennials want more of the same things. *European Management Review.* 2020;17(4): 901–14.

40. Hsieh HH, Huang JT. Exploring factors influencing employees' impression management feedback-seeking behavior: the role of managerial coaching skills and affective trust. *Human Resource Development Quarterly.* 2018;29(2): 163–80.

41. Knight R. How to handle difficult conversations at work. *Harvard Business Review*. 9 Jan 2015. https://hbr.org/2015/01/how-to-handle-difficult-conversations-at-work

42. Nikolić TM, Perić N, Bovan A. The role of feedback as a management tool in performance management program. *Calitatea*. 2020;21(177): 3–8.

43. Moore JR, Hanson W. Improving leader effectiveness: impact on employee engagement and retention. *Journal of Management Development*. 2022;41(7/8): 450–68.

44. Salvadorinho J, Teixeira L, editors. Leadership coaching framework tool-based to support worker engagement and retention in Industry 4.0. Proceedings of the International Conference on Industrial Engineering and Operations Management, 26–28 July 2022, Rome, Italy; 2022.

45. Barsh J, Lavoie, J. Lead at your best. *McKinsey Quarterly*. 2014. https://www.mckinsey.com/featured-insights/leadership/lead-at-your-best.

46. Fredrickson BL, Losada MF. Positive affect and the complex dynamics of human flourishing. *American Psychologist*. 2005;60(7): 678.

47. Friedman HL, Brown NJ. Implications of debunking the 'critical positivity ratio' for humanistic psychology: introduction to special issue. *Journal of Humanistic Psychology*. 2018;58(3): 239–61.

48. Baldwin D. How to win the blame game. *Harvard Business Review*. 2001;79(7): 55–143.

49. Weiss JA. *An examination of employee coachability and managerial coaching in organizations*. PhD thesis. De Paul University; 2019.

50. Lewis L. Creating the conditions for receptivity of feedback. *International Journal of Evidence Based Coaching and Mentoring*. 2015(9): 90–101.

51. Steelman LA, Wolfeld L. The manager as coach: the role of feedback orientation. *Journal of Business Psychology*. 2018;33(1): 41–53.

52. Burns R. To a Louse. 1786 [Available from: http://www.robertburns.org/works/97.shtml].

53. Ellinger AD, Bostrom RP. Managerial coaching behaviors in learning organizations. *Journal of Management Development*. 1999;18(9): 752–71.

54. Pronin E. How we see ourselves and how we see others. *Science*. 2008;320(5880): 1177–80.

55. McDowall A, Millward L. Feeding back, feeding forward and setting goals. In: Palmer S, McDowall A, editors. *The coaching relationship: putting people first*. Hove: Routledge; 2010. p. 55–78.

56. Biswas-Diener R. *Practicing positive psychology coaching: assessment, activities and strategies for success*. John Wiley & Sons; 2010.

57. Kauffman C. Positive psychology: the science at the heart of coaching. In: Stober DR, Grant AM, editors. *Evidence based coaching handbook: putting best practices to work for your clients*. Hoboken, NJ: Wiley; 2006, p. 219–53.

58. Seligman ME. Coaching and positive psychology. *Australian Psychologist*. 2007;42(4): 266–7.

59. Grant AM, O'Connor SA. Broadening and building solution-focused coaching: feeling good is not enough. *Coaching: An International Journal of Theory, Research and Practice*. 2018;11(2): 165–85.

60. Goldsmith M. Try feedforward instead of feedback. In: Goldsmith M, Lyons L, editors. *Coaching for leadership*. San Francisco: Pfeiffer; 2006.

61. Mrazek III JC. *Investigating and comparing the differences in feedback orientation between three generations*. PhD thesis. The University of the Rockies; 2015.

62. Ray P, Singh M. Effective feedback for millennials in new organizations. *Human Resource Management International Digest.* 2018;26(4): 25–7.

63. Chillakuri BK. Fueling performance of millennials and generation Z. *Strategic HR Review.* 2020;19(1): 41–3.

64. Delgado D, Hill N, Regalado A, Waldman N. Millennials leading the workforce. *Journal of Business Studies Quarterly.* 2020;10(2): 35–42.

65. Gabrielova K, Buchko AA. Here comes Generation Z: millennials as managers. *Business Horizons.* 2021;64(4): 489–99.

66. Lyons P, Bandura R. Employee learning stimulated by manager-as-coach. *Journal of Workplace Learning.* 2020;32(8): 627–40.

67. Meyer E. *The culture map*. New York: Public Affairs; 2015.

68. Settle-Murphy N. *Leading effective virtual teams*. Boca Raton, Fl.: CRC Auerbach; 2012.

69. Shin SY, Ulusoy E, Earle K, Bente G, Van Der Heide B. The effects of self-viewing in video chat during interpersonal work conversations. *Journal of Computer-Mediated Communication.* 2023;28(1): zmac028.

70. Stoeckli E, Uebernickel F, Brenner W, Weierich A, Hess S. Digital feedback for digital work? Affordances and constraints of a feedback app at InsurCorp. 14th International Conference on Wirtschaftsinformatik, 24–27 Feb 2019, Siegen, Germany.

71. Welch NM. *Team coaching: influencing work-team trust*. PhD thesis. Fielding Graduate University; 2021.

72. Center for Creative Leadership. Leading effectively. CCL. 10 April 2024. https://www.ccl.org/articles/leading-effectively-articles/what-is-psychological-safety-at-work/

73. Edmondson AC, Bransby DP. Psychological safety comes of age: observed themes in an established literature. *Annual Review of Organizational Psychology and Organizational Behavior.* 2023;10: 55–78.

74. Carr C, Peters J. The experience of team coaching: a dual case study. *International Coaching Psychology Review.* 2013;8(1): 80–98.

75. Frazier ML, Fainshmidt S, Klinger RL, Pezeshkan A, Vracheva V. Psychological safety: a meta-analytic review and extension. *Personnel Psychology.* 2017;70(1): 113–65.

76. Tkalich A, Šmite D, Andersen NH, Moe NB. What happens to psychological safety when going remote? *IEEE Software.* 2024;41: 113–22.

77. Candan RI. *Effects of sandwiched feedback versus direct feedback on performance*. PhD thesis. The Chicago School of Professional Psychology; 2023.

78. World Economic Forum Future of Jobs. World Economic Forum. 2023. https://www.weforum.org/publications/the-future-of-jobs-report-2023/.

79. Kross E, Ong M, Ayduk O. Self-reflection at work: why it matters and how to harness its potential and avoid its pitfalls. *Annual Review of Organizational Psychology and Organizational Behavior.* 2023;10: 441–64.

80. Du Toit A. Making sense through coaching. *Journal of Management Development.* 2007;26(3): 282–91.

81. Kolb D. *Experiential learning*. Englewood Cliffs, NJ: Prentice Hall; 1984.

82. Porter J. Why you should make time for reflection even if you hate doing it. *Harvard Business Review.* 21 March 2017. https://hbr.org/2017/03/why-you-should-make-time-for-self-reflection-even-if-you-hate-doing-it.

83.	Athanasopoulou A, Dopson S. *Developing leaders by executive coaching: practice and evidence.* Oxford: OUP; 2015.

84.	Hunt P. Keeping up-to-date with technology change. In: Passmore J, Diller SJ, Isaacson S, Brantl M, editors. *The digital and AI coaches' handbook: the complete guide to the use of online, AI, and technology in coaching.* Abingdon, Oxon.: Routledge; 2024. p. 49–63.

85.	Muff K, Liechti A, Dyllick T. How to apply responsible leadership theory in practice: a competency tool to collaborate on the sustainable development goals. *Corporate Social Responsibility and Environmental Management.* 2020;27(5): 2254–74.

86.	Hullinger A, DiGirolamo J, Tkach J. Reflective practice for coaches and clients: an integrated model for learning. *Philosophy of Coaching: An International Journal.* 2019;4(2): 5–34.

87.	Eurich T. Harvard Business Review. 2018. https://hbr.org/2018/01/what-self-awareness-really-is-and-how-to-cultivate-it.

88.	Jones RJ. *Coaching with research in mind.* Abingdon, Oxon.: Routledge; 2020.

89.	Cannon HM, Feinstein AH, Friesen DP, editors. Managing complexity: applying the conscious-competence model to experiential learning. Developments in business simulation and experiential learning. Proceedings of the annual Association for Business Simulation and Experiential Learning (ABSEL) conference. Little Rock, AR, 2010.

90.	Ruona WE, Gilley JW. Practitioners in applied professions: a model applied to human resource development. *Advances in Developing Human Resources.* 2009;11(4): 438–53.

91.	Luft J, Ingham H. The Johari Window. *Human Relations Training News.* 1961;5(1): 6–7.

92.	Freedman AM. Some implications of validation of the leadership pipeline concept: guidelines for assisting managers-in-transition. *The Psychologist-Manager Journal.* 2011;14(2): 140–59.

93.	Schoen D. *The reflective practitioner: how professionals think in practice.* Aldershot: Ashgate; 1983.

94.	Passmore J, Woodward W. Coaching education: wake up to the new digital and AI coaching revolution! *International Coaching Psychology Review.* 2023;18(1): 58–72.

95.	Moon JA. *A handbook of reflective and experiential learning: theory and practice.* Routledge; 2013.

96.	Brassey J, De Smet A, Kruyt M. *Deliberate calm: how to learn and lead in a volatile world.* HarperCollins; 2022.

97.	Ellis-Brush K. Augmenting coaching practice through digital methods. *International Journal of Evidence Based Coaching & Mentoring.* 2021;15: 187–97.

98.	Bridgeman J, Giraldez-Hayes A. Using artificial intelligence-enhanced video feedback for reflective practice in coach development: benefits and potential drawbacks. *Coaching: An International Journal of Theory, Research and Practice.* 2024;17(1): 32–49.

99.	Goodyear C. How self-coaching can work for you. *Nursing Management.* 2023;54(12): 56.

100.	Greif S, Rauen C. Self-reflection in coaching. In: Greif S, Moeller H, Scholl W, Passmore J, Mueller F, editors. *International handbook of evidence-based coaching: theory, research and practice.* Cham: Springer; 2022. p. 839–49.

101.	Graßmann C, Schermuly CC. Coaching with artificial intelligence: concepts and capabilities. *Human Resource Development Review.* 2021;20(1): 106–26.

102.	Drucker PF. *The practice of management.* New York: Harpers; 1954.

103.	Hawkins P. *Leadership team coaching: developing collective transformational leadership.* E-book ed.: Kogan Page; 2021.

Four

INTRODUCTION

In previous chapters, we discussed coaching skills in the context of individual coaching conversations, whether face to face or online. In this chapter, we will explore both face-to-face and online *team* coaching. We will discuss both formal team coaching and the use of coaching skills by team leaders.

Much of the research about team coaching is in the context of an external coach working with a team. Fortunately much of this research is also relevant for managers coaching their own teams. Team coaching by managers is less common than coaching of individuals (1) but it offers tremendous potential for amplifying the positive impact of coaching in organisations. Although individual coaching is very effective, research suggests that durable changes in leadership behaviour can best be achieved through coaching in the group context (2). Indeed even when every individual member of the team is coached, the team does not necessarily improve (3).

As Hooijberg and Watkins (4) point out, leading a hybrid team requires skills in addition to those required for leading a team that only works face to face. They suggest that in the virtual space, managers need excellent coordination skills including goal-setting and progress monitoring, while in the face-to-face space, the focus is more on collaboration, learning, emotional connections, and difficult conversations. If there are problems in a team in the face-to-face environment, research suggests that such problems will be amplified in the online space (5), making it all the more critical for team leaders to have the skills to manage in the online as well as in the physical workplace.

Coaching helps in both face-to-face and virtual contexts. However, there is limited research on virtual team coaching (6), particularly when the focus, as in this book, is on managers coaching their own teams, and

DOI: 10.4324/9781003239826-4

not on external coaches working with a team. In this chapter we explore what is currently known about coaching teams while the wider organisational context is discussed in Chapter Five.

TEAMS AND TEAM COACHING

The importance of teams has risen with the increase in complexity in organisations, the global challenges we all face, and the increased pace of change. This increased complexity, as highlighted in Chapter One, means that 'there is now a need for people to relate differently to each other in order to create new ways of thinking, being, working and organising' (7, C1). A hierarchical approach where people have to wait to be told what to do, and where cross-functional initiatives have to be approved by relevant authorities in each functional area, does not allow an organisation to be agile. In contrast, in organisations where there is a shared understanding and shared values, people can use their initiative, confident that their decisions will be in line with strategic priorities. Coaching team leaders empower team members to interact directly with each other and not refer each decision back to the team leader for approval. This enables the team to respond quickly when issues arise and creates a positive team culture as team members learn to rely on each other and deepen their relationships. Furthermore, the relationships developed through cross-functional teams help find ways around organisational obstacles.

A further reason for an enhanced appreciation of teams is the increase in volume and complexity of knowledge and the pace at which new knowledge is developed. It is increasingly difficult for any one individual to have a detailed grasp of all relevant knowledge. The benefits of diversity are well-known, sparking creativity and novel ideas (8). Diversity helps ensure that the team as a whole has sufficient understanding of the issues at stake and insights into the options possible. The range of perspectives and expertise of team members allow stronger strategies to be developed and implemented, with a better understanding of customer needs leading to more innovation and creative problem-solving.

Clear roles and responsibilities are important for all teams to function efficiently. Peter Hawkins (9, p. 18) lists the essential requirements for effective teams as:

core learning, coordinating and consolidating, reflecting, learning, integrating;
    clarifying, team charter, team KPIs, goals, objectives, roles;

commissioning, ensuring a clear commission for the team and contracting on what it must deliver, selection;
   co-creating, interpersonal and team dynamics team culture; and
   connecting and engaging all the critical stakeholders.

Team coaching addresses each of these requirements and thereby supports team effectiveness. It is a collective process that engages with the whole team, rather than, or not only, between individual team members and the team leader. Clutterbuck (10, p. 120) defines team coaching as 'Helping the team improve performance, and the processes by which performance is achieved, through reflection and dialogue'. Team coaching has also been described as a sustained series of conversations, with a focus on goal-setting, deepening awareness, actions, and accountability (11).

As team coaching research and practice have increased over the last few years, definitions of team coaching have evolved. Whereas Hawkins and Smith (12) initially defined team coaching as 'enabling a team to function as more than the sum of its parts, by clarifying its mission and improving its external and internal relationships', Hawkins (6, p. 80) later framed team coaching as being 'for any team, not just the most senior, where the focus is on how the team collectively gives leadership to those who report to them, and also how the team influences their key stakeholder groups'.

Just as coachability is important for effective coaching of individuals, so too is coachability important for team coaching. Welch (13, p. 69) highlights three aspects of coachability for team coaching: being open to exploring different perspectives, being open to change, and being emotionally available. Managers rarely have the opportunity to select a new team, and individual team members may be at different levels of willingness to engage in formal coaching (14). Hawkins (6) warns that if advocates push for team coaching to be adopted, the resistance of the sceptics will intensify. Instead, informal coaching can be used with the team, using the coaching skills discussed in Chapters Two and Three.

FORMAL TEAM COACHING

Formal team coaching comprises coaching the team collectively as well as coaching individual team members. There are three main applications, namely team goal-setting and action planning, addressing feedback and problem-solving, and reflection and learning. Each of these will now be discussed.

Goal-setting can be a great team-building activity as well as creating a shared understanding and shared priorities. These shared goals are the foundation for empowerment and enable team members to take decisions quickly in line with the agreed priorities. The process of the team working through organisational goals together cements a sense of common purpose.

A coaching team leader needs to be clear on the organisational goals to which their team contributes so that they can facilitate their team in determining how they will do so, in addition to identifying any additional goals of specific relevance to the team. Managers who align employee aspirations with organisational goals and facilitate the achievement of individual and team objectives have a greater impact on team effectiveness than pressure-based managers who apply extensive pressure to get results (15). The latter can achieve short-term benefits but damage long-term team performance outcomes, generating stress and tension within the team.

Considering organisational goals first of all, the leader as coach reviews relevant organisational goals with the team and, importantly, explains why they are relevant to this particular team. Research by Latham and Locke (16) stresses the importance of making the rationale clear. An open question asking team members to explore how they see (or do not see) the relevance is helpful in surfacing disagreements or lack of conviction about the relevance. Some organisations allow freedom in how organisational goals are worded at the unit level. This can be helpful in ensuring that the goals are understood by everyone across the organisation and fosters buy-in. The Objectives Key Results (OKR) process outlined in Chapter Three works well as a collaborative team approach to goal-setting (17), ensuring that the team has a shared understanding of priorities, that it is aligned on a shared direction and vision, and communication and transparency are improved.

In identifying additional goals for the team, the team leader might ask open questions such as 'What else do we need to focus on to make this our best year yet?'. In an online meeting, participants might be invited to add their suggestions in the chat. These suggestions can then be reviewed collectively. For example, if there is a pattern in complaints suggesting a need for upskilling, the team might agree on training on a specific topic, with the measure for success set as a reduction in complaints. If employee surveys suggest that more mentoring is needed, the team might agree on a target for mentoring. Short-term goals that lead towards long-term goals are helpful in making long-term goals tangible and directing effort towards things that are achievable. This increases the likelihood of success in achieving the long-term goals (18).

Once goals have been agreed, the team can move to planning specific actions to achieve the goals, such as organising training or mentoring and tracking the number of people attending training or engaging in mentoring. A shared team calendar can be used as a simple way to high-light deadlines. As mentioned in Chapter Three, there are now many goal tracking apps on the market. Some apps are also starting to emerge at the team level. Talability[1] provides a strategy map, allowing users to zoom in to individual teams or out to the organisational level, while ClickUp[2] combines collaboration, time management, and project management tools to track progress on goals. While it has long been known that follow-up increases the likelihood of agreed actions being implemented, it is only recently that we are seeing evidence that this follow-up can be undertaken effectively by software. This means that rather than following up on all the actions in a plan, the team leader can focus on actions that are at risk of, or are actually, falling behind. Most goal tracking software apps include visualisations to draw attention quickly to items of poten-tial concern.

Feedback, Problem-Solving, and Innovation

Feedback can be motivating and empowering as noted by Shave (19, p. 22) who says: 'Being proactive in monitoring team performance allows managers to provide feedback in real time, keeping the team on track, empowering, and encouraging remote workers and virtual team members.' Feedback on team performance can come from a variety of sources, such as from internal or external clients, from the manager's observations, or from the team's own reflections. There is a risk that team members who get on well with each other may be reluctant to raise difficult issues, not wishing to 'rock the boat' or offend each other. The team leader can emphasise the positive intent of feedback and help the team to address it as an opportunity for improvement rather than as criticism to be rejected (10).

One of the skills of the team leader is to know when feedback is best given individually and when best to the team as a whole. If feed-back about a negative issue does not apply to everyone in the team, those not contributing to the issue may resent being 'tarred with the one brush' if the feedback is given to everyone. If only one individual has contributed to an issue, that individual should be given feedback in private. In contrast, if there is an open and trusting environment, if feedback applies to the team as a whole and all team members can contribute to improvements, then discussing team feedback collectively is valuable. The same principles apply to team feedback as to individual feedback (see Chapter Three): feedback being specific, timely, and actionable. As with individual feedback, it may be useful to pause to reflect on the feedback before switching to creative collective problem-solving mode. Even where feedback is specific to an individual, once the issue has been identified, it may be useful to call on the team to help develop potential solutions.

Creative problem-solving, whether to address feedback or to develop new or improved products, services, or processes, is an energising activity for a team. Recent research has shown that managerial coaching has a positive impact on innovative work behaviour (20), which, given the increasing need for organisations to develop and improve their products, services, and processes, is of huge benefit. Appreciative Inquiry is a strengths-based approach which is consistent with team coaching, encouraging people to dream and to realise those dreams (21).

Collective brainstorming usually generates more ideas than from one person on their own. It is important for the team leader to ensure that all ideas are initially welcome, with judgement and prioritisation coming later. Although some of the ideas that emerge may not be practical, they may form the nucleus of a useful idea that might otherwise not have been voiced. An alternative form of brainstorming is for everyone to write their ideas on sticky notes without discussing them, writing one idea or question per note. These notes are then placed on a wall, and similar ideas grouped together (hence writing only one idea on each note which can be moved around). This gives equal weight to all ideas, regardless of the seniority of any individual. The original version of the rules for brainstorming recommended that some time should pass before reviewing ideas (22) – to enable ideas that had not emerged in the first meeting to be put forward and to allow a fresh look at the ideas that had been generated. The ideas are then discussed, with some ideas combined and others eliminated, until a consensus is reached, or a vote held, possibly applying a set of criteria which may or may not be weighted. This approach to brainstorming works in groups of all sizes, even with hundreds of people.

The online version of posting notes on a wall is easy to implement, using software like Miro or Mural. Many of these tools are integrated with collaboration platforms like Webex or Slack, allowing teams to chat and video conference as well as share their ideas. A further advantage to online is automatically generated captions, transcriptions, and in some cases translation. Even where the text needs manual editing in order to be fully accurate and grammatically correct, this still saves a huge amount of time. Some platforms such as Microsoft Teams now incorporate Artificial Intelligence and can summarise the discussion, or what a particular person has said, and draft the wording of any actions agreed. These platforms also offer a feature where the software recognises when a person joins a meeting late and gives them a summary of what has been discussed up to that point, any links shared, and any actions agreed. Chat and Q&A functions also provide a record which can be put through an Artificial Intelligence app to get a quick summary of the key points, taking care that nothing confidential is included.

Team Reflection and Learning

Self-awareness is as important for teams as it is for individuals (23, 24). The importance of reflection cannot be overstated, allowing teams to make sense of a range of data points, to learn from experience, to develop a shared worldview, and, at the same time, to guard against groupthink and bias. Indeed Welch (13, p. 108) describes reflection as 'an ongoing, integral component of team coaching'. Team coaching deepens the quality of team reflection, which helps teams to innovate and to maintain productivity during stressful times (7).

The Johari Window mentioned in Chapter Three can also be used to explore levels of team awareness in different teams. It can increase the size of what the team knows and what other people know about them and reduce the size of the blind and the hidden areas (i.e. those areas where the team has a blind spot about something that others can see or areas which the team is aware of but keeps hidden). Increasing self-disclosure leads to increased trust, which in turn makes people more comfortable about self-disclosure (25).

Reflection can take place 'in action', for example during a meeting, or 'after action', for example in an after action review or project wash-up meeting. After action reviews are perceived as more common as it may not be obvious to team members when the team leader is reflecting in action. After action reviews do not always take place, as teams are often eager to move onto the next project or under pressure to do so. Without reflection, the team loses the opportunity to learn for the next time and may repeat their previous way of approaching a project. As Clutterbuck (10, p. 12–13) points out, 'Teams are typically so busy doing that they have little time for reflection. Team coaching helps teams review performance, boost results, improve communication and build rapport.' Effective teams learn from a wide range of sources – experience, feedback, data, and external and internal stimuli as well as undertaking training together. Clutterbuck suggests that members of permanent teams join different project teams at least once a year so that they experience different approaches to teamwork.

Coaching managers have been found to have a significant impact on team learning, particularly in the case of high performance work teams (26). Attending training together virtually or face to face provides a common language and enables team members to support each other in applying what has been learned. Where training is online and completed independently, the team can discuss what each person learned in a later meeting, thereby reinforcing what has been learned. While learning is usually grounded in what has been learned from the past, Cooperrider uses the term 'anticipatory learning' to indicate discovery when teams work together (21). They suggest that setting a goal for complex challenges like sustainable development can lead to people arguing about specific targets and not doing anything, whereas a focus on learning can help people move forward. Team leaders who adopt a coaching approach explicitly prompt their team to learn.

Confirming the close relationship between coaching and learning, Clutterbuck (27, p. 280) identifies team coaching as 'a learning intervention designed to increase collective capability and performance of a group or team, through application of the coaching principles of assisted reflection, analysis and motivation for change'. Setting aside some time to learn together makes it more likely that teams will learn and improve. This can be a few minutes in a regular meeting or specific meetings for the purpose of learning. In this increasingly complex world, Hawkins (28, C3) writes: 'The world needs forms of team coaching that bring together the best that both coaching and organizational development have to offer in a new integrated approach that simultaneously enables the individual, team, organization and wider eco-system to learn and co-evolve together.' By fostering connections between team members, managers enhance knowledge sharing and team performance as well as positive relationships in the team, leading to trust and employee engagement (29). The role of the team leader is crucial in ensuring that the team makes time for collective learning and reflection, as otherwise teams tend to prioritise tasks (10). It is important for team members to take collective responsibility for the team's performance and for each other's learning, as well as integrating individual development plans with team goals (10). Teams can also set collective learning goals. For example, if team members agree on the importance of climate action, they might agree that they will all undertake a short course on carbon literacy, so that their collective discussions and decisions are well-informed.

Some learning styles limit the ability of the team to learn (6); there are teams which only operate on a trial and error basis, teams which restrict their learning to correcting a past mistake, teams which reflect without taking action, teams which analyse without piloting, and teams which have little engagement with the wider system. Team leaders should be alert to the possibility of these limitations and coach their team to embrace learning and development on an on-going basis.

USING COACHING SKILLS AS A TEAM LEADER

Coaching skills are useful in many of the responsibilities of a team leader, such as developing their team, monitoring team dynamics, chairing meetings, enabling sound decision-making, leading negotiations, and team communication. Team leaders can help the team not only to focus on completing tasks but to engage with each other and share responsibility for the team's success (5).

Developing Effective Teams

According to Clutterbuck et al. (8), team coaching can help a group to become a team, enhancing the collective function which leads to higher performance. In other words, a team coaching approach can help with team building as well as with team performance. A study in the UK and Greece found that skilful managerial coaching makes a significant difference to the team's performance (30). Team reflection helps build/re-build trust (31, p.29): 'Deep, shared reflection is a critical step in enabling groups of organizations and individuals to actually "hear" a point of view different from their own, and to appreciate emotionally as well as cognitively each other's reality. This is an essential doorway for building trust where distrust had prevailed and for fostering collective creativity.' When new people join an existing team, it takes time to establish connection and trust (8). This requires more than introducing the new person at the first meeting they attend. The coaching team leader can look for opportunities for the new person to work on a task with one or more other team members and to be the person who reports back to the whole team. This gives others the reassurance that they can depend on the new team member.

If it is possible for a team to meet face to face, as is the case for hybrid teams, this can help establish rapport initially, with later meetings held online or occasionally face to face. If the team only works together virtually, it is useful for the manager to meet virtually with each individual prior to the first team meeting to create a sense of connection and answer individual questions. Balancing the needs of the team, the individual, and the task was recommended many years ago by John Adair (32) and is as relevant in the hybrid or online space as in the physical workplace. One way to balance the needs of the individual and the team is to alternate whole team meetings with individual catch-ups. Team meetings allow the team to focus on shared goals, challenges, information sharing, and learning. Individual meetings can alternate between meetings focusing on the individual's areas of responsibility and meetings focusing on the individual's growth and development.

Not every task is best completed by a team. Criteria that may influence the decision about whether or not to assign a task to an individual or a team include:

- Does one individual possess all the knowledge and skills required?
- Does one individual have the time needed to complete the task on time?
- Could a team achieve additional benefits, such as a collaborative culture, or professional development of team members?
- What level of complexity or degree of inter-relatedness between task elements might suggest that a team is the better placed to address?

When a task needs to be completed, managers should make a conscious choice whether to assign the task to a team or to an individual, as outlined in Figure 4.1.

Team leaders can coach hybrid teams to think through which tasks can best be performed remotely and which are better done face to face. In making these decisions, we should challenge our assumptions. For example, if we think that relationship building is always best done face to face, what evidence do we have for that? Do all generations share this assumption or do employees who have grown up collaborating in online games see things differently?

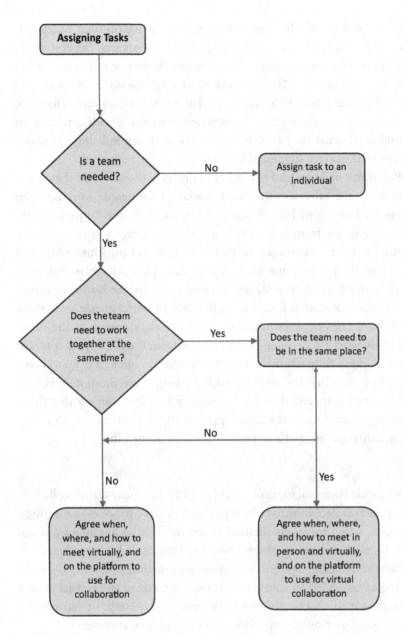

Figure 4.1 Assigning Tasks to Individuals or to Teams

Different teams have different needs. Hence, the frequency and length of meetings will vary. This can be agreed with the team at the outset and reviewed periodically to ensure that the selected frequency is still appropriate. Some teams have a short daily meeting to maintain connection (6) and to ensure that team members know what others are working on and where they may be able to help. Others thrive on their independence, happy with occasional meetings to share progress. Depending on the complexity and urgency of the task, the frequency might be weekly, monthly, or quarterly. Managers with more than one team cannot assume that what will work with one team will work with another. However, they can call on their previous experience to share with a new team examples of what they have found works well, while being genuinely open to alternatives suggested by members of the new team.

Proximity bias can lead managers to perceive those whom they regularly see in the office as more hard-working than people working from home. To lessen this bias, we need to be clear on the outputs we are expecting to see from our team members, encourage our remote team members to let us know about their activities and priorities (33), and recognise their achievements. It appears that proximity bias may now be reducing for hybrid workers. A recent study by the National Bureau of Economic Research found no difference in performance reviews or promotion rates between those working five days a week in the office and those working a couple of days a week from home (34). In contrast, those working fully remotely were promoted less often. It is up to managers to ensure that the most appropriate people are promoted. Hence, it is important to guard against proximity bias by ensuring that those working remotely have the same opportunities for interaction, development, achievement, and recognition as those in the office.

Team Dynamics

Observation is critical to team coaching (13). For many teams, collective action such as decision-making or problem-solving happens in meetings. However, when managers themselves are involved in discussions, it can be difficult for them to observe team dynamics and to see their own impact on the team. Options to gain insights include observing the team during a session led by another team member, asking an external person or facilitator to observe the interactions in the meeting, or recording a meeting for later reflection (with the permission of attendees).

Team coaching helps increase connection, trust, and cohesion, while at the same time lessening dysfunctional levels of conflict. Conflict can occur when there are competing priorities and when achieving one goal comes at the expense of one or more other goals (35). The value of diverse perspectives has been well documented in terms of quality of decision-making (36). Some conflict is productive, reducing the risk of groupthink. However, too much conflict can damage relationships and lessen the ability of the team to achieve its goals. Team coaching can bring issues to the surface in a respectful way and help the team as a whole to manage conflict and improve their performance (37).

Graen (38) suggests that team coaching helps create psychological safety, which subsequently increases the likelihood of team coaching being effective (10). Tkalich et al. (39) advise that making the most of days in the office, for example by having all members of a team in the office on the same day and developing routines such as regular celebrations of team achievements, helps contribute to psychological safety for hybrid teams. The core skill of coaches, according to Thornton (40), is 'holding', which she describes as 'the capacity to enable clients to feel safe enough to learn' (p. 28). Holding allows people to feel comfortable while being both curious and courageous (41). When managers are willing to be vulnerable, they not only pave the way for their own learning, they also show others that it is okay to do so (42). Role modelling and signalling what is regarded as positive behaviour are important in creating the psychological safety that will allow the team to thrive. When psychological safety is present, there are multiple benefits, from employees being more willing to give the team leader feedback, to employees being willing to put forward risky ideas, to speak up about problems at an early stage and to voice dissenting opinions while showing respect for all participants. Research about safety in an online coaching environment is mixed; some people felt safer opening up in digital coaching while others felt they needed at least to start their coaching relationship face to face (5).

There is a huge volume of research that demonstrates the importance of trust and the multiple benefits it brings, including positive impacts on team performance (43). It can take longer to build trust and rapport in group coaching than in individual coaching (8). Furthermore, trust is particularly important (and more difficult to establish) in a fully virtual environment where team members are reliant on each other and have no opportunity to meet in person (44). According to Huber (45, p. 67–8), 'Trust is the bedrock of any successful team, and in a remote environment, it takes on an even greater significance. Without the natural rapport that comes from in-person interactions, remote teams need to build trust deliberately and thoughtfully.' As Manfred Kets de Vries (2) points out, it is impossible to email a handshake or a smile. Managers therefore have to invest a huge amount of time in relationship building. Asking team members to share their progress, their knowledge, and where they would like support helps build cohesion and mutual respect. Practices which build trust in face-to-face contexts such as showing interest and concern, and being willing to be vulnerable, also help build trust in an online context (46). Empathy and authenticity are easier to build in the online space when people keep their cameras on (46).

Managers can use a coaching approach to help the team to agree their values and how they will be demonstrated. Such discussions help develop a shared understanding of norms and expectations. In large organisations, a set of values may be determined at a higher level. In this case, managers can help the team to think through what these organisational values look like in practice in their context. Having an agreed set of values means that both the team leader and the team members can reference the values if they believe someone is acting in a way that is inconsistent with the values.

Clutterbuck (10) recommends that teams agree on how to handle difficult situations. For example, if the team has agreed that they will be succinct, and someone regularly includes irrelevant information in making their point, one of the team members (not necessarily the manager) can give a reminder about the agreement to be succinct. The reminder is just that: a reminder about the agreed principles, not an attack on another team member. Referring to team values is a non-confrontational way of addressing issues, as illustrated in Box 4.1. Ignoring tensions between individual team members leads to worsening relationships between team members and deteriorating performance of the team over time.

Box 4.1 Team Values

When Fernando entered the meeting room, he immediately sensed the tension. Jack, who was normally upbeat and chatting with colleagues before meetings started, was sitting looking at his phone. Maeve was standing by the window and not talking to anyone. Donna on the other hand was giggling as she said something in a low voice to Michael sitting beside her. As team leader, Fernando reflected quickly and decided to bring forward an idea he had been mulling over.

Good morning everyone,' said Fernando. 'Before we start, I had an idea I wanted to share with you and see what you think. Basically I thought we might spend five minutes at the start of every monthly meeting, to reflect on one of our team values – we developed them last year, but we haven't really done much since then. What do you think?'

There was a moment's pause.

'Could be useful,' said Maeve. 'When we first came up with them, we were always pulling each other up if anyone said something that wasn't in line with them, and saying "that's not very collaborative", or whatever. But then we kind of forgot.'

'I wasn't here when they are developed,' said Jack. 'Can anyone remember what they are?'

'One of them was about respect,' said Maeve, looking directly at Donna, who looked away.

'I wasn't here either,' said Michael. 'But we did something at my last company that might be helpful. At the start of our monthly meeting, we set aside five minutes where someone on the team would reflect on one of our values and give an actual example of someone demonstrating that value in the team.'

'That sounds good,' said Jack.

'And we should pull people up when they aren't behaving in line with the values, like we used to before,' said Maeve.

'Okay,' said Fernando. 'Let's do both of those, we'll have a "Value of the Month" reflection, and we won't put up with people not behaving in line with our values. Are we all agreed?'

Everyone including Donna nodded and murmured agreement. Some of the tension that Fernando had sensed before was still there but there was a sense of positive energy that the team was going to move forward. It would be interesting to see how things developed. He would also take the opportunity for one-on-one conversations over the next week to see if any other concerns emerged or if other actions were needed to help the team to gel.

Sometimes it is helpful to ask a team explicitly what is not being said and what is holding them back (40). The team leader can bring conflicting positions and gaps in reasoning to the surface, allowing emotions to be expressed while ensuring that all team members feel safe and are not attacked for stating their position. The leader can then coach the team to agree on an ideal position and work out how to get there.

Much of the collective work of teams is through meetings. And yet, many people find meetings less productive than they could be, if not an outright waste of time. The time people spend in meetings is a large investment by any organisation.

Listening in a group discussion ensures that information is shared, and a shared understanding developed. Respect is demonstrated through listening to each other, with only one person speaking at a time, not interrupting other speakers, and actively engaging with the content and purpose of the meeting. This in turn promotes positive relationships. Rogers (47) says that when people feel listened to, they also listen more to each other, and are more likely to adopt other people's points of view.

There is some debate around whether leaders should speak first or last. In Aboriginal Australian yarning circles, elders listen first and speak last. Hall and Hall (33) hold a similar view, arguing that when leaders give their opinion first, those with a different opinion are unlikely to speak up. They suggest instead that senior people in a meeting should give information and ask questions but avoid giving their own opinion too early. This allows others to be heard and a consensus to be reached. However, this only works where psychological safety exists and people trust that the leader is genuinely interested in their views, rather than having a pre-determined view. Otherwise, people may be reluctant to speak up in case their ideas are in conflict with those of the leader.

Some people may need specific encouragement to speak up. These people can be invited to share their expertise without putting them on the spot, for example they might be told in advance that they will be asked to report back on a particular task. Some team leaders use the 'chat' function in an online meeting or a separate chat platform to alert people that they will be called on next to speak, so that the person called on is ready. This is particularly helpful for a team member lacking in confidence.

The more that people listen respectfully to each other, the easier it is for all team members to speak up and for team meetings to be worthwhile. By listening carefully, the team leader can hear nuances that suggest there may be a disagreement, even if not overtly articulated. Disagreements are sometimes rooted in misunderstandings which can be brought to the surface and clarified during the meeting. On the other hand, some disagreements may be based on personality conflicts and may be best dealt with outside a whole team meeting.

Successful Coaching for Leaders and Managers

Depending on the size of the meeting, online break-out rooms may be useful, allowing smaller groups to work together and then come back to the plenary group. These break-out rooms can also be used for social breaks, with team members having a chat while having a tea or coffee, making time to connect as human beings (48). Sharma (49) suggests that in addition to having some social chat at the start of a meeting, teams can occasionally hold short meetings just for conversation. In physical workplaces, such gatherings are not uncommon in celebrating birthdays or cultural days. Similar gatherings can be held virtually but teams may have to experiment to find what works best for them, especially when people are under time pressure and any additional meetings are unwelcome.

Being purposeful in asking questions is particularly important in a team setting. Many of the purposes of the questions discussed in Chapter Two are also relevant in the team context. For example, questions for relationship building can be used before a formal meeting starts, to show interest and generate rapport. Asking questions in a team setting can increase interaction and engagement. However, some team members may become impatient and want to get straight to the point of the meeting. The coaching team leader may need to experiment and to be persistent in order to establish effective ways of working with their team or teams.

Asking an open question of the whole team can be problematic. For example, no one might reply. This might be for a variety of reasons – a blame culture or lack of trust, self-confidence, age, experience, or being one of a minority in the team. On the other hand, the same person might reply every time and some people might never speak. When people stay silent, it is not always clear whether they agree or disagree. Even if they agree, it may not be clear whether they have a shared understanding and agree for the same reasons. Listening and questioning skills help draw out the beliefs underlying people's reasoning. When people feel safe to speak up and know that they will be heard, the team and organisation benefit from stronger proposals.

Team members can play a number of roles that help make meetings worthwhile. For example, members might ask questions to raise an issue or ask clarifying questions to ensure a shared understanding of what is being discussed and what is agreed. A regular summary of where a discussion has reached can help keep everyone on the same page. It is easy for people to get distracted, whether in a face-to-face or online meeting. Team members can be champions for an idea, or, as mentioned below, play the role of devil's advocate. A team member might specific-ally invite other people to share their perspective or prompt the team to reflect. When teams self-manage like this, responsibility for how well the meetings work is shared, rather than assumed to be the sole responsi-bility of the team leader.

Online meetings can be organised as short meetings on specific agenda items rather than occasional long meetings. Hawkins notes that it is harder to hold people's attention as long in a virtual meeting (6). In hybrid meetings the team coaching leader can stay online during breaks or after a meeting, so that those who are based remotely do not per-ceive those based in the same location as the leader as always having an advantage, with more opportunities for relationship-building. Any per-ception of an 'in-group' can be detrimental to team morale and exacer-bate perceptions of proximity bias.

Where both face-to-face and virtual meetings are possible, teams can decide which format to use for which purpose. Dinnocenzo and Morwick (50) suggest that shorter meetings by phone 'can be a wel-come relief to team members with video burnout'. Hybrid teams can have some face-to-face social interactions to help team bonding. How-ever, team leaders need to pay attention to the possible blurring of work and home boundaries and ensure that all team members have access to the support and technology they need to succeed (51).

There is rarely a pause in online meetings for people to interrupt a speaker. Coaching leaders monitor body language to see people sitting forward or someone who has unmuted their microphone because they want to speak, and notice if someone has raised their real or virtual hand. However, the larger the meeting, the smaller the picture size of each par-ticipant, and the more difficult it is to see these indicators, particularly if someone is also screensharing. It can be helpful for one of the team to monitor the chat and hand signals, to ensure that any questions are addressed. A record of questions and comments posted in the chat is available when the meeting ends, allowing the manager to follow up on any unanswered questions.

The team leader can pause periodically to check for people who want to speak or specifically invite people to comment on the issue under dis-cussion. Some people are reluctant to speak up unless invited to do so. Another challenge, as mentioned in Chapter Two, is that it can be more difficult to maintain silence in an online meeting; unless the team leader explicitly signals that they are allowing silence for people to process or think about the issue at hand, participants may assume the connection has frozen. People can also misinterpret a pause as meaning that the other person has finished speaking, leading to a colleague feeling cut off or interrupted. If everyone holds silence for a little longer than in a face-to-face meeting, this can help make sure that people have finished speaking before the next person starts. This may also lead to people volunteering additional ideas.

Visual aids and programs where participants can record ideas and progress are useful for team coaching meetings. They ensure a shared understanding of what has been agreed and demonstrate transparency. A collaborative team spirit can be nurtured through the use of chat platforms, virtual whiteboards, online brainstorming tools, and other forms of sharing ideas and information. Setting norms for technology use promotes positive team dynamics (51).

To listen well, everyone in a meeting should be there for the purpose of the meeting, and not completing emails or other tasks at the same time (52). If people are not expected to engage throughout the meeting, they should only attend for their specific item. However, if team members are expected to coach each other, listening attentively and asking pertinent questions or information, managers can make it an explicit expectation that those attending will remain focused for the duration of the meeting. They can then have follow-up conversations with anyone who only contributes to their item. Citrin (53) warns that multi-tasking during video meetings exacerbates cognitive fatigue. Little steps like turning off notifications from instant messaging platforms help avoid distractions.

Each team can agree on what will make their meetings most effective and worthwhile. For example, a team might agree that the norm is to have their cameras on, with exceptions where needed. Another team might decide that this is purely at the discretion of participants. Some people find it stressful to see themselves on camera and even though there is an option on most platforms to switch off self-view, this may not be enough (54).

'Zoom fatigue' is a phenomenon that garnered a great deal of attention during the pandemic, with employees tiring from looking at computer screens all day (55). Other than meetings, many people's work is computer-based, such as when report writing or modelling financial outcomes. When meetings are also online, people can find it less tiring to turn off their cameras. However, as Turner et al. (56, p. 190) warn, not having cameras on in virtual meetings makes it more difficult to 'read' the room. The authors also note that when cameras are off, participants in the meeting may be more likely to multi-task rather than be fully engaged in the meeting. Coaches and mental health practitioners have reported finding online sessions more draining than face-to-face sessions (57), although this may have been exacerbated by pandemic conditions.

To lessen screen fatigue, team leaders should allow time between meetings – as we do when travelling to or from physical meetings. Travel time provides a much-needed opportunity to process what has happened in one meeting and to prepare for the next. With virtual meetings, it is technically possible to go from one meeting to another without a pause, but this is to underestimate the power of reflection, the ability to learn from what has happened, to think about what needs to happen next, and simply to allow a mental break between one meeting and another. Calendar software like Microsoft Outlook allows users to change the default start and end time of meetings; for example, starting ten minutes after the hour or finishing five minutes before the hour builds in processing time. For meetings longer than an hour, it is helpful to include breaks to allow participants to move away from their screens, close their eyes, stretch their legs, or whatever will help them rejoin the meeting with fresh energy. Diller (57) also advocates mindfulness as a way to help reduce the exhaustion that can be generated by online coaching.

It is important to be alert to signs of stress or burnout and to promote self-care, breaks, and taking leave. Coaching managers should role-model self-care and signal when leaving the office or taking breaks that they will not be attending to emails when on leave. The latter can be achieved by nominating someone else to be the team leader in their absence and providing contacts for people who can advise if unexpected difficulties emerge. This builds capacity in the organisation and gives others the chance to decide if they would like a leadership role in the future. When someone is in an acting capacity, the manager should trust them and let them do the job without hovering in the background. The hardest part for some managers is letting go and having a genuine 'digital de-tox'. Some do this by checking their email to satisfy themselves that there is nothing that needs their attention. However, if the team leader is perceived as 'always on', others may see this as an implicit expectation or an illustration of what is needed to succeed in the organisation. When well-being suffers, so too do engagement and productivity, leading to underperformance across the whole organisation. A checklist for effective virtual and hybrid teams is provided in Table 4.1.

Table 4.1 Team Coaching Leader's Guide to Effective Virtual and Hybrid Teams

Team Coaching Leader's Guide

1. Have a clear purpose for the team, with clear roles. Agree team goals and how to track progress.
2. Encourage respectful open communication that helps build a sense of connection and trust among team members.
3. Agree on regular individual check-ins which allow the coaching team leader to satisfy themselves as to the progress being made, to offer support, and help work out how to address any challenges. The purpose is not to micro-manage employees but to stop any obstacles getting in their way.
4. Ensure that all team members have access to relevant software, know when and how to use it, and what to do when the technology fails.
5. Show your care for your team members.
6. Seek feedback and adjust how the team works in order to make best use of people's precious time.

Team Decision-Making

While team leaders ultimately have responsibility for decision-making, many decisions benefit from input from their teams. Good decision-making requires evidence, an understanding of context, creative options, and clear criteria for prioritisation of options. Team coaching can help with each of these. First of all, the team listens carefully to those providing data relating to the question on which a decision is needed and asks questions to clarify the data and the context. Then the team uses brainstorming techniques to generate creative options using resources such as physical or virtual sticky notes, in a face-to-face or virtual meeting. The next step is to prioritise the options identified.

A useful prompt is to think about what needs to be done now, what needs to be done in the short term, and what needs to be done for the medium or longer term. Postponing the last of these means that it may never be achieved, so it is important for the team leader to have the discipline to set aside some time for longer-term thinking, even when there is a huge amount of work to be done in the short term.

As mentioned in Chapter Two, scaling questions (58) can be used to help decide how to move forward towards a goal. For example, a manager might ask their team where they are now, if achieving their goal is a ten. The aim is to develop a shared understanding of what success looks like and how to get there. Different team members might assess the situation differently, as they take different factors into account.

Some people might even suggest a minus number for the current position. Through sharing the reasons for the numbers they give, the team develops a shared understanding of their current situation. The manager can then encourage the team to come up with ideas to move up the scale.

The criteria for decision-making should be developed in advance to avoid later tailoring of these criteria to achieve an outcome the team leader thinks desirable. Brainstorming techniques can be used to develop a long list of criteria. If a criterion is so important that if it is not met, the idea does not go ahead, this can form a first-stage gate, and only ideas that pass that gate are then prioritised. All criteria may be weighted equally, but it often happens that some criteria are more important at a particular point in time. The discussion of the relative importance of different criteria helps surface unspoken assumptions about what is important to the team. Careful questioning helps elicit these assumptions, identifying potential barriers to success and potential sources of support for an idea. In this way, team coaches maximise the chances of an idea succeeding.

Coaching leaders experiment with ways to surface disagreements or reservations in a constructive way. This is important as people may not speak up when they have concerns if they are in teams that are keen to support each other. One option is for team members to take turns being a 'devil's advocate', someone who actively looks for potential flaws in an idea, not to attack the person proposing it but to help make the idea stronger by identifying and addressing the flaws. This helps avoid the situation where one team member is always seen as the naysayer and consequently earns a reputation for being negative. Another option is to bring in stakeholders for a scenario planning exercise to help think through consequences and impacts. This is particularly useful where stakeholders have not been involved in generating ideas, as they bring a fresh perspective and sometimes new data and new ideas. Nowadays, stakeholders are often involved in prioritising projects (59).

Team Negotiations

Team discussions with other teams, both within an organisation and externally, often turn into negotiations, whether or not they are intended as such. Examples include process improvements, partnerships, and service-level agreements. Coaching skills are invaluable, allowing underlying concerns to emerge, enabling people in a meeting to feel genuinely heard, and mutually satisfactory options to be developed. Silence is powerful in negotiations, and although sometimes regarded as a way of eliciting concessions from the other party, recent research suggests that silence prompts reflection and leads to added value, with neither party seeing silence negatively (60). As noted in Chapter Two, it can be more difficult to hold silence in an online discussion. As already mentioned, it is useful for the team leader to signal a pause, to avoid the pause being misinterpreted as a technical glitch.

Team Communication

Coaching leaders can help their team(s) agree communication protocols such as preferred channels for communication which can help team effectiveness. For instance, a team might agree that telephone, video conversations, or instant messaging will be used for informal or urgent queries, and emails where a record of responses is useful. Informal messages on a chat platform where personal information and photos can be shared as well as questions asked and answered can help virtual teams feel connected. Side chats on a video call or some informal conversation at the start of a meeting can also form some of the social 'glue' that helps a team work well together.

Similarly a team might decide how often some types of communication will be used (e.g. a daily meeting, a weekly email, ad hoc informal messaging). Research has shown that it is the quality rather than the quantity of communication that matters, and in fact over-communicating can have a negative effect, even leading to increased burnout (61). Getting the balance right can be difficult as different team members may have different expectations about what is the 'right' amount of communication. Agreeing as a team on what is appropriate can help manage expectations.

Email is useful for sharing information quickly, but as De Rosa and Citrin (53, p. 82) point out, if you want to coach or deal with conflict, 'video meetings are infinitely superior to email.' If a meeting is purely for information giving, then, as Hall and Hall (33) observe, moving that meeting online will probably just bore more people more quickly. Instead, the authors suggest only holding meetings where audience participation is integral to the purpose and outcomes of the meeting. Otherwise, some form of asynchronous communication, where team members can respond when it fits with their schedule, is more efficient and productive.

Coaching leaders can also prompt teams to agree expectations about response times and any meeting-free times, such as no meetings, emails, or messages in the evening or at weekends. Teams might decide to keep one day a week which is meeting-free and/or email-free. The example managers set is critical as people may feel obliged to answer an email sent by a manager at the weekend or they may want to impress their manager, even if the manager explicitly notes that a reply the following week will suffice. Some managers choose to reply to emails their team members send at weekends but not to initiate an email chain. Managers can hold emails in their drafts folder or use the 'delayed send' option in order not to send an implicit message that the manager is working at the weekend and hence expects others to do so also. The unintended consequence of holding emails for the start of the following week can be a flurry of emails all at once which can be overwhelming. Some employees prefer to deal with emails at a time of their choice even if this is over the weekend. Rather than make assumptions about what works best, managers and employees can discuss individual preferences and find ways of working that suit both. This is increasingly important as countries both in Europe and Australia start to enshrine employees' right to switch off in legislation.

Even though technology allows employees to be contacted 24/7, managers should ensure that they allow employees time to switch off and re-charge. Workplace regulations vary in different countries, and it is both morally right and makes good business sense not to expose employees to the risks of harm to mental or physical health that can result from being 'always on' (62). Setting realistic expectations of when employees need to be available is now an expected part of workplace arrangements that support employee well-being. Hybrid teams and teams working across time zones should take local work patterns into account. Agreement on working hours when teams are in different time zones demonstrates respect for people's time and their work-life balance (45).

Team leaders should encourage team members to communicate with each other and not only with the team leader or the team as a whole. This helps build strong relationships across the team. It also helps when the team leader changes, as the team can continue to self-manage. Team leaders also need to be mindful of how to make new team members feel included; it can be hard to break into a team which already has strong relationships.

Regular communication and support are important, particularly in geographically dispersed teams (51). Managers do however have to take care that, in providing support, they do not fall into the trap of micro-management. As mentioned in Chapter Three, micro-management has been shown to lessen employee engagement, increase team conflict, and reduce productivity and innovation (63). Even when managers mean well and want to motivate their teams, they can achieve the opposite if they are controlling and constantly give direct instructions, rather than helping their employees to think for themselves (64). Sometimes this is because managers feel comfortable in a technical space where they have expertise, as illustrated in Box 4.2.

Box 4.2 Why Does He Keep Ringing Us Up?

Sarah looked at the caller's name on the Webex app. 'Not Joe again,' she said to Ling who was sitting beside her. 'Why does he keep ringing us up?'

It was Tuesday afternoon, and their manager was on the phone again. And just as Sarah was in the middle of inserting formulas into a complex spreadsheet that she was working on with Ling.

'Hi Joe,' said Sarah.

'Oh hi Sarah,' said Joe. 'Just wondering how you're getting on with the data for tomorrow. If you need any help, you just have to ask.'

'I will, Joe,' Sarah replied. 'But it's all good for now. Ling and I are working on it together. I'm thinking of putting "Do not disturb" on Webex so that I don't get interrupted.'

'Good idea,' said Joe. 'Now where are you up to with the spreadsheet?'

Sarah told him, knowing what would happen next and dreading it.

'Well you're doing well so far, Sarah,' said Joe. 'Now, what I would do is this ...' and he began to tell her in detail how to do what she was already doing.

Twice she tried to interrupt to say that was what they were doing but Joe wasn't listening. He obviously didn't sense that she had mentally switched off and continued to talk enthusiastically about the Excel formulas he loved so dearly. And he seemed to think his input was welcome, signing off with a happy 'Glad I could help, Sarah' followed by the even more de-motivating 'I'll check in later to see how things are going'.

'Oh no,' thought Sarah. 'How do I stop him doing that? He's not helping, he's slowing us down. And it just feels like he doesn't trust me or thinks that he would do it better himself. I can't carry on working like this. It's getting me down and I don't feel like I am being given the chance to stretch myself.'

She resolved to start job hunting once she had got the data ready. It was a pity really, she liked working with Ling and the other people on the team, but she couldn't see any likelihood of Joe changing his behaviour. He thought he was being helpful and would be very offended if she told him otherwise. And that wouldn't do her career any good either.

Traps to Avoid

Focusing only on the team can lead managers to ignore the fact that different team members may be at different stages of learning and may need different support. Instead, managers should balance the needs of the team with the needs of individual team members.

If the manager does not set aside time for the team to learn and think together, the team will be less innovative in the solutions they develop. Allowing even a short amount of time for the team to work together (not just listen to each other presenting information) will help the team to become more cohesive and effective.

Getting Better at Team Coaching

Here are three activities which can help you get better at leading teams in the virtual and hybrid workplace:

1. Do a 360° survey and compare your self-assessment with how your team view you. Share your results with your team. Use the feedback to improve.
2. Ask an observer to note the amount of time each person is speaking, and whether their contributions to group discussions are constructive or otherwise; for example, are they proposing ideas or building on other people's ideas, are they including others in the conversation or blocking them, are they praising or criticising? This analysis can then be used in a collective reflection on how the team's meetings may be made more effective. There may be individuals who require

specific feedback or training. For example, if the analysis shows that one person repeatedly dominates discussions or that a person often raises irrelevant or inappropriate points, the team leader can discuss the specific issue with the individual in a one-on-one conversation. Alternatively, an app such as Ovida[3] can be used to record and analyse a team meeting, giving the team real data to reflect on.

3. Set aside one meeting or part of a meeting periodically to reflect collectively on what is working well and where the team might try to improve.

IN CLOSING

Just as there is debate around whether a manager can truly coach their direct reports, as discussed in Chapter One, there is also debate around whether a manager can coach their own team. Recent research shows that it is certainly possible. According to Clutterbuck (10), experiments conducted with several organisations in the UK show that 'line managers can be effective coaches to their teams, as long as they are able to develop a safe coaching culture and climate' (p. 140).

It might be argued that it is enough for managers to coach individuals and to use traditional management skills with teams. This would be to underestimate the power of team coaching. In this, as in many aspects of leadership in today's complex hybrid workplace, we are in a time of experimentation. More research into effective team coaching by managers will emerge over the next few years. In the next chapter we will go beyond the team level to discuss coaching at the organisational level.

NOTES

1 See https://www.tability.io/ fpr further information.
2 See https://clickup.com/ for further information.
3 See https://ovida.io/ for further information.

REFERENCES

1. Mäkelä L, Kangas H, Korkiakangas E, Laitinen J. Coaching leadership as a link between individual-and team-level strength use at work. *Cogent Business & Management*. 2024;11(1): 2293469.
2. Kets de Vries MF. Leadership group coaching in action: the zen of creating high performance teams. *Academy of Management Perspectives*. 2005;19(1): 61–76.
3. Clutterbuck D, Megginson D, Bajer A. *Building and sustaining a coaching culture*. London: Kogan Page; 2016.
4. Hooijberg R, Watkins M. The future of team leadership is multimodal. *MIT Sloan Management Review*. 2021;62(3): 1–4.

5. Erdös T. Coaching the team in digital workplaces. In: Passmore J, Diller SJ, Isaacson S, Brantl M, editors. *The digital and AI coaches' handbook: the complete guide to the use of online, AI, and technology in coaching.* Abingdon, Oxon.: Routledge; 2024. p. 313–27.

6. Hawkins P. *Leadership team coaching: developing collective transformational leadership.* E-book ed.: Kogan Page; 2021.

7. de Haan E, Stoffels D. *Relational team coaching.* E-book ed.: Taylor & Francis; 2023.

8. Clutterbuck D, Gannon J, Hayes S, Iordanou I, Lowe K, MacKie D. *The practitioner's handbook of team coaching.* E-book ed.: Routledge; 2019.

9. Hawkins P. *Leadership team coaching in practice: case studies on creating highly effective teams.* Kogan Page; 2022.

10. Clutterbuck D. *Coaching the team at work: the definitive guide to team coaching.* 2nd ed. E-book ed.: Nicholas Brealey; 2020.

11. Britton JJ. Expanding the coaching conversation: group and team coaching. *Industrial and Commercial Training.* 2015;47(3): 116–20.

12. Hawkins P, Smith N. *Coaching, mentoring and organizational consultancy: supervision and development.* Maidenhead: Open University Press; 2006.

13. Welch NM. *Team coaching: influencing work-team trust.* PhD thesis. Fielding Graduate University; 2021.

14. Ellam-Dyson V, Palmer S. Leadership coaching? No thanks, I'm not worthy. *Coaching Psychologist.* 2011;7(2): 108–17.

15. Weer CH, DiRenzo MS, Shipper FM. A holistic view of employee coaching: longitudinal investigation of the impact of facilitative and pressure-based coaching on team effectiveness. *The Journal of Applied Behavioral Science.* 2016;52(2): 187–214.

16. Locke EA, Latham GP. The development of goal setting theory: a half century retrospective. *Motivation Science.* 2019;5(2): 93.

17. Zasa FP, Buganza T. Developing a shared vision: strong teams have the power. *Journal of Business Strategy.* 2023;44(6): 415–25.

18. Höchli B, Brügger A, Messner C. How focusing on superordinate goals motivates broad, long-term goal pursuit: a theoretical perspective. *Frontiers in Psychology.* 2018;2(9): 1879.

19. Shave L. Executive management and teams: a hybrid model for workplace, remote working and virtual team management. *IQ: The RIMPA Quarterly Magazine.* 2022;38(1): 20–4.

20. Viitala R, Laiho M, Pajuoja M, Henttonen K. Managerial coaching and employees' innovative work behavior: the mediating effect of work engagement. *The International Journal of Entrepreneurship and Innovation.* 2023. https://doi.org/10.1177/14657503231221693

21. Grieten S, Lambrechts F, Bouwen R, Huybrechts J, Fry R, Cooperrider D. Inquiring into appreciative inquiry: a conversation with David Cooperrider and Ronald Fry. *Journal of Management Inquiry.* 2018;27(1): 101–14.

22. Osborn AF. *Applied imagination.* New York: Scribner; 1953.

23. Sutton A, Crobach C. Improving self-awareness and engagement through group coaching. *International Journal of Evidence Based Coaching & Mentoring.* 2022;20(1): 35–49.

24. Kross E, Ong M, Ayduk O. Self-reflection at work: why it matters and how to harness its potential and avoid its pitfalls. *Annual Review of Organizational Psychology and Organizational Behavior.* 2023;10: 441–64.

25. Bucaloiu I. Criteria for efficiency of internal communication. *Annals of the Academy of Romanian Scientists New Series on Economy, Law and Sociology Sciences.* 2019;5(2): 25–32.
26. Hagen M, Gavrilova Aguilar M. The impact of managerial coaching on learning outcomes within the team context: an analysis. *Human Resource Development Quarterly.* 2012;23(3): 363–88.
27. Clutterbuck D. Team coaching. In: Cox E, Clutterbuck DA, Bachkirova T, editors. *The complete handbook of coaching.* 3rd ed. London: Sage; 2018. p. 279–94.
28. Hawkins P. Systemic team coaching. In: Clutterbuck D, Gannon J, Hayes S, Iordanou I, Lowe K, MacKie D, editors. *The practitioner's handbook of team coaching.* E-book ed.: Routledge; 2019. p. 36–52.
29. Hendriks M, Burger M, Rijsenbilt A, Pleeging E, Commandeur H. Virtuous leadership: a source of employee well-being and trust. *Management Research Review.* 2020; 43(8): 951–70.
30. Nyfoudi M, Shipton H, Theodorakopoulos N, Budhwar P. Managerial coaching skill and team performance: how does the relationship work and under what conditions? *Human Resource Management Journal.* 2023;33(2): 328–45.
31. Senge P, Hamilton H, Kania J. The dawn of system leadership. *Stanford Social Innovation Review.* 2015;13(1): 27–33.
32. Adair JE. *Action-centred leadership.* New York: McGraw-Hill; 1973.
33. Hall K, Hall A. *Leading remote and virtual teams: managing yourself and others in remote and hybrid teams or when working from home.* Crowthorne, Berks.: Global Integration; 2021.
34. Bloom N, Han, R. Liang, J. *How hybrid working from home works out.* Cambridge, MA: National Bureau of Economic Research Working Paper 30292; 2023.
35. Gaba V, Joseph J. Content and process: organizational conflict and decision making. *Frontiers in Psychology.* 2023;14. https://doi.org/10.3389/fpsyg.2023.1227966
36. Elgoibar P, Armstrong R, Euwema M. *Conflict management in the workplace.* Oxford University Press; 2022.
37. Hayes S, Popp N. Constructive-developmental theory: a lens for team coaching. In: Clutterbuck D, Gannon J, Hayes S, Iordanou I, Lowe K, MacKie D, editors. E-book ed.: *The practitioner's handbook of team coaching.* Routledge; 2019. p. 1.
38. Graen G, Canedo JC, Grace M. Team coaching can enhance psychological safety and drive organizational effectiveness. *Organizational Dynamics.* 2020;49(2): 100697.
39. Tkalich A, Šmite D, Andersen NH, Moe NB. What happens to psychological safety when going remote? *IEEE Software.* 2022(Jan–Feb);41: 113–22.
40. Thornton C. *Group and team coaching.* London: Routledge; 2016.
41. Petriglieri G. The psychology behind effective crisis leadership. *Harvard Business Review,* 22 April 2020. https://hbr.org/2020/04/the-psychology-behind-effective-crisis-leadership
42. Kegan R, Lahey L, Fleming A, Miller M. Making business personal. *Harvard Business Review.* 2014;92(4): 44–52.
43. Breuer C, Hüffmeier J, Hibben F, Hertel G. Trust in teams: a taxonomy of perceived trustworthiness factors and risk-taking behaviors in face-to-face and virtual teams. *Human Relations.* 2020;73(1): 3–34.
44. Morrison-Smith S, Ruiz J. Challenges and barriers in virtual teams: a literature review. *SN Applied Sciences.* 2020;2: 1–33.

45. Huber T. Leading teams: unlocking the power of collaboration: E-book ed.: Amazon; 2023.

46. Schilling H, Kauffeld S. Building empathy and trust in online environments. In: Passmore J, Diller SJ, Isaacson S, Brantl M, editors. *The digital and AI coaches' handbook: the complete guide to the use of online, AI, and technology in coaching.* Abingdon, Oxon.: Routledge; 2024. p. 154–65.

47. Rogers CR, Farson R. Active listening. In: Newman RG, Danziger MA, Cohen M, editors. *Communication in business today.* Washington, D.C.: Heath and Company; 1957.

48. Hawley R, Turner E, Iordanou I. Managing ethics online. In: Passmore J, Diller SJ, Isaacson S, Brantl M, editors. *The digital and AI coaches' handbook: the complete guide to the use of online, AI, and technology in coaching.* Abingdon, Oxon.: Routledge; 2024. p. 212–26.

49. Sharma PN, D'Innocenzo L, Kirkman BL. Why leaders resist empowering virtual teams. *MIT Sloan Management Review.* 2021;63(1): 1–6.

50. Dinnocenzo DA, Morwick J. Remote leadership: successfully leading work-from-anywhere and hybrid teams. Bedford, TX: Walk the Talk Company; 2021.

51. Bell BS, McAlpine KL, Hill NS. Leading virtually. *Annual Review of Organizational Psychology and Organizational Behavior.* 2023;10: 339–62.

52. Ferrazzi K. Getting virtual teams right. *Harvard Business Review.* 2014;92(12): 120–3.

53. DeRosa D, Citrin JM. *Leading at a distance: practical lessons for virtual success.* E-book ed.: John Wiley & Sons; 2021.

54. Rodriguez C, Telloian C. Zoom anxiety is more common than you think. PsychCentral, 25 June 2021. https://psychcentral.com/anxiety/zoom-anxiety-is-more-common-than-you-think-heres-why#recap

55. Ngien A, Hogan, B. The relationship between Zoom use with the camera on and Zoom fatigue: considering self-monitoring and social interaction anxiety. *Information, Communication & Society.* 2023;26: 2052–70.

56. Turner T, Tan, SH. *Shared leadership disciplines: a better way to lead & coach.* E-book ed.: Amazon; 2023.

57. Diller SJ. Ethics in digital and AI coaching. *Human Resource Development International.* 2024;27(4): 548–96

58. Visser CF. The origin of the solution-focused approach. *International Journal of Solution-Focused Practices.* 2013;1(1): 10–17.

59. Andersen PD, Hansen M, Selin C. Stakeholder inclusion in scenario planning—a review of European projects. *Technological Forecasting and Social Change.* 2021;169: 120802.

60. Curhan JR, Overbeck JR, Cho Y, Zhang T, Yang Y. Silence is golden: extended silence, deliberative mindset, and value creation in negotiation. *Journal of Applied Psychology.* 2022;107(1): 78.

61. Shockley KM, Allen TD, Dodd H, Waiwood AM. Remote worker communication during COVID-19: the role of quantity, quality, and supervisor expectation-setting. *Journal of Applied Psychology.* 2021;106(10): 1466.

62. Büchler N, ter Hoeven CL, van Zoonen W. Understanding constant connectivity to work: how and for whom is constant connectivity related to employee well-being? *Information and Organization.* 2020;30(3): 100302.

63. Ryan S, Cross C. Micromanagement and its impact on millennial followership styles. *Leadership & Organization Development Journal.* 2024;45(1): 140–52.

64. Milner J. The motivational micromanager. *Organizational Dynamics.* 2024;53(3): 101054.

Five

INTRODUCTION

In this chapter we go beyond managers coaching individuals and teams to explore the organisational context, looking at what it means to have a coaching culture, the importance of systems thinking, and the challenges of coaching in multi-cultural and multinational organisations, including creating an environment where people accept that change will continue to happen.

As discussed in Chapter One, we live in a time of increasing complexity and change, the Volatile Uncertain Complex and Ambiguous (VUCA) environment first identified by leadership researchers over 30 years ago (1). These days it is difficult for any one individual to have a complete grasp of all the relevant data and the nuances of each location where their organisation is based or the markets they serve. Attempting to do so can be overwhelming. To support leaders working at the organisational level, we draw upon research from several different strands of leadership research, all of which are consistent with a coaching approach.

CULTURE

Culture can be hard to define but is often described as 'the way we do things around here' (2). People often work out for themselves what they think the culture of an organisation is, by interpreting the many signals sent consciously or unconsciously by the organisation's leaders. These signals include stories about the heroes or villains of an organisation (when people are recognised for doing something above and beyond expectations), rituals and routines such as a weekly stand-up meeting, as well as structures and systems such as organisation charts and performance dashboards (3). Feedback mechanisms reinforce the desired behaviour and discourage behaviour not in line with the organisation's values.

In some organisations there is a difference between the espoused values and the values which are actually experienced in the workplace

DOI: 10.4324/9781003239826-5

(4). There can also be conflicting values between different parts of an organisation or between an organisation and its partners or stakeholders (5). Many people are members or leaders of more than one team; for example, there is a functional team they lead, a functional team they are a member of, and often other project teams as well. Deploying coaching across the organisation and its ecosystem can help create a shared culture.

Coaching Culture

Definitions of coaching cultures typically include formal and informal coaching being widely deployed in an organisation as the common approach to leading and relating to colleagues (6). One requirement of a coaching culture is that managers use a coaching style as their normal leadership approach (6). Clutterbuck and co-authors define a coaching culture as one 'where the principles, beliefs and mindsets driving people's behaviour in the workplace are deeply rooted in the discipline of coaching (7).

The hallmarks of a coaching culture are illustrated in Figure 5.1.

As illustrated in Figure 5.1, where there is a coaching culture, it is the norm that people adopt a coaching approach (8) and senior leaders role-model coaching (9). Coaching dialogues are common with an emphasis on feedback, reflection, and learning. The effectiveness of coaching is measured and there are stories of successful coaching

Figure 5.1 Hallmarks of a Coaching Culture

outcomes. Recognition of individuals and teams engaged in coaching signals to the organisation that coaching is valued.

Clutterbuck (7) suggests that the most obvious indication of a coaching culture are behaviours such as actively listening to each other, supporting and challenging team members, exploring choices and options, frequent seeking and giving of feedback which is acted upon, and taking time to reflect and learn. Put simply, managers who coach their employees help develop a coaching culture (10). Kapoutzis et al. (11) conclude that leadership buy-in, formalised processes, and a coaching style of management are foundational elements that are necessary for the development of a coaching culture.

Benefits of a Coaching Culture

Numerous benefits of coaching have been identified by researchers (12, 13), including:

- individuals being empowered and transformed through personal growth;
- alignment between individuals and organisations;
- relationships between managers and employees leading to employees being more willing to discuss issues relating to their performance and to try new things,
- increases in employee engagement, innovation, performance, and productivity;
- and managers experiencing sheer joy at the transformation they see in their employees.

By making coaching the default approach across an organisation, these benefits are amplified. Coaching can help support the mission, vision, and values of an organisation (7). Every coaching conversation is an opportunity to reinforce shared values and strategic priorities, even something as apparently simple as a manager listening to an employee outlining an idea. When such conversations take place daily, managers reinforce the behaviours, the values, and the performance expectations of the organisation. When all or most managers across an organisation are engaged in coaching, there are improvements in creativity, learning, trust, and employee engagement, which in turn result in innovation, readiness for change, productivity, reduced absenteeism, enhanced staff retention, and achieving organisational goals. The benefits gained from individual coaching are enhanced through team coaching, leading in turn to significant benefits for the organisation, as shown in Table 5.1.

In some organisations, only senior leaders are coached (14). This is perhaps because of an assumption than an external coach is needed or is better in some way. Hiring external coaches incurs a cost but that is not the only factor to be considered when deciding on who should coach and be coached. In a coaching culture, everyone has some experience of being coached, because that is the style of leadership adopted across the

Table 5.1 Individual, Team, and Coaching Outcomes

Individual Coaching Outcomes

- Personal growth, competence, individual performance improvement, achievement
- Confidence, motivation, self-esteem, self-efficacy
- Role clarity
- Alignment

- Positive relationships, feeling valued and cared for, psychological safety enhanced well-being, reduced stress
- Trust
- Readiness for change
- Innovation, problem-solving
- Empowerment

Team Coaching Outcomes

- Relationships
- Morale
- Psychological safety
- Readiness for change

- Engagement
- Innovation, problem-solving
- Empowerment

Organisational Coaching Outcomes

- Alignment and achievement of organisational goal and strategy
- Enhanced morale, employee engagement, empowerment
- Ease of attracting new employees, higher employee retention
- Reduced absenteeism, presenteeism, and sick leave

- Innovation, improved processes, quality, efficiency, and cost savings
- Improved customer relations and supply chain partnerships
- Improved stakeholder relations
- Improved performance and productivity

organisation. This has led to what has been termed the coaching ripple effect (15), where people who are coached often begin to self-coach, developing a habit of asking themselves the questions their coaching manager would ask. In turn, they listen to their own direct reports and ask them similar questions. Over time, coaching conversations become the norm. When new managers are hired or promoted these days, their ability to coach is often one of the criteria considered. In the UK 80% of managers say they are expected to coach (12).

Although coaching cultures can emerge organically, coaching is likely to remain haphazard and not achieve its full potential unless there is a formal plan to develop a coaching culture over time. Megginson and Clutterbuck (16) describe four stages of developing a coaching culture, from 'nascent' where there is little coaching taking place, to 'tactical' where there is ad hoc coaching, 'strategic' where formal coaching takes place regularly, and 'embedded' where people at all levels of an organisation are engaged in formal and informal coaching. In their more recent work they stress the importance of developing a vision for a coaching culture (7). Hunt and Weintraub (8) suggest that when a coaching culture is fully developed, the coaching manager may actually spend less time formally coaching as coaching is happening throughout the organisation.

Coaching may not always be called coaching (17) but managers regularly use the coaching skillset of active listening, asking helpful questions, and giving constructive feedback, leading to the positive outcomes of enhanced leadership capability and employee engagement (18). Not calling this coaching can be for various reasons, perhaps because of a previous experience of being badly coached (or something being called coaching which was not), or earlier attempts to introduce coaching to an organisation which were unsuccessful (7).

In describing the Ershad coaching framework, Van Nieuwerburgh stated that he used the terms 'facilitator' and 'learner' rather than 'coach' and 'coachee' in order to emphasise the centrality of learning in Ershad coaching, a form of coaching based on Islamic principles. Van Nieuwerburgh describes Ershad coaching as 'a learner-led conversation that is supported by a facilitator who is skilled at listening, asking questions and providing a safe and respectful environment for reflection'. Using language that is appropriate to the culture helps ensure that the behaviours are enacted. This is more important than being pedantic about which terms are used.

While one of the hallmarks of a coaching culture is that coaching conversations are the norm, researchers have found that not all managers want to coach, whether formally or informally (17, 19). There are several reasons why this may be so. For example, managers may feel that they do not have the skills or the time to coach their own employees. Employees may respond negatively to constructive feedback and therefore managers sometimes avoid confronting issues. This leads to poor performance going unchallenged, which in turn leads to resentment on the part of other employees. The commitment of managers to coaching is important in developing a coaching culture (20).

In a coaching culture there is an emphasis on learning. Managers are committed to their own learning and facilitate learning in their organisations (21). Decisions are evidence-based and high performance is expected. Innovation is encouraged, with the understanding that not everything will work the first time. Instead of punishing failure, the approach in a coaching culture is to learn from it and work out how to improve. This assists organisations in being agile and able to respond to the challenges of a VUCA environment in ways that traditional command and control hierarchies cannot achieve.

Encouraging managers to coach requires organisations to ensure that managers have the ability to coach, the motivation to coach, and the opportunity to coach (12). The Ability Motivation Opportunity framework dovetails neatly with Self Determination Theory (SDT), which taps into people's inner motivation, focusing on their autonomy, competence, and social relatedness.

Considering the motivation for managers to coach first of all, it sometimes helps the initial implementation to show how coaching fits with the organisation's values. For example, if the organisation has a set of values which include listening respectfully to employees as well as recognising good performance and encouraging learning, it would be difficult for any manager to say they disagreed. In contrast, requiring managers to coach is problematic as managers who do not believe in the efficacy of coaching and merely go through the motions mechanically will damage the understanding and positive experience of coaching in an organisation. It is also not consistent with autonomy which is a core tenet of SDT.

Other ways to motivate managers to coach include explaining the benefits, citing examples of successful coaching by credible colleagues, and recognising managers who adopt a coaching approach (12).

Researchers agree that top management support is vital (7, 22). This includes senior leaders themselves adopting a coaching approach as well as voicing support for coaching and investing in training and resources to equip managers to coach. Successful pilots generate positive word of mouth, leading to a demand for more coaching and supporting the business case for investing in coaching.

With regards to competence, organisations can support managers to adopt a coaching approach by providing training tailored for coaching by managers (22). The coaching skills discussed in Chapters Two and Three are deployed by both external coaches and coaching managers, but the context is so different that different training is required. Coaching managers face a number of challenges that the external coach does not experience, such as confidentiality issues when an employee reveals something to their coaching manager that they would not normally tell their manager (23). Coaching managers also have valuable opportunities for coaching that external coaches do not have, such as on-going interactions and deep familiarity with the employee's context.

Unfortunately the focus in many coaching programs is often on applying a generic model, such as the GROW (Goals, Reality, Options, Will) model (24–26). The simplicity of the GROW model means that it is sometimes assumed that people can apply it with little effort. In some courses, participants are taught to move through each step of the model in strict order, regardless of the stage the other person is at in their thinking. This does not make sense and much of their organisation's investment will be wasted. A coaching conversation should be a helpful dialogue, unique to a particular conversation, not mechanically going through a series of steps in a set order.

For managers, some of the most valuable learning takes place when they listen attentively to their employees. Informal coaching conversations transform organisations, raising morale and engagement when people feel heard and creating a buzz of excitement when more and more employee ideas are implemented. Tailored coaching programs for managers help to develop the mindset and skillset to adopt a coaching approach, and the confidence to try these skills in the workplace.

Support is needed both when managers first start to coach and on an on-going basis. Recent research found that Human Resources professionals often support the introduction of managerial coaching through providing training for formal coaching but could do more to provide on-going support (10). As with any desired change in behaviour, there is a need for encouragement to ensure that coaching behaviours become the manager's default approach to leadership (16, 27).

Implementing a coaching approach requires on-going support for managers in face-to-face, online, or hybrid contexts, just as coaching supervisors provide support for external coaches (22, 28). Human Resources/People, Culture Departments, and coaches, both internal and external (22, 32), offer different perspectives to challenge and support. Supervision is increasingly common in executive coaching and encouraged by professional coaching associations. This notion of super-vision which is familiar to psychologists and counsellors does not trans-late well to managerial coaching. Nevertheless, having one's own coach or mentor, peer, or Human Resources professional is helpful in a number of contexts. For example, managers may need advice when exploring ethical dilemmas or working with challenging employees. Such advisors also provide support for tackling issues such as confidentiality, conflicts of interest, and power imbalance (33), as well as by assisting managers to reduce their own stress levels and preventing burnout (34). There are also online coaching resources, both in the form of on-going training and information, and apps that help prompt or prepare for coaching sessions. The extent of support available varies with the size of the organ-isation. Local business chambers or small business support organisations sometimes provide assistance.

The social-relatedness element of SDT can be addressed through establishing a peer coaching network of managers who have been trained in managerial coaching together. This also addresses competence, as managers can practise coaching skills and ask questions about their coaching experience in a safe place.

Peer coaching encourages reflection (29) and has the added advan-tage of not having any power imbalance between the person coaching and the person being coached. Whether done in pairs or as a group, managers who coach each other develop positive relations with each other and always have colleagues they can call on when tackling tricky situations. Peers can give each other feedback on how effectively they are listening or asking questions, giving feedback, or on any of the other coaching skills discussed in Chapters Two and Three, thereby contrib-uting to increasing competence.

One of the reasons that peer coaching helps is because of the Solomon Paradox, the fact that we are not always very good ourselves at applying the advice we give to others (30). Reflecting with someone else can make us more realistic in our self-assessment and more committed to doing something about it. People tend to discount some of the feedback they receive or fail to notice what other people see so clearly (31). If other people feel safe sharing their observations, the feedback recipient's self-awareness benefits enormously.

Identifying opportunities to coach is a judgement call by managers. Scenarios can be explored in tailored programs to help managers think through how they would tackle a range of coaching conversations with different purposes and with different people. Managers may be reluctant to try informal 'corridor coaching' because they are uncertain about how an employee might respond (17). To enable managers to take advantage of opportunities to coach, research recommends not only training managers but also providing coaching awareness training for all employees to ensure a shared understanding of coaching and how it will be used (12). It is also important to ensure that organisational training, systems, and processes are aligned in identifying coaching by leaders as a leadership approach valued in the organisation.

Respecting people's autonomy in deciding whether to coach, motivating them to coach, and ensuring they have the competence and on-going support to coach is a sustainable way to develop a coaching culture. Managers who are initially sceptical may be convinced by their experience of being coached themselves. They may then try a coaching approach and genuinely buy in to the process. Over time, as people see that coaching adds value in terms of the outcomes these early adopters achieve, as well as being recognised by the organisation and hence good for their careers, more managers start to engage.

The combination of managers coaching up, down, and across all levels of an organisation with leadership support, systems thinking, and partnerships with stakeholders helps elevate coaching from an individual practice to a systemic leadership approach, amplifying the benefits for the organisation as well as for managers and their teams.

Systems Thinking and Coaching

A systems thinking approach helps organisations to address evolving community expectations. 'Corporate leaders are expected to take care not only of their business and their direct stakeholders, but also to contribute to society,' according to Muff, Liechti, and Dyllick (35) in their analysis of responsible leadership. By adopting a coaching approach, managers can work effectively with their peers, their teams, and with stakeholders inside and outside their organisation, making good use of technology, and reflecting and learning from experience in order to adjust their approach where needed.

In these complex and rapidly changing times, leaders need to develop their capacity to see the whole system, the big picture as well as the detailed local picture, making use of data analytics and software to support their understanding of rapidly changing events. Goodman's model of reflection (36, 37) includes systems thinking, exploring patterns where similar events have happened before, structures underpinning the pattern identified, and the mental models which may be contributing to the existing structures. Clutterbuck (7) applies this model to the development of a coaching culture, using the example of a company where a coaching course for managers was organised. The organiser noticed that almost a third of managers did not attend. In looking for patterns, the organiser could see where this had happened before and if the managers who cancelled shared any characteristics, for example if they were from the same part of the company. By working at the pattern level, the organiser was able to tackle underlying causes. Clutterbuck then suggests how the organiser could investigate structural issues – in this case, whether the way targets were set was a barrier to people attending training. Finally, in exploring mental models the organiser can assess whether some managers have unspoken negative attitudes towards coaching which can be brought out into the open and discussed. Applying systems thinking in this way helps to avoid dealing with symptoms in order to identify and address underlying causes.

According to Senge (38), the core capabilities of systems leaders include:

- deep listening, which helps develop relationships, trust, and collaboration;
- deep shared reflection, willingness to understand other people's point of view emotionally as well as cognitively, which also leads to trust; and
- focusing on co-creating the future, rather than on only on reactive problem-solving.

These core capabilities can be demonstrated through the application of a coaching skillset. Systems thinking provides a lens for coaching managers to think holistically about their organisation and its eco-system.

Modern organisational life is multi-layered, meaning that the team coach must be able to think about those different layers (39). With a spirit of curiosity and a willingness to learn, the coaching leader can move between the big picture and the detail, between global and local, ready to adjust as new information and perspectives come to light. In adopting a systems perspective, the coaching leader considers the links between different elements of the system as well as the different elements themselves. The ability to see the big picture makes it easier to resolve conflicts which often arise from people focusing narrowly on their own perspective (38).

Lawrence (40) recommends that team coaches become familiar with systems theory, complex adaptive systems, and complexity theory, and apply that understanding when working with stakeholders. More recently, Lawrence (41) has warned that the systems label may not always be helpful, and that a more agile and flexible approach may be needed.

The importance of stakeholders for effective teams has been a constant theme in Hawkins's work from the inclusion of 'external and internal relationships' in the 2006 (42) definition of team coaching through to the 2021 definition of leadership team coaching as 'focusing on how the team enact collective leadership in relation to all their stakeholders' (43). The coaching manager considers not only the team and the individuals in the team, but also the relationship between the team and with other teams or stakeholders (44). Stakeholders include staff, customers, suppliers and partner organisations, investors, investors, regulators, communities in which the organisation operates, professional or trade associations and others as well as the natural environment in which the team operates. The systems coach fosters collaboration with stakeholders, within and outside the organisation, transforming relationships through dialogue, and developing shared goals with stakeholders to optimise outcomes for all partners.

Figure 5.2 illustrates how coaching at the organisational level includes interactions with stakeholders.

Figure 5.2 prompts us to think not only about each element in the system but also about the interactions between the elements. For example, there may be interactions with other teams at the same level, interactions between the team and individuals, between the team and the organisation as a whole, or between the team and the external environment. The ability to simultaneously think about the world in different ways helps the manager to cope with complexity. An interesting example is a Canadian study of 'Two-Eyed Seeing', which McKinnon and Long (45) describe as a collaborative way of tackling wicked problems by

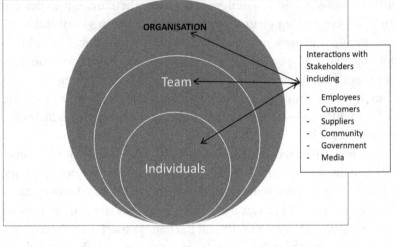

Figure 5.2 The Coaching System in Organisations

seeing the world through both an Indigenous and a Western perspective. To take an example from nature, the anableps is a fish which has one pair of eyes for seeing above water and another pair for seeing below water. If managers adopt a similar approach (46), they will track both the big picture and the small details, taking care of the people and of the tasks that need attention.

A stakeholder map helps managers understand where and how a team interacts with its stakeholders and helps each team develop a shared understanding of its place in the world. It identifies what is important to each stakeholder, which can suggest ideas for how to improve relations with each stakeholder. A stakeholder map can be used, regardless of whether a team interacts only with internal stakeholders or has a wide-ranging ecosystem, including external stakeholders such as local government politicians and officials, community organisations, suppliers, customers, and media. It is important for the stakeholder map to be reviewed and updated regularly as new players in the ecosystem emerge.

Employees are vital stakeholders and, as such, they need to be included in forward planning. How this is done varies in different countries and organisations. Regardless of the legal framework, adopting a coaching approach in developing strategy, innovation, and change leads to stronger implementation. Organisations also need to consider former employees and potential future employees as stakeholders. Former employees who have left on good terms are wonderful ambassadors for the organisation. A good reputation and positive word of mouth makes it easier to attract the best employees, who in turn contribute to the culture and performance of the company.

Sometimes stakeholders have competing priorities. The coaching leader asks questions to identify areas of overlapping interest and to identify possible solutions, some of which may be developed to satisfy all sets of stakeholders. Awareness of how stakeholders interact minimises the likelihood of unintended consequences when changes are introduced. Without this understanding, new solutions may either not work or only partially succeed because those who came up with them did not understand the whole system. Clutterbuck (47) suggests that new behaviours are less likely to become embedded if the environment is not supportive, that is, if peers, direct reports or managers do not really support the implementation. Listening to diverse perspectives can help develop solutions in a way that addresses any concerns.

The complexity of the VUCA world means that it is not always easy to determine a clear long-term strategy. The Cynefin framework (48) suggests that the way we respond to external events can and should vary. When the external environment is clear and simple, we can compare what we are doing with best practice and make improvements. When things are more complicated but still predictable, the framework suggests that we need more data to identify good options. The authors warn that in a complex environment, no matter how much data we analyse we may not be able to find an answer but instead need to pilot possible solutions, understand that not all our ideas will work, and keep experimenting. Finally, in a chaotic environment in the Cynefin framework, leaders have to act quickly and take quick decisions. The COVID-19 pandemic fits with their description of a chaotic environment (49). Post-pandemic, in Cynefin terms, we are in a complex environment requiring experimentation. Whether we will ever get to a simple or merely complicated environment again seems unlikely given the continuing rapid changes, particularly the application of artificial intelligence to the business world. Strategy nowadays needs to be 'guided by audacious questions at the top level, but also actualized by people working much closer to the front line' (50). Snowden and Boone (48) suggest that in parallel with managing a crisis, leaders should set up a team to seek opportunities for innovation. Experimenting with small steps helps move the organisation forward, even though some of those steps are likely to fail (51).

Systems thinking emphasises learning. Argyris (52) distinguishes between 'single loop' learning where people learn to correct a mistake and 'double loop' learning where we also learn about underlying or systemic issues to try to prevent an issue recurring. Argyris found that many professionals are not used to failure and become defensive when problems are identified. Their defensiveness becomes a block to learning. In contrast, when managers and teams are honest about the issues, it is easier to solve the right problem and to generate solutions. Where there is an expectation of continuous improvement, employees are more likely to continue learning and to develop their skills (53). Implementing coaching enables an organisation to become a learning organisation (54).

Coaching managers encourage reflection and learning, with regular feedback a feature of a coaching culture. Learning benefits from reflection (55). Researchers in India experimented with two teams, where both teams went through the same training (56). One team was given 15 minutes at the end of every working day to reflect on what they had learned that day. That team outperformed the other team in a test at the end of the month. Clutterbuck (7) suggests that teams provide a bridge between individual and organisational learning. Organisations should do more to promote the value of reflection if they want to increase the impact of training and the value they receive from their investment in training. Coaching has long been associated with increases in employees taking what they have learned in training and applying it in their workplace (57).

Feedback is vital for learning and improvement (58). For teams to be willing to try new things and learn from the experience, psychological safety is essential (59). Eurich (60) notes that people do not always learn from experience and warns that being experienced can in fact make us overconfident about our performance and our level of self-awareness. This links to the Dunning-Kruger effect mentioned in Chapter Three.

The coaching skills outlined in previous chapters can be applied in extended relationships with stakeholders, as suggested in Table 5.2.

Traps to Avoid

In their enthusiasm to spread the joy of coaching, some organisations send all their managers to coaching training and mandate that everyone implement coaching. Managers who do not see the benefit of coaching and are forced to coach may simply go through the motions, tick the required boxes, and fill in the required forms. This risks damaging the credibility of coaching within their team and more broadly. A better approach is to establish a shared understanding of coaching and its benefits and then provide dedicated managerial coaching training and support for those who wish to engage.

Table 5.2 Coaching Skills in the Wider System

Coaching Skill	Examples in a systems approach
Observation	Rather than relying on second-hand data, the coaching team leader might take a team to see how their product is used by customers before engaging with customers on their feedback and collaboratively developing improvements. Coaching leaders adopt a strengths-based approach, noting what is working and building on it.
Listening	In a meeting with stakeholders, the coaching leader listens carefully to each stakeholder, summarising and paraphrasing to make sure they have understood the issue correctly.
Asking Questions	Coaching leaders ask questions initially to map stakeholders and processes to gain a deep understanding of the system. The map is updated as new information emerges.
Goal Setting	Coaching leaders set goals with partnership teams to ensure that there is buy-in from all companies represented in the partnership.
Feedback	Coaching leaders address any tension they observe arising in a partnership team, stopping any attempts to blame the other company/companies in the partnership and ensuring the focus is on the future.
Reflection	Time is set aside in meetings for quick reflections on what is working well and what could work better. Time is set aside after a project is completed for a deeper reflection on the lessons to be learned.

Relying on outdated stakeholder maps is a risk, which at best sub-optimises the organisation's response and relationships and, at worst, may lead the organisation to make bad decisions because it either misses some stakeholders completely or underestimates the significance of some stakeholders' perspectives. Adopting a systems coaching approach ensures that all stakeholders are regularly considered.

CROSS-CULTURAL COACHING

The way that managers coach their employees has to take account of culture. The impact of globalisation means that even small companies often have a multi-cultural workforce. Communication varies in different cultures (61) and coaching relies on how we use words. This is about more than sharing a common language. It is also about being humble and empathetic, and not arrogantly assuming that our way is the best way (62). The characteristics of a coaching culture where people are open to multiple perspectives, respectful of others, and regularly reflect and learn can also help leverage cultural differences (7).

There have been many extensive studies of culture over time, with some of the best known being the work of Hofstede (63–66), Trompenaars (67–69) and, more recently, Project Globe (70–72). There have also been criticisms of these studies and how they were conducted. For example, Hofstede's original study was conducted between 1967 and 1973 within a single company (IBM), albeit in over 50 countries. It is unlikely that everyone in a particular country would share the same views as those who were surveyed and it is likely that employees of a single large company may share some characteristics, regardless of where they are based. While each of these studies provides useful insights, they do not provide a simple answer or recipe for how to work with people from different cultural backgrounds and create a risk of people adopting beliefs based on invalid stereotypes. Instead, a coaching manager might use one of the dimensions identified in these studies such as power distance as a starting point for reflection and questions about how that dimension might influence leadership and coaching in a particular context.[1] A framework that is particularly relevant to coaching is Rosinski's Cultural Orientation Framework (73).[2]

Expectations of coaching and the way coaching is enacted vary in different cultures. For example, if a coaching manager sits in on a meeting or activity with the specific intention of observing, then in a participative culture there would usually be a conversation with the employees to be observed, explaining the intent of the observation and what will happen post-observation. Employees might have the opportunity to withdraw from the meeting if they do not wish to be observed or to suggest ways in which the observation might be best undertaken (e.g. for a particular segment of a meeting). Such conversations might also be held in a culture of high power distance, but with the intent to inform rather than consult employees.

Culture influences the way we ask and answer questions (74). Some cultures are more hierarchical than others and there is greater power distance between managers and employees. This in turn influences both the type of questions we ask and how acceptable it is to ask questions. In countries with high power distance, it may not be seen as acceptable for employees to ask their managers any questions. What we ask about may also vary. To establish rapport in a British company, it is not uncommon to ask about a local football match, whereas in another country that might be seen as a waste of valuable time. Asking about someone's weight may be a sign of caring in some cultures, but offensive or seen as an intrusion into an employee's personal life in others. There are also differences in how we use our body language, such as in how much direct eye contact is expected. If our native language is different from that of the other person, we should think of simple ways of posing our questions. Learning more about other cultures and asking respectful questions helps to avoid misinterpreting what we see based on the assumptions we make.

Goal-setting also varies in different cultures (75). Some cultures have a long-term orientation whereas others are more short term in their planning, and hence the time horizons for goal-setting vary. In cultures which prefer to avoid uncertainty, people may be uncomfortable with brainstorming options but keen to tie down details in order to reduce uncertainty. Countries with a collectivist orientation are more likely to define and reward shared goals than individual goals. In countries with high power distance, employees may be more likely to accept and expect that the manager will set goals. However, if they are encouraged to frame their goals in ways that are genuinely meaningful to them and not just what they think the manager wants to hear, the motivational impact can be powerful. Particularly in a high power distance country it is helpful to separate goal-setting and performance evaluations from coaching conversations focusing on career and capability development (32).

How we give feedback – in public or private, to individuals or teams, direct or indirect – also varies. For example, in China, where Confucian values include respect for social status and loss of face is to be avoided (76), a coaching manager would make sure that any feedback that might be construed as criticism is given in private. In the Middle East, reference is sometimes made to a third party whom the person being coached respects, as this can help the person consider a new perspective on their behaviour. Data gathered from key stakeholders can help an individual to accept feedback and address it (77, 78). Interestingly, people's willingness to defer to someone of perceived higher status has been found to lessen when conversations are held online (47). In low power distance countries it is more common for employees to give team leaders feedback than in countries with high power distance.

Adopting a coaching approach which is culturally compatible with those being coached can help ensure that coaching is successful. For example, Ershad coaching which is based on Islamic principles has been found to be effective with Muslims in the UK (79), with participants valuing the fact that the coaching process was aligned with their faith and that they shared values with the coach.

A study of managerial coaching in 51 countries (80) found that women were more likely to coach than men. The authors suggested that this could help women address double standards, where women who were assertive were not always perceived as positively as their male counterparts displaying similar behaviour. Coaching, in contrast, allows women to be both rigorous in the performance they expect of their employees and supportive of their employees' development. The study also found that managerial coaching was more common in collectivist rather than individualistic cultures. The study's authors recommend that expatriate managers from individualistic countries should be prepared to coach their employees if they move to a country with a more collectivist orientation. Another study, of Chinese managers coaching employees in a subsidiary in Zambia, found that learning outcomes were enhanced when managers adopted a coaching approach, particularly where the managers showed cultural sensitivity (81). How people regulate their emotions is not always the same in different cultural contexts, adding to the complexity of developing appropriate leadership approaches in multicultural organisations (82). A study in Malaysia found that managerial coaching was effective in encouraging employees, particularly women, to 'take charge', in other words, to be proactive in initiating self-improvement and improvements in the workplace (83). Another Malaysian study found that coaching worked well with a young workforce (84).

Learning about different cultures helps managers to hold coaching conversations in appropriate ways. Hawkins (43) emphasises the importance of developing frameworks in which people can work together and encouraging a dialogue in which both parties participate in learning. Similarly, Kliewer (85) advocates a reciprocal approach to coaching, where information and experiences are shared, and new ways of working developed together. Approaching coaching in multi-cultural workplaces in a spirit of respectful curiosity and being willing to learn about other cultures helps the coaching manager to make fewer mistakes than they might otherwise do. This is also a useful focus for team learning. When managers have developed positive relationships, employees will be more tolerant of mistakes and more likely to give feedback to their manager about approaches or processes that might work better. The relative importance of prioritising relationships versus prioritising tasks varies in different countries (86) but both are important in achieving organisational outcomes as well as helping individuals and teams to grow.

Leadership in a multi-cultural context is a constant learning journey as not everyone from a particular culture will react in the same way. Furthermore, cultural norms change over time, especially when there is interaction with other cultures through migration, trade, and, nowadays, the influence of cinema, streaming services, and the Internet. In large countries like China there are many cultures, not a single culture. For example, the culture in a rural area in China may be more different from the culture in a large city in China than the culture of that large city is from other large cities. Learning about cultural norms is the start of a conversation and not a permanent description that applies to everyone from that culture.

In the context of an international merger, investing in cross-cultural training for everyone can reduce the risks and costs of misunderstandings and increase the chances of the merger succeeding. Where there is a coaching culture, Clutterbuck (7) suggests that people are more likely to reflect on experiences, to be curious, to question how cultural preferences might influence their interactions, to be open to different perspectives, to respect others, and to be driven by the need to grow and learn rather than by the need to be right. Intercultural competence is highly congruent with VUCA leadership requirements (87).

Nurturing diversity and inclusivity has multiple benefits for the organisation. Diverse perspectives lead to more innovative solutions, better quality decision-making, and better understanding of customer and other stakeholder needs, leading to better company outcomes (88, 89). Taking the opportunity to appreciate the strength of different ideas helps organisations to gain from diversity by improving their processes and products, as well as by widening the talent pool from which the organisation can draw. There are also potential difficulties. For example, decision-making may be slower as it takes time to consider each perspective in a genuine rather than tokenistic manner (90). The benefits of diversity will only be realised where there are positive relationships, trust, and psychological safety ensuring that people feel safe speaking up. To give a simple example, if someone puts forward an idea that has little chance of success, a manager (or colleague in an environment where people give each other feedback respectfully) might find some small component of the idea which could form the basis of a workable idea. When a person's idea is built on they are more willing to put forward more ideas, whereas if their idea is shot down they may be reluctant to speak out again.

Of course diversity does not just relate to culture. There are many other forms of diversity in today's workplaces. The same attitude of learning and receptiveness to feedback helps the coaching manager appreciate the nuances and provide the leadership each team member needs, while nurturing relations with the team as a whole. With regard to age diversity, research shows that coaching works with different generations, including millennials who have sometimes been reported as a source of frustration for older managers (91).

Inclusion is important for health and well-being. Diversity can take many forms and employees should feel safe in sharing as much or as little about themselves as they wish. People thrive when they can bring their whole selves to work and feel a sense of belonging. In an organisation where there is overt or covert discrimination, people protect themselves by concealing part of their identity. Minority Stress Theory shows that having to constantly cover up how we feel is exhausting and can lead to mental health issues (92). A coaching culture where each individual feels valued and heard is a sound foundation for a healthy workplace. Furthermore, fostering an inclusive workplace is known to enhance employee engagement (93). A study of managerial coaching in the UAE found that coaching helped reduce bullying and alienation (94).

Coaching in Multinational Organisations

Multinational organisations are by their nature dispersed and multi-cultural. Having discussed the cultural influences which influence coaching, we will now consider the additional challenges created when a team is working across different countries.

Multinational companies have long been used to bringing teams together from around the world one or more times a year, for example for strategy sessions or team building (43). However, the pandemic created a circuit breaker that made people realise that these large meetings might not always be necessary. This, says Hawkins (43, p. 179), means that 'with the increasing globalization of all forms of organization, and the cost of travel in terms of money, time and world resources, team coaches have needed to evolve ways of building trust with less face-to-face time than we have previously been used to'.

There are challenges in trying to ensure that people across an organisation have equal opportunities for development and recognition. When a virtual team operates across several countries, each of the team members may be in a different legal entity and subject to different employment regulations. Asking questions and exploring options in a culturally sensitive way can help develop a shared understanding of what is possible so that the best choices can be made. Technology options also exist that can be applied globally, for example recognition apps such as Nectar[3] and Reward Gateway.[4]

There are many technology options for the remote and hybrid workspace, including software for videoconferencing and text messaging (e.g. Zoom, Microsoft Teams, Webex and Slack), for collective brainstorming (Mural, Miro), for working on shared documents (Google Drive and Dropbox), and for project management and goal tracking (Microsoft Project, Asana, Trello, and Jira). Used well, they can help teams work efficiently and cohesively to resolve queries and facilitate social interactions that at least partially compensate for the lack of face-to-face casual conversations.

Large Meetings

Much of the work in organisations today is done in meetings. Just as the purpose of team meetings needs to be clear, as discussed in Chapter Four, so too with the purpose of large group meetings. Technology now makes it easy for leaders to 'meet' huge numbers of staff online, allowing a consistent message to be given throughout an organisation. This can help promote a sense of belonging and unity (95). In synchronous meetings, there should be some form of interaction, such as questions and answers, polls, or side conversations on the same or a different channel to the main meeting to make it worthwhile for people to meet at the same time.

For example, in a Town Hall meeting, where senior leaders update employees on an organisation's progress on its strategy and key activities, people can post their questions on a wall if the meeting takes place in a physical location or on apps such as Slido or Pigeonhole. Questions can be posed anonymously, meaning that those who lack the confidence to speak up in large meetings can still have input. If all the questions posed cannot be answered in the meeting, it is important to give and keep a commitment to respond to all questions (including any tricky ones) soon after. Recording the meeting helps ensure that all employees hear the same information directly from senior leaders. A video response to questions that could not be answered during the meeting can also be shared on the company's intranet.

Online meetings also bring additional difficulties if they use a webinar format where only the speaker(s) can be seen, thus providing fewer of the visual cues that suggest whether people are engaged and following what is being said. Platforms which allow attendees at virtual meetings not only to participate in the main meeting but to have side conversations and break-out groups can also be used effectively. As we became more proficient at using meeting platforms, we can optimise the way we run online meetings.

Deciding whether a meeting should be face to face or online is an important choice, particularly in hybrid multinational or geographically dispersed companies. One of the advantages of online meetings is that they can be scheduled differently to traditional in-person meetings. In a large multinational, it is time-consuming and costly to bring people together from around the world, and hence a three-day agenda makes sense. If such a meeting is held online, the meeting can be split into different elements, and a series of meetings set up, each of which focuses specifically on each element. This has the added advantage of holding people's attention because of the shorter time span and of being easier to slot into people's diaries. And of course there are cost, time, and pollution savings as well as less time away from one's home and family.

Because of these considerations, there needs to be a strong rationale for face-to-face meetings. Pure information-giving can be done very well online with the added bonus of recordings and transcriptions. People's increasing familiarity with videoconferencing and other collaboration applications has led to an increase in the amount of work that is now done remotely, with some teams switching to fully remote, whereas in the past they also held some face-to-face meetings.

Care must be taken to find times that work for all attendees, or at least to avoid the worst inconveniences. Depending on the time zones involved, it may be possible to find a time that is after 6 am in one country and before 8 pm in another. There are numerous Internet sites that make it easy to find overlapping times. Flipped meetings, where people have information in advance, whether in written or video format, allow the meeting time to be spent in interactive debate.

Despite the advantages of online meetings, there are still some advantages to meeting face to face, in particular in relation to relationship-building and the ability for multiple informal chats to take place alongside a face-to-face meeting. There are often things that people do not think are important enough to arrange a meeting about and hence they hold on to them until there is a face-to-face opportunity.

If it is decided to meet face to face, then it is important also to decide where to hold the meeting and not default to everyone coming to the head office. If meetings are held at different locations where a company has employees, head office staff meet not only the senior leaders of a particular location but also those who work with them. They get a feel for the local context (using the manager's observational, listening, and questioning skills). Similarly, virtual team meetings can alternate between meetings of the team itself and meetings that also include the direct reports of the team members. This again builds a wider network of relationships. Some of the extended team members may have useful information to contribute to the meeting in their particular area of expertise. Assuming that discussions in these meetings are collegiate, and any disagreements handled respectfully, attending these meetings can give those next in line for leadership roles better insights into the transparency of decision-making; this is a positive for trust and morale and also motivates them to apply for leadership positions that arise. In other words, this approach helps with leadership capacity-building.

Clutterbuck (47) warns that the risk of conflict is likely to be higher in a virtual team and that this risk may be higher again if the virtual team is culturally diverse. Using sports metaphors with which only some members of a team are familiar can create the perception of an in-group and an out-group. This is particularly the case when a sport is strongly identified with the home country of the headquarters of an organisation. Indeed, the very fact of some people being located at a headquarters location and others not can make those others feel that they are less likely to be listened to and so may be less likely to speak up. Proximity bias can lead to employees based in the head office having an advantage in terms of their opportunities to impress the organisation's senior leaders. A coaching approach can be used to guard against this risk by ensuring that the strengths of all employees in the organisation are recognised.

While not intentionally excluding people in other parts of the organisation or those working remotely, it can be easy for those at head office to forget about other locations (47). This can exacerbate a sense of an in-group and an out-group and that power and information are concentrated in one location, thereby disadvantaging those at other parts of the organisation. Clutterbuck (43) recommends strong and effective mechanisms to remind people about the need to communicate with their remote colleagues, noting that it is in fact even more important to communicate with virtual team members because those who are co-located can pick up a lot of information from informal conversations.

Centralisation versus Decentralisation

Many organisations alternate between high degrees of centralisation and decentralisation, rarely stopping at a point of equilibrium mid-way between the two. Both have benefits. In a highly centralised organisation, everyone is very clear on where decisions are made. Highly centralised also often means hierarchical, resulting in systems and processes that are not sufficiently agile to cope with a rapidly changing context.

Decentralised systems can be inefficient as some resources are duplicated. However, they have the advantage of local empowerment and are more in keeping with a coaching culture than a highly centralised organisation. Excellent communication skills are needed to ensure collegiality, coordination, and collaboration combined with a focus on achieving the overall organisational goals as well as the goals of the local unit.

The centralisation versus decentralisation debate is one of the paradoxes faced by leaders in today's organisations (96). Others include the tensions between being a global player and serving local markets, being people-focused while optimising the use of technology, and between staying true to the organisation's mission and being nimble and agile. Adopting a coaching mindset helps managers navigate these paradoxes with their teams, balancing the needs of the organisation, the team, and the individual, and constantly fine-tuning their approach.

Matrix Management

One way that organisations have tried to create an effective combination of local and global expertise is through matrix management. In a typical matrix structure, a team member has reporting lines to more than one manager, a primary reporting line, and so-called 'dotted lines' to other people. For instance, an operations manager in a factory in one country might report to the local general manager or managing director while also reporting to the global vice president of operations. Matrix management is fraught with tension as each of the reporting lines believes that it should take priority. Coaching helps team leaders and teams define clear roles and responsibilities, agree on shared priorities and how to measure them, as well as on how conflict will be managed. In this VUCA world, leaders can leverage coaching to develop and implement shared leadership in matrix organisations (97).

Readiness for Change

It has long been said that 'The only constant is change'. Change is now continuous rather than something that happens periodically. The pace of change has accelerated, with developments in information and communications technology allowing ideas to spread rapidly around the world.

There has been a great deal of research into how to manage change effectively. One of the best known change models is Kotter's Eight Steps (98). These steps include building a guiding coalition, forming a strategic vision, enlisting volunteers, and generating short-term wins (or picking low-hanging fruit). When managers adopt a coaching approach, they help develop a shared understanding of the current situation and the need for change, develop a strategic vision with input from stakeholders, identify barriers by listening to employee feedback, and identify options for removing barriers and implementing positive change. Researchers recommend training managers in coaching skills in order to develop employee engagement and have a positive influence on employees' ability to cope with change (99). Listening to employees and stakeholders helps identify potential problems with proposed changes and strengthens implementation.

While managing change well is important, recent research suggests that when managers have a coaching relationship with their employees, this has a positive impact on employees' readiness for change as well as on employee engagement (12, 100). Readiness for change is about people's willingness to accept, embrace, and implement change. Research over the last 30 years shows that readiness for change comprises three aspects: emotional readiness (people's affective response to change), intentional readiness (people's willingness to do something about the change), and cognitive readiness (people's beliefs and thoughts about the change) (101, 102).

Traditional change management processes address the cognitive aspects by explaining why the change is important. This helps reduce resistance to change. Sense-making is critically important in times of change, as people try to make sense of what is happening and what its impact might be (103). Coaching helps with sense-making (104) and it is therefore not surprising that coaching helps with readiness for change. Rolfe (105, p. 301) claims that 'coaching is an instrument or tool that can stabilize the constancy of change'.

Many studies have shown that change often arouses negative emotions such as anxiety, fear, and anger (106–108). Attempting to convince people who are fearful of change purely with rational arguments rarely succeeds (109). An approach that helps address the emotional as well as the cognitive aspects of change management is needed (110). This is where coaching helps. A coaching relationship has a positive impact on trust, creating a climate where employees feel safe and their concerns acknowledged, which in turn helps with employee well-being and resilience during change (111). Furthermore, coaching helps develop commitment to action through goal-setting and follow-up, thus addressing the intentional element of readiness for change. The ability to consider multiple perspectives also helps coaching managers to anticipate and address potential issues with change implementation, drawing on the wisdom of their teams and diverse stakeholders.

Traps to Avoid

It can be the case in a multinational company that those who speak the language of the parent company find it easier to get promoted than those who are highly competent and credible with their peers, but less fluent in the parent company language. This risk is particularly apparent during mergers and acquisitions, when people are getting to know each other and do not yet have other performance measures to use. The coaching manager helps by getting to know each team member and their strengths, sharing performance criteria in a transparent manner, and helping all team members, including their quieter colleagues, to be seen and recognised.

IN CLOSING

Moving beyond the individual and team coaching level to deploy coaching at the organisational level creates a genuinely inclusive coaching culture. Combining a coaching culture with a systems thinking approach amplifies the benefits. However, some organisations may simply not be ready or not have enough senior leaders with a coaching mindset to make this a reality. If that is the case, coaching leaders are best advised to implement coaching within their sphere of influence and ensure that informal coaching dialogues become the norm. Coaching dialogues underpin respectful collaboration across cultures and across multinational organisations, leading to positive outcomes for the organisation as well as for individuals and teams, including in times of change.

NOTES

1 Readers can explore the cultural dimensions in each of these studies at the following links:

Hofstede https://www.hofstede-insights.com/country-comparison-tool

Trompenaars https://www.thtconsulting.com/culture-factory/culture-explore/compare-countries/

Globe Project https://globeproject.com/study_2014.html

2 See https://www.cofassessment.com/ for further information.
3 See https://nectarhr.com/ for further information.
4 See https://www.rewardgateway.com/au/solution/peer-to-peer-recognition for further information.

REFERENCES

1. Bennis W, Nanus B. *Leaders: strategies for taking charge.* New York: Harper & Row; 1985.
2. Deal TE, Kennedy AA. Culture: a new look through old lenses. *The Journal of Applied Behavioral Science.* 1983;19(4): 498–505.
3. Johnson G, Whittington, R., Scholes, K. *Exploring strategy.* 9th ed. Harlow: Pearson; 2011.
4. Gopinath M, Nair A, Thangaraj V. Espoused and enacted values in an organization: workforce implications. *Management and Labour Studies.* 2018;43(4): 277–93.
5. Tong YK, Arvey RD. Managing complexity via the competing values framework. *Journal of Management Development.* 2015;34(6): 653–73.
6. Milner J, Milner T, McCarthy G. A coaching culture definition: an industry-based perspective from managers as coaches. *The Journal of Applied Behavioral Science.* 2020;56(2): 237–54.
7. Clutterbuck D, Megginson D, Bajer A. *Building and sustaining a coaching culture.* London: Kogan Page; 2016.
8. Hunt JM, Weintraub JR. *The coaching manager: developing top talent in business.* 3rd ed. Los Angeles: Sage; 2017.
9. Gormley H, van Nieuwerburgh C. Developing coaching cultures: a review of the literature. *Coaching: An International Journal of Theory, Research and Practice.* 2014;7(2): 90–101.
10. Jones J, Lundgren H, Poell R. 'I love and dream of a future where we're all coaches' – an analysis of multiple perspectives on managerial coaching. *European Journal of Training and Development.* 2024. https://doi.org/10.1108/EJTD-11-2023-0181
11. Kapoutzis N, Whiley LA, Yarker J, Lewis R. Coaching culture: an evidence review and framework for future research and practice. *Coaching: An International Journal of Theory, Research and Practice.* 2024;17(1): 50–76.
12. McCarthy G, Milner J. Ability, motivation and opportunity: managerial coaching in practice. *Asia Pacific Journal of Human Resources.* 2020;58(1): 149–70.
13. Cooper PR. *An investigative pursuit of managerial coaching, its effectiveness and the potential Impact it has on ROI indicators and employee productivity indicators in a call center environment.* PhD thesis. Sullivan University; 2018.
14. Anderson MC, Frankovelgia C, Hernez-Broome G. Business leaders reflect on coaching cultures. *LIA.* 2009;28(6): 20–2.
15. O'Connor S, Cavanagh M. The coaching ripple effect: the effects of developmental coaching on wellbeing across organisational networks. *Psychology of Well-Being: Theory, Research and Practice.* 2013;3(1): 1–23.
16. Megginson D, Clutterbuck D. Creating a coaching culture. *Industrial and Commercial Training.* 2006;38(5): 232–7.
17. Turner C, McCarthy G. Coachable moments: identifying factors that influence managers to take advantage of coachable moments in day-to-day management. *International Journal of Evidence Based Coaching and Mentoring.* 2015;13(1): 1–13.

18. Moore JR, Hanson W. Improving leader effectiveness: impact on employee engagement and retention. *Journal of Management Development.* 2022;41(7/8): 450–68.

19. Clutterbuck D, Megginson D. *Making coaching work: creating a coaching culture.* London: CIPD Publishing; 2005.

20. Mansor NA, Mohamed A, Idris N. Determinates of coaching culture development: a case study. *Procedia-Social and Behavioral Sciences.* 2012;40: 485–9.

21. Adele B, Ellinger AD. Managerial coaches' enacted behaviors and the beliefs that guide them: perspectives from managers and their coachees. *Frontiers in Psychology.* 2024;14: 1154593.

22. Milner J, McCarthy G, Milner T. Training for the coaching leader: how organizations can support managers. *Journal of Management Development.* 2018;37(2): 188–200.

23. McCarthy G, Ahrens J. Managerial coaching: challenges, opportunities & training. *Journal of Management Development.* 2013;32(7): 768–79.

24. Whitmore J. Business coaching international. *Coaching: An International Journal of Theory, Research and Practice.* 2009;2(2): 176–9.

25. Whitmore J. *Coaching for performance.* 4th ed. London: Nicholas Brealey; 2009.

26. Alexander G. Behavioural coaching – the GROW model. In: Passmore J, editor. *Excellence in coaching: the industry guide.* London: Kogan Page; 2006. p. 61–72.

27. Grant AM. It takes time: a stages of change perspective on the adoption of workplace coaching skills. *Journal of Change Management.* 2010;10(1): 61–77.

28. Oreg S, Berson Y. Leadership and employees' reaction to change: The role of leaders' personal attributes and transformational leadership style. *Personnel Psychology.* 2011;64(3): 627–59.

29. Van Nieuwerburgh C. *An introduction to coaching skills: a practical guide.* London: Sage; 2017.

30. Lin H, Zheng H, Wang F. Do bystanders always see more than the players? Exploring Solomon's paradox through meta-analysis. *Frontiers in Psychology.* 2023;14: 1181187.

31. Hay J. *Reflective practice and supervision for coaches.* Maidenhead: McGraw-Hill; 2007.

32. Carvalho C, Kurian PO, Carvalho S, Carvalho FK. Managing managerial coaching: the role of stakeholders. *Industrial and Commercial Training.* 2023;55(2): 295–305.

33. Milner J, Milner T, McCarthy G, da Motta Veiga S. Leaders as coaches: towards a code of ethics. *The Journal of Applied Behavioral Science.* 2023;59(3): 448–72.

34. She Z, Li B, Li Q, London M, Yang B. The double-edged sword of coaching: relationships between managers' coaching and their feelings of personal accomplishment and role overload. *Human Resource Development Quarterly.* 2019;30(2): 245–66.

35. Muff K, Liechti A, Dyllick T. How to apply responsible leadership theory in practice: a competency tool to collaborate on the sustainable development goals. *Corporate Social Responsibility and Environmental Management.* 2020;27(5): 2254–74.

36. Goodman M. *The iceberg model.* Hopkinton, MA: Innovation Associates Organizational Learning; 2002.

37. Monat JP, Gannon TF. What is systems thinking? A review of selected literature plus recommendations. *American Journal of Systems Science.* 2015;4(1): 11–26.

38. Senge PM. *Systems principles for leadership.* Working Paper (Sloan School of Management); 1758–86. Cambridge, MA: MIT; 1985.

39. Thornton C. *Group and team coaching.* London: Routledge; 2016.

40. Lawrence P, Whyte A. What do experienced team coaches do? Current practice in Australia and New Zealand. *International Journal of Evidence Based Coaching and Mentoring.* 2017;15(1): 94–113.

41. Lawrence P. Team coaching: systemic perspectives and their limitations. *Philosophy of Coaching.* 2021;6(1): 52–82.

42. Hawkins P, Smith N. *Coaching, mentoring and organizational consultancy: supervision and development.* Maidenhead: Open University Press; 2006.

43. Hawkins P. *Leadership team coaching: developing collective transformational leadership.* E-book ed.: Kogan Page; 2021.

44. Hawkins P. *Leadership team coaching in practice: case studies on creating highly effective teams.* London: Kogan Page; 2022.

45. McKinnon MN, Long BS. Leading with two eyes: leadership failures and possibilities in the management of a pulp mill's wicked problem. *Qualitative Research in Organizations and Management: An International Journal.* 2022;17(3): 318–39.

46. Steiner W. Manage like the four-eyed fish: 4 questions to help you look above and below the surface of things. Executive Coaching Concepts, 7 July 2014. https://executivecoachingconcepts.com/manage-like-the-four-eyed-fish/.

47. Clutterbuck D. *Coaching the team at work: the definitive guide to team coaching.* 2nd ed. E-book ed.: Nicholas Brealey; 2020.

48. Snowden DJ, Boone ME. A leader's framework for decision making. *Harvard Business Review.* 2007;85(11): 68.

49. Okoli J, Arroteia NP, Ogunsade AI. Failure of crisis leadership in a global pandemic: some reflections on COVID-19 and future recommendations. *Leadership in Health Services.* 2023;36(2): 186–99.

50. Brown S, Conn, C, McLean, R. Why strategists should embrace imperfection. *McKinsey Quarterly,* 8 April 2024. https://www.mckinsey.com/capabilities/strategy-and-corporate-finance/our-insights/why-strategists-should-embrace-imperfection.

51. McLean R, Conn, C. *The imperfectionists: strategic mindsets for uncertain times.* Hoboken: Wiley; 2023.

52. Argyris C. Teaching smart people how to learn. *Harvard Business Review.* 1991;69(3): 99–109.

53. Christensen U. How to teach employees skills they don't know they lack. *Harvard Business Review,* 29 Sept 2017. https://hbr.org/2017/09/how-to-teach-employees-skills-they-dont-know-they-lack

54. Ellinger AD, Ellinger AE. Providing strategic leadership for learning: optimizing managerial coaching to build learning organizations. *The Learning Organization.* 2020;28(4): 337–51.

55. Boser U. Learning is a learned behaviour. Here's how to get better at it. *Harvard Business Review,* 2 May 2018. https://hbr.org/2018/05/learning-is-a-learned-behavior-heres-how-to-get-better-at-it

56. Gino F, Staats B. Why organizations don't learn. *Harvard Business Review.* 2015;93(11): 110–18.

57. Olivero G, Bane KD, Kopelman RE. Executive coaching as a transfer of training tool: effects on productivity in a public agency. *Public Personnel Management.* 1997;26(4): 461–9.

58. Chamorro-Premuzic T, Bersin J. Four ways to create a learning culture on your team. *Harvard Business Review*, 12 Jul 2018. https://hbr.org/2018/07/4-ways-to-create-a-learning-culture-on-your-team

59. Edmunson A, Bohmer R, Pisano G. Speeding up team learning. *Harvard Business Review* [repr. 2019 special issue]. 2001;79: 125–34.

60. Eurich T. What self-awareness really is and how to cultivate it. *Harvard Business Review*, 4 Jan 2018. https://hbr.org/2018/01/what-self-awareness-really-is-and-how-to-cultivate-it

61. Hofstede G. National differences in communication styles In: Brzozowska D, Chłopicki W, editors. *Culture's software: communication styles*. Newcastle upon Tyne: Cambridge Scholars Publishing; 2015.

62. Youssef-Morgan CM, Luthans F. Positive leadership: meaning and application across cultures. *Organizational Dynamics*. 2013;42(3): 198–208.

63. Hofstede G. National negotiation styles. In: Mautner-Markhof F, editor. *Process of international negotiations*. New York: Routledge; 2019. p. 193–201.

64. Hofstede G, Kolman L, Nicolescu O, Pajumaa I. Characteristics of the ideal job among students in eight countries. In: Grad H, Blanco A, Georgas J, editors. *Key issues in cross-cultural psychology*. Boca Raton, FL: Garland Science; 2021. p. 199–216.

65. Hofstede G. Understanding culture: the unwritten rules of the game. *Psychology Review Magazine*. 2020;25(3): 12–5.

66. Hofstede G, Van Deusen C, Mueller C, Charles T. What goals do business leaders pursue? A study in fifteen countries. In: DiDomenica ML, Vangen S, Winchester N, Boojihawon DK, Mordaunt J, editors. *Organizational collaboration*. Abingdon, Oxon.: Routledge; 2020. p. 35–48.

67. Hampden-Turner C, Trompenaars F. *Riding the waves of culture: understanding diversity in global business*. London: Hachette UK; 2020.

68. Trompenaars F. Did the pedestrian die? Ethics across cultures. *Journal of Intercultural Management and Ethics*. 2018;1(1): 5–9.

69. Trompenaars F, Greene RJ. *Rewarding performance globally: reconciling the global-local dilemma*. E-book ed.: Taylor & Francis; 2016.

70. House R, Javidan, M. Lessons from project GLOBE. *Organizational Dynamics*. 2001;29(4): 289–305.

71. Javidan M, Dastmalchian A. Managerial implications of the GLOBE project: A study of 62 societies. *Asia Pacific Journal of Human Resources*. 2009;47(1): 41–58.

72. Den Hartog DN, De Hoogh AH. Cross-cultural leadership: what we know, what we need to know, and where we need to go. *Annual Review of Organizational Psychology and Organizational Behavior*. 2024;11(1): 535–66.

73. Gilbert K, Rosinski P. Accessing cultural orientations: the online cultural orientations framework assessment as a tool for coaching. *Coaching: An International Journal of Theory, Research and Practice*. 2008;1(1): 81–92.

74. Mosteo LP, Maltbia TE, Marsick VJ. Coaching for cultural sensitivity: content analysis applying Hofstede's framework to a select set of the International Coach Federation's (ICF) Core Competencies. *International Coaching Psychology Review*. 2021;16(2): 51.

75. Valverde-Moreno M, Torres-Jimenez M, Lucia-Casademunt AM. Participative decision-making amongst employees in a cross-cultural employment setting: evidence from 31 European countries. *European Journal of Training and Development*. 2020;45(1): 14–35.

76. Percy W, Dow K. The coaching dance applied: training Chinese managers to coach. *Coaching: An International Journal of Theory, Research and Practice.* 2021: 1–16.

77. Palmer T, Arnold VJ. Coaching in the Middle East. In: Passmore J, editor. *Diversity in coaching: working with gender, culture, race and age.* 2nd ed. London: Kogan Page; 2013. p. 111–26.

78. Mathew P, Hakrob AN. Coaching in a higher education institution in the Middle East: reflections on the obstacles and the way forward. *International Journal of Evidence-Based Coaching and Mentoring.* 2022;20(1): 66–82.

79. Kamel M, van Nieuwerburgh C. How Muslims in the UK experience coaching using the Ershad framework – an interpretative phenomenological analysis. *International Journal of Evidence-Based Coaching and Mentoring.* 2023;21(2): 179–94.

80. Ye R, Wang X-H, Wendt JH, Wu J, Euwema MC. Gender and managerial coaching across cultures: female managers are coaching more. *The International Journal of Human Resource Management.* 2016;27(16): 1791–812.

81. Niu X, Zhang B, Simasiku M, Zhang R. Managerial coaching behavior and subordinates' learning effects in cross-cultural context: a moderated mediation study. *Chinese Management Studies.* 2022;16(4): 885–903.

82. Haver A, Akerjordet K, Furunes T. Emotion regulation and its implications for leadership: an integrative review and future research agenda. *Journal of Leadership & Organizational Studies.* 2013;20(3): 287–303.

83. Ngo MSM, Mustafa MJ, Lee C, Hallak R. Managerial coaching and taking charge at work: the mediating roles of work engagement and role breadth self-efficacy. *Journal of Organizational Effectiveness: People and Performance.* 2024; Ahead of print. https://doi.org/10.1108/JOEPP-02-2023-0041.

84. Kuan CM, Abu Bakar H. Managerial coaching to improve on organizational performance: a case study of a multinational company. *Global Business Management Review.* 2023;15(2): 1–19.

85. Kliewer BW, Ndirangu BW. Advancing reciprocity in cross-cultural leadership coaching. *Journal of Leadership Education.* 2019;18(4).

86. Meyer E. *The culture map.* New York: Public Affairs; 2015.

87. Rath CR, Grosskopf S, Barmeyer C. Leadership in the VUCA world – a systematic literature review and its link to intercultural competencies. *European Journal of Cross-Cultural Competence and Management.* 2021;5(3): 195–219.

88. Tamunomiebi MD, John-Eke EC. Workplace diversity: emerging issues in contemporary reviews. *International Journal of Academic Research in Business and Social Sciences.* 2020;10(2): 255–65.

89. Garg S, Sangwan S. Literature review on diversity and inclusion at workplace, 2010–2017. *Vision.* 2021;25(1): 12–22.

90. Cicea C, Marinescu C, Pintilie N, editors. Organizational culture in different environments: evidence From Japan. Proceedings of the International Management Conference 'Managing People and Organizations in a Global Crisis'. 4–5 Nov 2021, Bucharest, Romania. Academy of Economic Studies, Bucharest.

91. Ndungu PK, Karimi J. Managerial coaching and millenials in the workplace In: Ngari Karimi JM, editor. *Topical issues in strategic human resource management.* Eldoret, Kenya: Utafiti Foundation; 2023. p. 158–71.

92. Smith IP, McCarthy G. The Australian corporate closet: why it's still so full! *Journal of Gay & Lesbian Mental Health.* 2017;21(4):327–51.

93. Goswami S, Goswami BK. Exploring the relationship between workforce diversity, inclusion and employee engagement. *Drishtikon: A Management Journal*. 2018;9(1): 65–89.

94. Al-Nasser A, Behery M. Examining the relationship between organizational coaching and workplace counterproductive behaviours in the United Arab Emirates. *International Journal of Organizational Analysis*. 2015;23(3): 378–403.

95. Pawar S, Dhumal V. The role of technology in transforming leadership management practices. *Multidisciplinary Reviews*. 2024;7(4): 2024066-.

96. Lewis MW, Smith WK. Today's most critical leadership skill: navigating paradoxes. *Leader to Leader*. 2023;2023(107): 12–18.

97. Kennedy RL. *Shared leadership in a matrix organization: an exploratory study*. PhD thesis. Fielding Graduate University; 2017.

98. Kotter JP, Akhtar V, Gupta G. *Change: how organizations achieve hard-to-imagine results in uncertain and volatile times*. John Wiley & Sons; 2021.

99. Van den Heuvel M, Demerouti E, Schaufeli W, Bakker A. Personal resources and work engagement in the face of change. In: Leka JHS, editor. *Contemporary occupational health psychology: global perspectives on research and practice*. Hoboken, NJ: Wiley Blackwell; 2010. p. 124–50.

100. McCarthy G, Bird, S., Milner, J. Change is the new normal – how does managerial coaching relate to engagement and promote readiness for change? Accepted for the 37th Australian New Zealand Academy of Management (ANZAM) Conference, 2–5 Dec 2024, Wollongong, Australia

101. Armenakis AA, Harris SG. Reflections: our journey in organizational change research and practice. *Journal of Change Management*. 2009;9(2): 127–42.

102. Armenakis AA, Harris SG, Mossholder KW. Creating readiness for organizational change. *Human Relations*. 1993;46(6): 681–703.

103. Weick KE. Enacted sensemaking in crisis situations. *Journal of Management Studies*. 1988;25(4): 305–17.

104. Du Toit A. Making sense through coaching. *Journal of Management Development*. 2007;26(3): 282–91.

105. Rolfe J. Change is a constant requiring a coach. *Library Management*. 2010;31(4/5): 291–303.

106. Bickerich K, Michel A, O'Shea D. Executive coaching during organisational change: a qualitative study of executives and coaches perspectives. *Coaching: An International Journal of Theory, Research and Practice*. 2018;11(2): 117–43.

107. Galli BJ. Change management models: a comparative analysis and concerns. *IEEE Engineering Management Review*. 2018;46(3): 124–32.

108. Neves P, Almeida P, Velez MJ. Reducing intentions to resist future change: combined effects of commitment-based HR practices and ethical leadership. *Human Resource Management*. 2018;57(1): 249–61.

109. Aiken C, Keller S. The irrational side of change management. *McKinsey Quarterly*. 2009;2(10): 100–9.

110. Cameron E, Green M. *Making sense of change management: a complete guide to the models, tools and techniques of organizational change*. London: Kogan Page Publishers; 2019.

111. Wilson W, Lawton-Smith C. Spot-coaching: a new approach to coaching for organisations operating in the VUCA environment. *International Coaching Psychology Review*. 2016;11(1): 24–38.

Six

INTRODUCTION

In this chapter we first consider how to evaluate the effectiveness of coaching at the individual, team, and organisational level. We then discuss how to improve our coaching skills. Basically the questions we ask ourselves are:

- How do we know if we are using our coaching skills well?
- How can we get better?

We conclude by exploring how Generative Artificial Intelligence (GenAI) can support and transform the way managers coach their employees. As will be discussed, GenAI has tremendous power to help managers improve, but it is vitally important that managers continue to prioritise human relationships and apply their judgement, wisdom, and empathy in making ethical use of emerging technology.

EVALUATING COACHING

Coaching may be evaluated at the individual, team, or organisational level. However, it must be recognised that organisations are not controlled laboratories and hence improvements at the organisational level may be due to many factors and not only attributable to managers adopting a coaching approach.

Assessing Individual Coaching

A quick way to assess if employees recognise that their managers are using a coaching approach is the short version of Ellinger's Managerial

DOI: 10.4324/9781003239826-6

Coaching scale (1). This simply asks employees the extent to which they agree with the following statements:

- My supervisor sets expectations with me and communicates the importance of those expectations to the broader goals of the organisation.
- My supervisor encourages me to broaden my perspective by helping me to see the big picture.
- My supervisor provides me with constructive feedback.
- My supervisor solicits feedback from me to ensure that his/her interactions are helpful.
- My supervisor provides me with resources so I can perform my job more effectively.

Alternatively, similar statements can be incorporated in a 360° coaching manager survey to be completed by the manager, their own manager,

Table 6.1 Coaching Manager Survey

Coaching Manager Survey
On a scale of 1–10, where 10 is outstanding and 1 is very poor, how would you rate your manager?
1. My manager helps me set goals aligned with the organisation's goals.
1   2   3   4   5   6   7   8   9   10
2. My manager enables me to understand stakeholder expectations.
1   2   3   4   5   6   7   8   9   10
3. My manager encourages me to seek feedback from stakeholders.
1   2   3   4   5   6   7   8   9   10
4. My manager listens to my ideas.
1   2   3   4   5   6   7   8   9   10
5. My manager asks me questions that make me think.
1   2   3   4   5   6   7   8   9   10
6. My manager encourages me to learn.
1   2   3   4   5   6   7   8   9   10
7. My manager gives me helpful feedback.
1   2   3   4   5   6   7   8   9   10
8. My manager makes time to review my progress with me.
1   2   3   4   5   6   7   8   9   10
9. My manager helps me to reflect.
1   2   3   4   5   6   7   8   9   10
10. My manager supports me to act on feedback and reflection.
1   2   3   4   5   6   7   8   9   10

their direct reports, and their peers, with the wording adapted depending on the respondent. An example is shown in Table 6.1.

Rather than measure coaching as a whole, it can be helpful to measure and improve the specific coaching skills discussed in Chapters Two and Three. For example, if a manager has scored low on Item Four in Table 6.1, *My manager listens to my ideas*, they might initially think that this is not true. They may genuinely believe that they do listen to their employees' ideas. Nevertheless, employees' perceptions matter. If they perceive that they are not being listened to, then the benefits anticipated when managers listen to their employees will not materialise. The manager needs to address the perception if they are correct in their belief that they do in fact listen to their employees.

Recording (with permission of the participants) allows a manager to re-play a conversation and focus on specific aspects that they wish to improve. This is particularly easy with online meetings which now come with the option of automatic transcription. AI apps can be used (again with participants' permission) to analyse how much of the time the manager is speaking in a coaching session, how much of the time the other person is speaking, and how much silence is allowed. This data can heighten a manager's self-awareness and feed into improvement actions.

There are many ways to evaluate individual coaching skills. Examples are listed in Table 6.2.

Measuring Progress in Team Coaching

Several measures can be used to assess whether team coaching is effective and where there is room for improvement. Examples include the attainment of team goals, measuring the effectiveness of team meetings through a survey of participants, or a 360° survey of the team leader. Identifying one or two key measures and making improvements as a result is far more valuable than measuring several items and not doing anything with the data. On the other hand, if a team collectively decides on what to measure, reviews the data together, reflects, and agrees on ways to improve, then this transparency and activity can develop trust and help the team to grow.

While Clutterbuck's book *Coaching the Team at Work* (2) focuses primarily on an external coach coming into an organisation to coach a team, he devotes a chapter to the self-coaching team. The characteristics of a self-coaching team can be used to confirm progress in how well the team is working together, for example, whether the team generates its own

Table 6.2 Evaluating Coaching Skills

Coaching Skill	Examples of Evaluation
Observation	Take notes in a meeting. Compare your notes with those of participants and with a recording of the meeting. Seek feedback from peer, coach, or mentor on your observation skills.
Listening	Leadership 360° survey including questions about listening. Seek feedback from peer, coach, or mentor on the quality of your listening.
Questioning	Reflect on the types of question you ask, e.g. are they open questions that encourage others to develop their thinking? Do you always ask the same questions? Are your questions genuine and do they aim to help the employee? Seek feedback from peer, coach, or mentor on the quality of your questions. Use an AI app to record and analyse a coaching session. Conversation dynamics software which is typically used to analyse sales calls can be used for managers' conversations also.
Goal-setting	Review how aligned the goals you set are with organisational goals. Seek feedback from peer, coach, or mentor on the quality of your goal-setting.
Feedback	Reflect on times when you have given feedback and whether that feedback has been actioned by the feedback recipient. Can you identify anything you do or that the employee does that makes it more likely that the feedback will be taken on board and addressed? Seek feedback from peer, coach, or mentor on the quality of your feedback.
Reflection	Track how often you make time for reflection and go beyond a simple description of the facts of a situation to include different perspectives, emotions, and impact. Consider how you often you reflect on what has happened over a period of time and move beyond single incidents to identify patterns. Note to what extent you take action based on your reflections.

feedback, internally and from others, whether the team is self-motivated to learn, whether the team reviews the quality of its coaching regularly, and whether the team asks itself difficult questions.

Many managers are used to 360° leadership surveys where they get feedback from peers, from their own manager, and from their direct reports. Similar to the coaching manager survey in Table 6.1, an example of a 360° survey for a Team Coaching Manager is listed in Table 6.3.

Table 6.3 Team Coaching Manager Survey

Team Coaching Manager Survey

On a scale of 1–10, where 10 is outstanding and 1 is very poor, how would you rate the leader of this team?

1. Our team leader facilitates the team in setting goals and tracking progress.

   1   2   3   4   5   6   7   8   9   10

2. Our team leader enables us to understand our stakeholder expectations.

   1   2   3   4   5   6   7   8   9   10

3. Our team leader encourages us to seek feedback from stakeholders.

   1   2   3   4   5   6   7   8   9   10

4. Our team leader listens to the team's ideas.

   1   2   3   4   5   6   7   8   9   10

5. Our team leader prompts us to listen to each other and build on each other's ideas.

   1   2   3   4   5   6   7   8   9   10

6. Our team leader asks us questions that make us think.

   1   2   3   4   5   6   7   8   9   10

7. Our team leader encourages us to learn together.

   1   2   3   4   5   6   7   8   9   10

8. Our team leader makes time for us to review our progress as a team.

   1   2   3   4   5   6   7   8   9   10

9. Our team leader helps us to reflect together.

   1   2   3   4   5   6   7   8   9   10

10. Our team leader supports us to act on feedback and reflection.

   1   2   3   4   5   6   7   8   9   10

The outcome of the team coaching manager survey in Table 6.3 can help the manager to focus on a particular area to improve. For example, a team coaching manager might do really well at setting goals and tracking progress, but less well at encouraging the team to learn together. Managers might decide first to learn more themselves about the benefits of a team learning together before addressing the issue with their team and deciding what they might do collectively.

Measuring Progress at the Organisational Level

Numerous scales have been tested by researchers to confirm that they are valid measures for employee engagement, readiness for change, and other outcomes which may be of interest to organisations in addition to measures such as revenue, productivity, and profit. These scales can be used as leading indicators of progress towards what the organisation has determined is important, providing early warning if the organisation is at risk of not achieving its goals. For example, we know that trust (a leading indicator) leads to better performance (3, 4). Therefore, if leading indicators suggest a drop in trust, rather than waiting for financial results (a lagging indicator) to be released, we should identify and address the causes. Otherwise, we can expect financial outcomes to deteriorate over time. Understanding the reason for a drop in any indicator is important. Once again coaching skills can help make sense of the data and agree on options to address.

There is a risk that organisations may spend more time measuring progress than actually taking action to achieve progress. When organisations develop a coaching culture, they usually have some specific aims in mind (5). Instead of trying to measure every aspect of a coaching culture, it is more useful to measure specific aims which are important to the organisation. This is sometimes described as Return on Expectations (6), an alternative to Return on Investment. For instance, if an organisation wants to reduce absenteeism, and absenteeism comes down in a department where managerial coaching is being piloted and not in other departments, there is an indication that coaching may be making a difference. Tavis and Woodward (7) suggest adapting measures used to measure the effectiveness of Learning and Development initiatives and give examples of how organisations can measure the desired outcomes of coaching, such as changes in behaviour or achieving goals.

Measuring the impact of coaching at the organisational level is challenging as there may be other contributory factors. For example, if the managers in a department undertaking a pilot of managerial coaching already have a coaching mindset, coaching might be expected to have a positive impact. As managerial coaching is deployed in more and more departments, the indicator can be monitored to see if coaching makes a difference in other departments also. Nyfoudi et al. (8) urge organisations to go beyond 'happy sheets' to evaluate the added value of coaching in an organisation. The indicators chosen should be relevant and meaningful to the organisation and can be ascribed a monetary value if needed. A discussion among teams about what success would look like and what indicators might be used is another way to develop a shared understanding about what matters, the strengths the team already has, and the strengths the team members want to develop.

Megginson and Clutterbuck (5) provide a questionnaire which organisations can use to measure their progress towards developing a coaching culture. For example, at the nascent stage, employees may be coached if their managers are keen but there is no discussion of coaching by senior leaders. At the tactical stage, employees are coached as part of performance management and senior leaders talk about being coached. At the strategic stage, people expect to be coached at all stages of their career and senior leaders talk about the challenges of coaching or being coached. Finally, at the embedded stage, employees seek coaching internally and externally and the top team seeks and uses feedback on their coaching. The authors also suggest questions that can be used to assess visible manifestations of a coaching culture, such as whether coaching is continuous rather than spasmodic, whether people respond positively to feedback, and whether coaching is more about developing potential than fixing problems.

If an organisation is genuinely committed to developing a coaching culture, there are several ways to assess where they are on that journey, from one-to-one interviews to focus groups and surveys (5). When a team completes a coaching self-assessment together, they reach a consensus on the extent to which their organisation currently has a coaching culture. This helps develop a shared understanding of coaching and how it can be further developed.

The data we gather is only ever a starting point for reflection and conversations leading to improvements, not an end point in itself. Beautifully presented charts based on in-depth analysis have no value unless they deepen our understanding and help us work out what, where, and how we can make positive changes. We next suggest some ways of making improvements in our coaching practice.

COACHING AS A LEADER – HOW TO GET BETTER

Managers should be wary of trying to improve too much at the same time. Working on one or two things is sensible. After all, the manager will not want to over-survey stakeholders or drown in data. One way to lessen the temptation to tackle everything at once is to recognise that many issues are inter-related and therefore improvements in one area will lead to improvements in another. Some activities are suggested in Chapters Two, Three, and Four to help managers improve their coaching skills with individuals and with teams.

Reflection is the key to improving our coaching skills. Using the conscious competence model discussed in Chapter Three, rather than being content to be an 'unconscious competent' operating on autopilot, reflection allows us to enhance our reflective competence, with an on-going focus on personal and professional development. We use feedback to raise our self-awareness and help us identify opportunities for our own growth just as we help others identify opportunities for theirs.

If, for example, a manager has noticed, or has had feedback, that they are not good listeners, they can ask someone to observe a meeting and note when they interrupt someone else or do not allow enough time for the other person to articulate their thoughts. They might record a meeting and make notes themselves. They might ask people whether they feel heard. In a team where there is psychological safety, people may be willing to give such feedback directly. In other teams a short anonymous survey might elicit the feedback needed. The data gathering can be repeated, three to six months after the manager has adopted new practices, to see if there is any noticeable change. As we can all fall into bad habits, it is worth repeating the survey periodically.

Technology can help with reflection in many ways. With participants' agreement, it is now easy to record online meetings and use that as the basis for a reflection on how to improve our interactions, perhaps combined with analytics enabled by artificial intelligence. To improve how we give feedback, we can note how often we give feedback. We can ask both independent colleagues and team members to rate us on a simple survey against the criteria for good feedback discussed in Chapter Three, for example, do we give specific feedback? do we give feedback in a timely manner? A team can have a useful discussion on what good feedback looks like. For example, people may have different expectations of what 'timely' means in practice, with Gen Z typically expecting much faster/instant feedback. By welcoming feedback ourselves, we normalise the giving and receiving of feedback as something that is not a personal attack but intended to help us improve.

Reflection on goal-setting is best done collaboratively, with the people we set goals with and with stakeholders. This allows us to hold ourselves and others to account for what we have committed to achieve, to understand the reasons for any goals that have not been achieved, and how goals might be reframed if necessary to be relevant, realistic, meaningful, and challenging. This helps avoid the danger of goals being seen as a tick-box exercise and makes it more likely that the motivating potential of goal-setting will be achieved.

In the busyness of everyday life, managers may continue to lead as they always have done unless they make time to reflect on the questions and situations that arise every day and take action to improve. Leadership is a lifelong journey that requires dedication and commitment. Coaching helps managers enact leadership every day and also supports managers in continually improving their leadership capability.

TECHNOLOGY-SUPPORTED COACHING FOR LEADERS

As highlighted throughout this book, there are many ways in which technology can support leaders as coaches, from simply enabling coaching at a distance to supporting innovation, goal-setting, and reflection through dedicated apps. Apps are available 24 hours a day and, if made available to all employees, can provide on-going support for simple questions, allowing managers to spend their time where it is most needed. Apps do not suffer from fatigue or memory lapses, making them powerful allies in coaching (9).

The rise of Generative Artificial Intelligence (GenAI) has simultaneously worried and excited people. For coaching managers, GenAI offers the potential to support managers with their own leadership development. It can provide an automated assistant to keep track of progress towards goals, offer prompts for reflection, and suggest approaches that managers can tailor for different circumstances.

GenAI can be helpful in supporting leaders in systematically addressing the needs of all employees, providing that we mitigate the bias built in to the apps, and that we apply AI recommendations discerningly, with human judgement, ethically, and to best serve our people and our organisations.

AI has enormous potential to free up managerial time spent on repetitive tasks such as summarising long reports or preparing presentations, allowing them instead to put time into thinking strategically or coaching individuals or teams. Here we will review some of the ways coaching managers can use AI as part of their leadership toolbox.

AI-powered coaching chatbots or coachbots are becoming more common.[1] One of the early examples of a conversational coaching bot is Rocky.Ai,[2] which aims to help people define and achieve their goals. Another example is Bunch,[3] which tailors its advice to the individual leader and their goals (10). Weber (11) found that participants coached by a coachbot, Coach M,[4] made significant progress towards their goals, although they found that human coaching excelled in significant and transformational change. Other researchers have also found that for a specific purpose such as defining goals and following up on a person's progress, a chatbot can be very effective, leading to bigger increases in goal attainment compared with employees who were not coached (12).

However, employees working with the chatbot did not show increases in resilience or well-being, or reductions in stress.

Goal-tracking apps, such as ClickUp,[5] AI Coach Bud,[6] and Reclaim.ai,[7] work with calendar apps as well as videoconferencing and collaboration tools, blocking out time for goal-related activities, issuing reminders, charting progress, and generating reports. They provide a virtual nudge or nag, which even though it comes from an app rather than a person, increases the likelihood of people doing something about it. Weber (11) found that coachbots could effectively handle surface-level questions on progress towards goals while the human coach could go deeper. It may be that coachbots are particularly useful at the point in goal-setting where SMART goals are used to make measures explicit, as they can help pin down specifics and follow up progress towards the goals. Larger conversations about defining meaningful goals are currently still best undertaken with a human coach. Wearable technology can be combined with goal-tracking for some purposes, such as encouraging managers to look after their own well-being through physical activity, meditation, and so on (13). Wearable technology may be particularly acceptable for younger generations.

While the way that managers give feedback can be impacted by a manager's fatigue or emotions, an AI coachbot will consistently give feedback in line with the research-based principles incorporated in its programming (14). This can lessen the subjectivity of managers who may have favourites or less positive relations with some of their staff but it does of course depend on the fairness of the algorithm and the dataset on which the app was trained. AI-powered chatbots can now foster connection and create a sense of belonging, for example by wording emails empathetically (15). This may help overcome some of the disadvantages of remote and hybrid working, when people can feel isolated and disconnected (16). AI apps can pair feedback with gamification and appreciative communication, in a way that is difficult for human leaders to match consistently, with research suggesting that many people think that algorithms are fair and fast, and consequently people are more open to negative or development feedback from an app rather than from a human whom they see as judging them (15).

Other applications of coaching, such as generating options, considering consequences, prioritising against known criteria, visualisation, and evaluating implementation, can also be assisted by GenAI (17). For example, Motivational Coach Chatbot[8] can provide motivating commentary, advice, and encouragement as well as generating action plans to achieve a goal.

There are many other AI tools which can assist managers. Some software is designed to support scenario planning and develop strategy (e.g. Strategy-Pro Coachbot[9]), while other apps (e.g. Figma) are useful in online brainstorming as they not only record but group ideas and synthesise the output for the team to review. AI applications can analyse and summarise vast amounts of information, collate it in a structured format and make recommendations for strategic initiatives. Used with care, AI can save managers huge amounts of time, time they can use for the human relationships that underpin their effectiveness as coaching leaders.

GenAI can also help us refine our coaching skills. For example, as illustrated in Table 6.4, AI apps can suggest how to improve how we ask questions.

Table 6.4 Examples of Recommendations Generated by AI Apps for Managers on How to Improve How They Ask Questions

How Can a Coaching Manager Improve How They Ask Questions?

Gemini (Bard)	ChatGPT	Claude	Copilot
Silence is golden: Don't rush to fill every quiet space. Give your coachee time to reflect and formulate their thoughts. Variety and balance: Use a mix of question types to keep the conversation engaging and avoid predictability. Show genuine interest in their answers by asking follow-up questions that delve deeper into their thoughts and feelings.	Give team members time to process and respond to questions. Frame questions starting with 'What' or 'How' to encourage detailed responses and insights. Demonstrate that you value the team member's feelings and experiences. Help them see the connection between their current actions and their desired outcomes. Encourage team members to reflect on what is working well and how those successes can be built on.	Ask one question at a time to avoid overloading the person. Allow time to reflect and respond. Be patient with silence. . Clarify role dilemmas by probing assumptions: 'In an ideal situation, what process would you envision?' Know when to re-direct or refocus a wandering dialogue by restating your original question or goal for the discussion. Always ask permission to probe sensitive issues.	Empower self-reflection: Ask questions that prompt introspection: 'What insights have you gained from this experience?' 'How do your values align with your decisions?' Balance support and challenge: Mix questions that provide support and encouragement with those that challenge assumptions or behaviours: 'What strengths can you leverage?' 'What blind spots might be hindering your progress?'

Similarly as shown in Table 6.5, AI can suggest ways to improve our goal-setting approach, drawing on vast amounts of data to identify good practice. Some apps such as Copilot provide sources for readers to follow up on the original.

With the permission of the person being coached, the transcript of a coaching session can be uploaded to an AI app and the app asked to suggest alternative ways of framing the questions. Natalie Ashdown (18) gives an example of how effective this can be, when the app is then asked to give suggestions that match the competency statements of different levels of accreditation of the International Coach Federation (ICF). There are also programs that combine video with analysis against the ICF competencies, e.g. Ovida.[10]

GenAI can thus act as a source of ideas and a pocket reminder of good practice. AI apps are improving constantly, and new apps continue to come on the market. It is important not to stop once an app has made a suggestion but to ask the app further questions and to use its suggestions to reflect deeply on our practice, what is working well, and how the suggestions might or might not be used to improve. Used wisely, AI apps can give us food for thought and inspire us to improve.

As noted throughout this book, relationships are key to success in managerial coaching. GenAI offers powerful ways to support managers but should not take over from managers in conversations where the human element is needed. Hunt (19) warns that while it is crucial for coaches to develop their knowledge and skills in using technology, it is equally important not to allow technology to overshadow the coaching approach. As managers, we know our employees and thus can tailor a message in a way that makes it most likely that the feedback will be taken on board, whereas AI apps offer a generic form of wording, the appropriateness of which will depend both on the level of detail in the prompts we provide, and on the way the app has been programmed and trained.

Just as we experiment with remote and hybrid forms of leadership, so too we need to figure out how best to work with GenAI. The more specific the prompts we use, the more likely it is that the apps will suggest actionable recommendations. However, in being specific we should not provide confidential information relating to people or an organisation.

Researchers suggest that prompts should include standard terminology, context, desired outcome, and evidence-based best practice recommendations (20). They also suggest verifying recommendations by using follow-up questions such as whether any of the suggestions

Table 6.5 Examples of Recommendations Generated by AI Apps for Managers on How to Improve How They Help Team Members Set Goals

How Can a Coaching Manager Help a Team Member Set Goals?

Gemini (Bard)	ChatGPT	Claude	Copilot
Have open-ended conversations to understand the team member's aspirations, strengths, and any potential obstacles.	Explore the team member's personal and professional motivations.	Ask open-ended questions to explore what motivates them, what they're excited to accomplish or become, and what they want their future work, role, or impact to look like.	Empathy builds trust and encourages open communication. Con-sider their personal and professional context when discussing goals.
Align with bigger goals: Discuss how individual goals connect to team and department objectives, fostering a sense of purpose and contribution.	Understanding what drives them will help align goals with their values and aspirations.	Have them write down 5–10 possible goals and then narrow those down to two or three short-term goals and one stretch goal that gets them excited. Having too many goals can be overwhelming.	Collaborative goal-setting:
Encourage the team member to generate various options, exploring different possibilities before narrowing down to a specific goal.	Involve the team member in the goal-setting process. Collaboratively discuss and define the objectives, making sure they feel ownership and commitment to the goals.	Help them realistically brainstorm potential obstacles, pitfalls, or challenges so you can identify how to address those. Review their existing strengths and resources as well.	Involve team members in defining their goals. Ask, 'What outcomes do you want to see?'
Schedule regular one-on-one sessions to track progress, offer guidance, and celebrate achievements.	Identify and provide the necessary resources, training, or support needed for the team member to achieve their goals.	Consider what skills, tools, knowledge, or other resources they might need from you or the organisation to achieve the goals. Offer to help with access or introductions.	Discuss alignment with team and organizational goals. How does their work contribute?
Empower the team member to take ownership of their goals and decisions, fostering independence and accountability.	Help the team member prioritise goals based on importance and impact.	Decide on a consistent meeting cadence to review progress and challenges on goals.	Encourage ownership by asking, 'How committed are you to achieving this goal?'
Acknowledge and celebrate milestones and accomplishments, reinforcing motivation and commitment to the goal.	Be open to adapting goals as needed.		Discuss potential obstacles and how to overcome them.
	Help the team member identify opportunities for skill enhancement that align with their goals.		Balance challenge and realism:
	Recognise and celebrate the team member's achievements along the way.		Goals should stretch team members without overwhelming them.
			Avoid setting goals that are too easy or too ambitious.
			Adaptability:
			Goals may evolve based on changing circumstances.
			Be flexible and adjust as needed.

came from authoritative sources (e.g. textbooks, journals, or professional associations), as well as verifying these recommendations with human professionals. Using follow-up prompts enables the user to get increasingly relevant answers. For example, if you ask an AI app to suggest possible scenarios for a plan that you are considering, you might then ask it to critique the plan, to identify risks, and how to mitigate them. As Maslach (21) reflects, sometimes simply asking questions helps us get 'unstuck' in a similar way to when we talk to a human coach. Nonetheless, AI apps are still prone to errors, drawing on unreliable Internet sources and even inventing sources to back up their responses. Ochis (22) advises leaders to question the validity, reliability, and fairness of the outputs of AI and to ensure that the way it is used is transparent, accountable, and aligned with the organisation's values and goals. This is a rapidly advancing area that will no doubt see huge developments in the coming years.

In addition to individual coachbots, there are also team coachbots which can assist a team and a team leader in numerous ways, from organising agendas for individual and team meetings, generating prompts for typical difficulties that can arise with team work, including a space for reflections, providing team coaching resources, documenting and following up on agreed actions, making a dashboard of progress visible to all, sharing a whiteboard for brainstorming, and hosting a team chat room (23). GenAI can synthesise resources from a huge array of information including free text feedback to give the team a shared view of the world, in a way that does not preference any individual perspective on the team. The team can then explore the information together (24). Future developments in team coachbots are likely to include instant analysis of conversational dynamics and team interactions, as well as more data on team performance (2).

GenAI does not replace human intelligence but it can help spark thoughts and connections. Combined with big data analytics, it can free up human thinking time. This comes with a warning as there is also a risk that its use may lead to flawed decision-making because of biases in its algorithms or in the datasets on which the AI program was trained (25). For example, rather than relying on job applicants being selected by an AI application, we need to satisfy ourselves that the best applicants are shortlisted and selected. The AI program will make its recommendations and findings based on its training data, regardless of whether or not that data set was representative (26). It is up to us to decide which of its outputs are helpful and how to use AI ethically and responsibly. A useful framework listing issues to consider when making decisions around the use of AI is the Aletheia framework.[11]

GenAI may also pose risks to mental health and well-being, depending on how it is implemented (27). In a well-known example, one app suggested to someone feeling depressed to jump off a bridge (28). Increased use of AI may lead to decreased contact with human peers. Monitoring of workers can reduce their autonomy and increase anxiety and stress. Coaching managers can help mitigate these risks by ensuring that we continue to value human contact, understand employee motivation, and maintain positive relations. Where there is little social support, people's physical as well as mental health suffers (29).

GenAI can support managers in keeping track of morale and employee engagement on an on-going basis, rather than by a periodic survey (15). In fact, Van Quaquebeke and Gerpott (15) suggest that in the future, AI will be better able to address employees' psychological needs than many human leaders, by addressing the fundamental aspects of motivation identified in Self-Determination Theory (10), namely autonomy, competence, and social relatedness. According to the authors, algorithms can increase an employee's experience of autonomy by giving them information about options and asking questions about the employee's choices.

Difficulties with AI arise when we use vague criteria, leaving it to the software to decide for example what exactly we mean by 'strong leadership skills' in a job description. Leadership can look very different in different organisations, in different cultures, and for different genders. A discussion of what sort of leadership we want in our organisations is an interesting conversation to have prior to recruiting new employees, bringing implicit beliefs to the surface. Problems can also arise if the algorithm is given the resumés of successful leaders in an organisation and told to find applications that are similar. This mimics what happens in some selection processes run by human beings and typically results in continuing to recruit the same sort of people, without appreciating the value that diversity brings in meeting the evolving needs of our communities and stakeholders. We can use AI programs themselves to help identify alternative perspectives and potential biases (30).

While AI can help managers, directors, and investors understand the challenges of a particular industry, users should sense-check any information from AI with people in the industry. There are some interesting challenges relating to the non-use of AI in leadership. For example, Van Quaquebeke and Gerpott ponder the potential consequences if a leader decides not to adopt the recommendations of an AI program (15) which later prove to have been a better option. A leader's reflection on the rationale for their decision-making might even end up as evidence in a dispute.

Ethical and legal issues relating specifically to the use of technology and GenAI in coaching include transparency, disclosure, and data privacy, with legal requirements varying in different countries (31, 32). Employees should know if an AI coachbot is being used. Managers need to satisfy themselves as to how any data they upload to an app will be protected. They should request permission from any individuals whose data they upload, or alternatively not upload any real data, regardless of whether or not it is identifiable. As mentioned above, AI apps are prone to bias. Managers therefore need to critically review AI recommendations before deciding on a course of action.

Keeping up to date and experimenting with technology is important as new software or updates to existing software can offer new features which have genuine benefits for leaders and teams. For example, various forms of telepresence are emerging, using holograms, virtual or augmented reality, creating a more realistic sense of being together with other people even if they are at the other side of the world. Keeping up to date in a fast-moving field like GenAI is a never-ending task. It can also be challenging to decide which application is best suited for a particular context. All of these techno-stressors, including the possibility of being seen as available 24/7, have to be managed carefully to avoid emotional exhaustion and burnout (33).

In the virtual world, we can explicitly remind employees to take time away from their screens, to close their eyes or stretch their eyes from time to time, so that they know this is not only okay but actually expected by their team leaders. Conducting a Zoom call while walking in a garden, through a forest, or along the seashore can enhance our well-being, not only through physical activity but also because numerous studies have shown that connection with nature has a positive impact on our mental, physical, and social well-being, improving cognitive function and reducing stress (34–36). Interestingly, even images of nature used as a screensaver can also be beneficial (34). The rise in apps focusing on well-being and applications of positive psychology such as meditation and gratitude also help remind people of the benefits these practices can have while making it easy for people to apply these practices through mobile or wearable technology options (37). Making time for reflection is also linked with self-care (38).

While technology including GenAI has huge potential to support leaders, the focus for coaching managers is firmly on human relationships, in face-to-face, hybrid, and remote working environments. A coaching mindset helps us switch from thinking about people as human resources to valuing human relationships. It is these relationships that allow us to make the most of our coaching skills, optimising outcomes for individuals and organisations.

IN CLOSING

Coaching is a practical way to apply leadership, face to face, online and in the hybrid world of work that has emerged since the pandemic. Moving away from the old debate about whether leaders are born or made, we can confidently say that managers can indeed learn coaching skills and can apply them effectively with individual employees and teams, in large and small organisations, in single and multiple locations across the world, in person and online. Technology is improving at a staggering rate and, used wisely, can be a huge support in our practice as leaders as coaches.

This book has drawn on research from around the world to indicate how coaching can be used successfully by leaders and managers in the face-to-face, remote, and hybrid ever-changing world of work today. We hope you find it useful, that you continue to develop your own coaching mindset and skillset, and that you, your team, and your organisation all benefit.

NOTES

1 Examples of apps, chatbots and coachbots are provided in this book not as an endorsement but simply to illustrate the range of applications available. In such a fast moving space, it is likely that some of these links will no longer work by the time this book is published.
2 See https://www.rocky.ai/digital-coach for further information.
3 See https://bunch.ai/ for further information.
4 See https://transferoflearning.com/services/chatbot/ for further information.
5 See https://clickup.com/ for further information.
6 See https://topai.tools/t/aicoachbud for further information.
7 See https://reclaim.ai/ for further information.
8 See https://zapier.com/templates/motivational-coach-bot for further information.
9 See https://www.thelatitude.io/opt-in-ea4addde-7e98–4264-a01e-b7e53c614c31 for further information.
10 See https://ovida.io/ for further information.
11 See https://www.rolls-royce.com/innovation/the-aletheia-framework.aspx.

REFERENCES

1. Ellinger AD, Hamlin RG, B RS. Behavioural indicators of ineffective managerial coaching. *Journal of European Industrial Training.* 2008;32(4): 240.
2. Clutterbuck D. *Coaching the team at work: the definitive guide to team coaching.* 2nd ed. Nicholas Brealey; 2020.
3. Le BP, Tran QT. Leadership practice for building trust of followers: decisive factors of organizational performance. *SEISENSE Journal of Management.* 2020;3(2): 45–57.
4. Hendriks M et al. Virtuous leadership: a source of employee well-being and trust. *Management Research Review.* 2020;43(8): 951–970.
5. Clutterbuck D, Meggison D, Bajer A. *Building and sustaining a coaching culture.* 2016: Kogan Page.
6. McCarthy G. *Coaching and mentoring for business.* London: Sage; 2014.
7. Tavis A, Woodward W. *The digital coaching revolution: how to support employee development with coaching tech.* Kogan Page Publishers; 2024.
8. Nyfoudi M et al., Managerial coaching skill and team performance: how does the relationship work and under what conditions? *Human Resource Management Journal.* 2023;33(2): 328–45.
9. Nath RP. *Profitable digital coaching.* E-book ed.: Adhyyan Books; 2024.
10. Ryan RM, Deci EL. Self-determination theory and the facilitation of intrinsic motivation, social development and well-being. *American Psychologist.* 2000;55(1): 68–78.
11. Weber E. A chatbot coaching case study revealing surprising results. Lever; 2023. https://transferoflearning.com/a-chatbot-coaching-case-study-revealing-surprising-results/
12. Terblanche N et al. Coaching at scale: investigating the efficacy of artificial intelligence coaching. *International Journal of Evidence-Based Coaching & Mentoring.* 2022;20(2): 20–36.
13. Kamble A, Desai S, Abhang N. Wearable activity trackers: a structural investigation into acceptance and goal achievements of Generation Z. *American Journal of Health Education.* 2021;52(5): 307–20.
14. Passmore J, Tee D. Can chatbots like GPT-4 replace human coaches: issues and dilemmas for the coaching profession, coaching clients and for organisations. *The Coaching Psychologist.* 2023;19(1): 47–54.
15. Quaquebeke NV, Gerpott FH. The now, new, and next of digital leadership: how artificial intelligence (AI) will take over and change leadership as we know it. *Journal of Leadership & Organizational Studies.* 2023;30(3): 265–75.
16. Höddinghaus M, Nohe C, Hertel G. Leadership in virtual work settings: what we know, what we do not know, and what we need to do. *European Journal of Work and Organizational Psychology.* 2023;33(2): 188–212.
17. Graßmann C, Schermuly CC. Coaching with artificial intelligence: concepts and capabilities. *Human Resource Development Review.* 2021;20(1): 106–26.
18. Ashdown N, Jones-Hunt P. *How can AI improve a PCC level recording?*, in Coaching Cafe. 2024, Open Door https://opendoorcoaching.com.au/what-if-ai-can-make-my-coaching-better/.
19. Otte S et al. Attitudes of coaches towards the use of computer-based technology in coaching. *Consulting Psychology Journal: Practice and Research.* 2014;66(1): 38.
20. Aguinis H, Beltran JR, Cope A. How to use generative AI as a human resource management assistant. *Organizational Dynamics.* 2024;53(1): 101029.

21. Maslach D. Generative AI can supercharge your academic research. Harvard Business Publishing, 14 Dec 2023. https://hbsp.harvard.edu/inspiring-minds/generative-ai-can-supercharge-your-academic-research

22. Ochis K. Become a strategic AI leader: how AI is game-changing for leaders. *Forbes Leadership*, 28 Dec 2023. https://www.forbes.com/councils/forbescoachescouncil/2023/12/28/become-a-strategic-ai-leader-how-ai-is-game-changing-for-leaders/

23. Hawkins P. *Leadership team coaching: developing collective transformational leadership.* E-book ed.: Kogan Page; 2021.

24. Foussier WG, Haitoglou A, Harrison T. Casting a vision for human-AI hybrid coaching practice. Thought Leadership Institute: The Future of Coaching, 27 Oct 2023. https://thoughtleadership.org/casting-a-vision-for-human-ai-hybrid-coaching-practice/

25. Kordzadeh N, Ghasemaghaei M. Algorithmic bias: review, synthesis, and future research directions. *European Journal of Information Systems.* 2022;31(3): 388–409.

26. Akter S et al. Algorithmic bias in data-driven innovation in the age of AI. *International Journal of Information Management.* 2021;60: 102387.

27. European Agency for Safety and Health at Work. Impact of artificial intelligence on occupational health and safety. Policy Brief, 7 Jan 2021. https://osha.europa.eu/en/publications/impact-artificial-intelligence-occupational-safety-and-health

28. O'Brien M, Swenson A. Cats on the moon? Google's AI tool is producing misleading responses that have experts worried. *Sydney Morning Herald.* 2024 May 26.

29. Van den Broek K, Hupke M, Kuasz F. *Psychosocial risks and workers health.* 31 Mar 2012, European Agency for Safety and Health at Work: https://oshwiki.osha.europa.eu/en/themes/psychosocial-risks-and-workers-health

30. Newstead T, Eager B, Wilson S. How AI can perpetuate – or help mitigate – gender bias in leadership. *Organizational Dynamics.* 2023;52(4): 100998.

31. Diller SJ. Ethics in digital and AI coaching. *Human Resource Development International.* 2024;27(4): 584–96.

32. Hunt P. Keeping up-to-date with technology change. In: Passmore J et al., editors. *The digital and AI coaches' handbook: the complete guide to the use of online, AI, and technology in coaching.* Abingdon, Oxon.: Routledge; 2024. p. 49–63.

33. Michalik NM, Schermuly CC. Is technostress stressing coaches out? The relevance of technostress to coaches' emotional exhaustion and coaches' perception of coaching success. *Coaching: An International Journal of Theory, Research and Practice.* 2023;16(2): 155–72.

34. Menzel C et al. Knowing and experiencing the benefits: factors influencing restoration evoked by nature photographs. *Journal of Environmental Psychology.* 2024;96: 102322.

35. Barragan-Jason G et al. Psychological and physical connections with nature improve both human well-being and nature conservation: a systematic review of meta-analyses. *Biological Conservation.* 2023;277: 109842.

36. Silva A, Matos M, Gonçalves M. Nature and human well-being: a systematic review of empirical evidence from nature-based interventions. *Journal of Environmental Planning and Management.* 2023;67(14): 3397–454.

37. Ghandeharioun A et al. 'Kind and grateful': a context-sensitive smartphone app utilizing inspirational content to promote gratitude. *Psychology of Well-Being.* 2016;6: 1–21.

38. Hawley R, Turner E, Iordanou I. Managing ethics online. In: Passmore J et al., editors. *The Digital and AI Coaches' Handbook: The complete guide to the use of online, AI and technology in coaching.* Routledge: Abingdon, Oxon.; 2024. p. 212–26.

Printed in the United States
by Baker & Taylor Publisher Services

...ted in the United States
...er & Taylor Publisher Services